SAILING THE WINE-DARK SEA
WHY THE GREEKS MATTER

BY THOMAS CAHILL
THE HINGES OF HISTORY

INTRODUCTORY VOLUME:
How the Irish Saved Civilization

THE MAKING OF THE ANCIENT WORLD:
The Gifts of the Jews
Desire of the Everlasting Hills
Sailing the Wine-Dark Sea

Three additional volumes are planned on the making
of the modern world.

ALSO BY THOMAS CAHILL

A Literary Guide to Ireland (with Susan Cahill)
Jesus' Little Instruction Book
Pope John XXIII

THE HINGES OF HISTORY

We normally think of history as one catastrophe after another, war followed by war, outrage by outrage—almost as if history were nothing more than all the narratives of human pain, assembled in sequence. And surely this is, often enough, an adequate description. But history is also the narratives of grace, the recountings of those blessed and inexplicable moments when someone did something for someone else, saved a life, bestowed a gift, gave something beyond what was required by circumstance.

In this series, THE HINGES OF HISTORY, I mean to retell the story of the Western world as the story of the great gift-givers, those who entrusted to our keeping one or another of the singular treasures that make up the patrimony of the West. This is also the story of the evolution of Western sensibility, a narration of how we became the people that we are and why we think and feel the way we do. And it is, finally, a recounting of those essential moments when everything was at stake, when the mighty stream that became Western history was in ultimate danger and might have divided into a hundred useless tributaries or frozen in death or evaporated altogether. But the great gift-givers, arriving in the moment of crisis, provided for transition, for transformation, and even for transfiguration, leaving us a world more varied and complex, more awesome and delightful, more beautiful and strong than the one they had found.

—THOMAS CAHILL

THE HINGES OF HISTORY

VOLUME I
HOW THE IRISH SAVED CIVILIZATION
The Untold Story of Ireland's Heroic Role
from the Fall of Rome to the Rise of Medieval Europe

This introductory volume presents the reader with a new way of looking at history. Its time period—the end of the classical period and the beginning of the medieval period—enables us to look back to our ancient roots and forward to the making of the modern world.

VOLUME II
THE GIFTS OF THE JEWS
How a Tribe of Desert Nomads
Changed the Way Everyone Thinks and Feels

This is the first of three volumes on the creation of the Western world in ancient times. It is first because its subject matter takes us back to the earliest blossoming of Western sensibility, there being no West before the Jews.

VOLUME III
DESIRE OF THE EVERLASTING HILLS
The World Before and After Jesus

This volume, which takes as its subject Jesus and the first Christians, comes directly after *The Gifts of the Jews,* because Christianity grows directly out of the unique culture of ancient Judaism.

VOLUME IV
SAILING THE WINE-DARK SEA
Why the Greeks Matter

The Greek contribution to our Western heritage comes to us largely through the cultural conduit of the Romans (who, though they do not have a volume of their own, are a presence in Volumes I, III, and IV). The Greek contribution, older than Christianity, nevertheless continues past the time of Jesus and his early followers and brings us to the medieval period. *Sailing the Wine-Dark Sea* concludes our study of the making of the ancient world.

VOLUMES V, VI & VII

These three volumes, to be published in the first decade of the twenty-first century, will investigate the making of the modern world and the impact of its cultural innovations on the sensibility of the West.

The series may be read in whatever order you like, since each volume is substantially complete in itself. In addition to the obvious order—starting with Volume I and continuing in numerical sequence—the author suggests that those who began with Volume II may find it convenient to continue with Volumes III and IV before reading Volume I.

THOMAS CAHILL

SAILING
THE WINE-DARK
❧ SEA ❧

WHY THE GREEKS MATTER

NAN A. TALESE
DOUBLEDAY
NEW YORK   LONDON   TORONTO
SYDNEY   AUCKLAND

PUBLISHED BY NAN A. TALESE
AN IMPRINT OF DOUBLEDAY
a division of Random House, Inc.

DOUBLEDAY is a registered trademark of Random House, Inc.

Pages 289–292 constitute an extension of this copyright page.

Book design by Marysarah Quinn
Map art by Jackie Aher

ENDPAPER: "Symposium," Tomba del Tuffatore, lastra nord,
480 B.C., Paestum, Museo Archeologico Nazionale,
© foto pedicini

Library of Congress Cataloging-in-Publication Data
Cahill, Thomas.
Sailing the wine-dark sea : why the Greeks matter /
Thomas Cahill.— 1st ed.
p. cm.— (Hinges of history ; v. 4)
Includes bibliographical references and index.
1. Greece—Civilization—To 146 B.C. 2. Civilization, Western—
Greek influences. I. Title.
DF77.C28 2003
909'.09821—dc21
2003050725

ISBN 0-385-49553-6

November 2003

1 3 5 7 9 10 8 6 4 2

FIRST EDITION

To

MADELEINE L'ENGLE

and

LEAH & DESMOND TUTU

and in memory of

PAULINE KAEL

mentors and models of life and art

ταὶς κάλαισιν ὕμμι νόημμα τῶμον

οὐ διάμειπτον

The heart within me never changes

toward you so beautiful

One can achieve his fill of all good things,
even of sleep, even of making love . . .

—HOMER

Once out of nature I shall never take
My bodily form from any natural thing,
But such a form as Grecian goldsmiths make
Of hammered gold and gold enamelling
To keep a drowsy Emperor awake;
Or set upon a golden bough to sing
To lords and ladies of Byzantium
Of what is past, or passing, or to come.

WILLIAM BUTLER YEATS

CONTENTS ❦

INTRODUCTION

THE WAY THEY CAME

Demeter's hair was yellow as the ripe corn of which she was mistress, for she was the Harvest Spirit, goddess of farmed fields and growing grain. The threshing floor was her sacred space. Women, the world's first farmers (while men still ran off to the bloody howling of hunt and battle), were her natural worshipers, praying: "May it be our part to separate wheat from chaff in a rush of wind, digging the great winnowing fan through Demeter's heaped-up mounds of corn while she stands among us, smiling, her brown arms heavy with sheaves, her ample breasts adorned in flowers of the field."

Demeter had but one daughter, and she needed no other, for Persephone was the Spirit of Spring. The Lord of Shadows and Death, Hades himself, the Unseen One, carried her off in his jet-black chariot, driven by coal-black steeds, through a crevice in the surface of Earth, down to the realms of the dead. For nine days, Demeter wandered sorrowing over land, sea, and sky in search of her daughter, but no one dared tell her what had happened till she reached the Sun, who had seen it all. With Zeus's help, the mother retrieved her daughter, but Persephone had already eaten a pomegranate seed, food of the dead, at Hades's insistence, which meant she must come back to him. In the end, a sort of truce was arranged. Persephone could return to her sorrowing mother but must spend a third of each year with her dark Lord. Thus, by the four-month death each year of the goddess of springtime in her descent to the underworld, did winter enter the world. And when she returns from the dark realms she always strikes earthly beings with awe and smells somewhat of the grave.

HISTORY MUST BE learned in pieces. This is partly because we have only pieces of the past—shards, ostraca, palimpsests, crumbling codices with missing pages, newsreel clips, snatches of song, faces of idols whose bodies have long since turned to dust—which give us glimpses of what has been but never the whole reality. How could they? We cannot encompass the whole reality even of the times in which we live. Human beings never know more than part, as "through a glass darkly"; and all knowledge comes to us in pieces. That said, it is often easier to encompass the past than the present, for it is past; and its pieces may be set beside one another, examined, contrasted and compared, till one attains an overview.

Like fish who do not know they swim in water, we are seldom aware of the atmosphere of the times through which we move, how strange and singular they are. But when we approach another age, its alienness stands out for us, almost as if that were its most obvious quality; and the sense of being on alien ground grows with the antiquity of the age we are considering. I first came in contact with people of another time and place in the sayings, stories, and songs my mother taught me when I was little. These were pieces of an oral tradition, passed on to her by her mother, who died before I was born, a countrywoman from the Galway midlands. So many of the words were strange to someone growing up in twentieth-century New York City: "When you've harrowed as much as I've ploughed, then you'll know something"; "You never know who'll take the coal off your foot, when it's burning you";

"Every old shoe finds an old sock." I had been to a farm once but had never seen harrow or plough in use, I knew what coal was but had never been warmed at an open coal fire, I surely knew what shoes and socks were but nothing of the archaic courting practices in the Irish countryside. My mother explained patiently that this last was meant as a hilarious sendup of old maids and their prospects. The sexual aspect of the imagery she doubtlessly left me to work out for myself. But her waves of words had a sort of triple (and simultaneous) effect: first, the experience of coming into contact with alien lives through the medium of the words they had left behind; then, an acknowledgment of the humanity I shared with these strangers from another time and place; and, last, the satisfying thrill that concentrated, metaphorical language can give its listener—the electric sensation at the back of the neck announcing the arrival of the gods of poetry.

It is through such wisps of words and such tantalizingly incomplete images that we touch the past and its peoples. When I attended a Jesuit high school in New York City and was taught to read Latin and ancient Greek, I had my first scholarly taste of the strangeness of other ages. In Homer's gods and heroes and in Ovid's *Metamorphoses*,^α I discovered the fleeting reflections of what was once a complete world: Odysseus putting out the giant's single eye, enormous in his forehead and balefully glistening; Niobe's many children, struck dead one at a time by the arrows of Apollo and Artemis, as Niobe stood by helpless, in mounting hysteria, finally consumed by insensate despair. Nothing like their plights had ever happened, or would ever happen, to me. I would never en-

α The *Metamorphoses*—a long narrative poem of pithy, sensuous episodes—was slipped to us by a teacher who seemed to understand how deadly was the assigned Latin curriculum for junior year, which consisted entirely of political speeches by the polysyllabic Cicero on topics that could only induce stupor.

counter a cyclops or be hunted by Apollo, but I could nonetheless feel as their victims felt: I could take on Odysseus's twitching anxiety in the face of an unbeatable enemy and the hopelessness of terminal captivity in the service of a monster (even if I had as yet but scant experience of being someone's employee); I could resonate with Niobe's heartsickness, fevered attempts to protect her children, and catatonic despair. I too had known impossible opponents; I too understood how much a mother loved her children.

Just around the corner from my school was the Metropolitan Museum of Art—which I discovered without the help of the Jesuits, who were verbal but not visual. There, in the old gallery of classical art, I first saw the faint traces of paint on the classical marble statuary and learned that the eyeless bronzes had once been fitted with lifelike irises. There I saw an accurate model of the Parthenon with its excited and boldly colored frieze of gods and heroes. I came to understand that ancient Greece had not been a collection of tasteful white marble statues but a place on fire with color. I made the connection between these astonishing figures that now lived along Fifth Avenue and the brilliant colors of Homer's metaphors: "the wine-dark sea," "the rosy-fingered dawn." I had, without knowing it, put the literature in a context.

I tell you these things now because my methods of approaching the past have scarcely changed since childhood and adolescence. I assemble what pieces there are, contrast and compare, and try to remain in their presence till I can begin to see and hear and love what living men and women once saw and heard and loved, till from these scraps and fragments living men and women begin to emerge and move and live again— and then I try to communicate these sensations to my reader. So you will find in this book no breakthrough discoveries, no cutting-edge scholarship, just, if I have succeeded, the feelings and perceptions of another age and, insofar as possible, real and rounded men and women. For me, the historian's principal task should be to raise the dead to life.

To keep a sense of how fragmented are the materials we are dealing with, I have set a story at the head of each chapter, such as the story of Demeter with which this introduction began. These fragments, which we usually call "myths," are pieces of the elaborate mythology of the Greeks, a mythology woven from many sources over the course of Greece's (largely un-knowable) prehistory and with many adumbrations of sights and sounds still to be found faintly in our own world. (In Demeter's story, for instance, the attentive reader may catch dark prefigurings of the Christian Mother of Sorrows and the novenas—penitential nine-day cycles—commemorating her pain at the loss of her magical Child, who rises from the grave in late March or early April.) These fragments also give the reader another way of approaching the material in the body of the chapter, another dark glass to look through.

At times, however, the fragments I lay out for your inspec-tion may seem not to fit well together, as if they were stray pieces from separate puzzles. In such cases, I would counsel pa-tience. There are moments when a large enough fragment can become a low wall, a second fragment another wall to be raised at right angles to the first. A few struts and beams later, and we may have made ourselves a rough lean-to in which to take mo-mentary shelter from the contrary buffetings of raw history. But it can consume the better part of a chapter to build such a lean-to; and as we do so the fragment we are examining may seem unconnected to the larger whole. Only when we step back can we see that we have been reassembling something that can stand in the wind.

◆ ◆ ◆

T HEIR ORIGINS LIE in mystery. Who the Greeks were
to begin with and where they came from are matters ob-
scured by the thick mists that envelop our understanding of
prehistoric Europe. Without written records, we must make do
with the clues that linguistics and archaeology can offer. The
likelihood is that the mounted warriors who rode into the valleys of Greece in the middle of the second millennium B.C. had
their origins in the Caucasus Mountains between the Black and
Caspian Seas. Gradually, these aggressive equestrians made their
way southwest through the Balkans till they reached the rugged
peninsulas, striated with mountains not unlike their mountains
of origin, and the volcanic isles and inlets of the Aegean Sea
that would serve as their permanent home. The language they
spoke was a cat's cradle of Indo-European roots, which means
that their speech betrayed their distant links to other bellicose
bands—the haughty Aryans of India; the rocklike Slavs with
their great joys and even greater sorrows; the crazy Celts of
Galatia, Central Europe, Gaul, Britain, and Ireland; the icy, relentless Germans and Vikings—who before and after them ride
out of the dim north to terrify and subdue farming cultures un-
prepared to do battle with armed men on horseback.

Of the indigenous farming folk they encountered we know
even less, save that they worshiped not sky-dwelling Zeus of
the thunderbolts but the fecund Earth herself, source of their
bounty—"the earth that feeds us all," as Homer will call her.
The primeval presence of Greece's aboriginal natives may still
be sensed in stories, such as Demeter's, of the annual death and
rebirth of the natural world. However woeful their clashes with
the Caucasians may have been, farmers and invaders became in
time one culture, united in language, religion, and custom.

There are hints in archaeological strata uncovered in the late nineteenth and early twentieth centuries of how this unified culture might have come to be.

At Cnossos in north-central Crete, the English archaeologist Sir Arthur Evans found the long-abandoned capital of a civilization he dubbed "Minoan" (after the legendary King Minos), a court of graceful buildings designed to withstand earthquakes and shelter sophisticated living. Brightly colored frescoes give us entrance to a strange world of long-haired, lightly clad Minoans, beardless men in belts and codpieces, women in skirts and corsets that leave the breasts exposed, naked young acrobats of both sexes who sportingly somersault over the backs of bulls. The Minoans had the rudiments of a written language, known to scholars by a few fragmented examples and called Linear A.β So far as we can tell, the writing is pictographic and syllabic, like the writing of the Mesopotamians and the Egyptians, but the symbols seem to have been employed only to make inventories that kept account of the Minoans' extensive commercial endeavors, never for more literary purposes. The symbols almost certainly do not represent Greek, for the Minoans were the acme of an indigenous culture that worshiped the Great Mother. They flourished from about

β According to a recent and controversial study, *Mysteries of the Snake Goddess* by Kenneth Lapatin, Sir Arthur and his "restorers" may themselves have created these frescoes or at least enhanced them considerably, as well as set up a veritable factory of "Minoan" objects for export. The English archaeologist was indeed an eccentric straight from the pages of Evelyn Waugh, both punctilious and batty, but was he capable of wholesale deception? No doubt much scholarly ink will be spilled before we can be sure of the truth of this matter. Whatever the final consensus (which might be difficult to reach, given the considerable investment that museums and private collections throughout the world have in objects that came to them under Sir Arthur's imprimatur), Linear A will remain part of the valid archaeological record, as will influential elements of Minoan religion and architecture, since examples of these have been uncovered at sites with no link to Sir Arthur.

2000 to 1400 B.C., at which point they were destroyed, why or how we can't be sure but probably in the overflow from a stupendous volcano on the isle of Thera (modern Santorini), which lies just north of central Crete. This island, which before its catastrophic eruptions was much larger, may well have given rise to the legend of the lost "continent" of Atlantis.

The discovery of the Minoans in the early 1900s had been preceded by other discoveries that electrified Europe. In the 1870s, Heinrich Schliemann, a self-made German businessman and Barnum-like promoter, declared that he had discovered the remains of ancient Troy, the city described in the *Iliad* as besieged for ten years by Greek forces who are finally able to destroy it through the famous ruse of the Wooden Horse. Schliemann discovered as well a horde of treasure, which he proclaimed to be "the treasure of Priam," king of the Trojans. He decked out his slinky Greek-born wife in the ancient trinkets, photographed her, and proclaimed her a dead ringer for Helen of Troy. Even if the "treasure of Priam" belongs to a period that predates the setting of the *Iliad* by a millennium or more, there is general consensus that Schliemann did indeed discover Troy just where it ought to be—on the coast of Asia Minor at the entrance to the Hellespont (today the Dardanelles).

Though the discovery of Troy won the biggest headlines, Schliemann's more important discovery—at least from the point of view of understanding Greek origins—was his unearthing of shaft graves in the area of Mycenae in the northeast Peloponnese. Here Agamemnon, leader of the Greek forces at Troy, had ruled; and here, according to legend, he had been slain on his return from the war by his wife, Clytemnestra, and her lover, Aegisthus. Once again, the irrepressible Schliemann overshot, claiming that the graves contained the soldiers of Agamemnon and even the legendary king himself, masked in

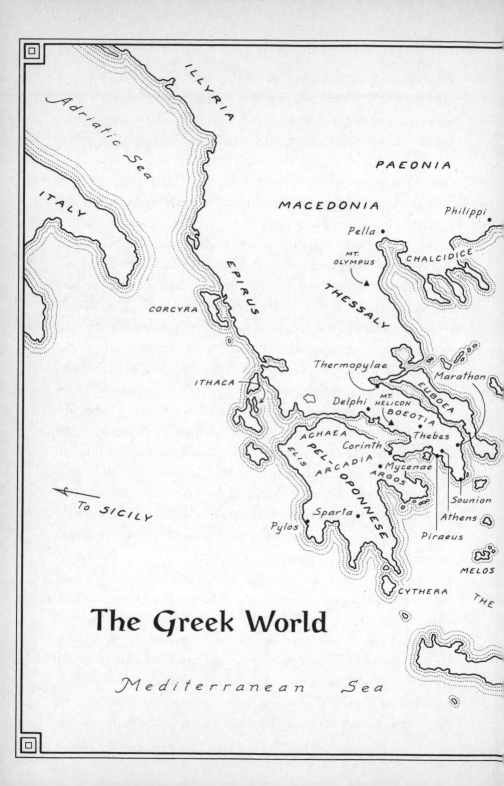

The Greek World

Black Sea

Byzantium

THRACE

SAMOTHRACE

THASOS

LEMNOS

PHRYGIA

HELLESPONT

TENEDOS

Troy

Aegean

Mytilene

LESBOS

LYDIA

ASIA
MINOR

CHIOS

Smyrna
Clazomenae
Colophon

Sea

SAMOS

Ephesus

ICARIA

CARIA

Miletus

DELOS

Cnidus

PAROS

NAXOS

COS

LYCIA

THERA

CYCLADES

RHODES

CRETE

Cnossos

0   50   100 miles

0   50   100 kilometers

gold. "I have looked upon the face of Agamemnon," said Schliemann. Though both mask and graves proved to have been fashioned centuries before Agamemnon and the Trojan War, the find yielded much information about the gradual marriage of Greek invader with indigenous farmer.

Long before Agamemnon had ruled, his ancestors, buried in the shafts—"there in the tomb stand the dead upright," Yeats had written of similar Bronze Age burials in Ireland—showed themselves to be typical Indo-European warriors, tall, bristling with weapons, in love with precious metals and their display, but already in their symbolic pottery and jewelry adopting the native cult of the Mother Goddess. The ruined court of this Mycenae of the Heroes likewise shows admired borrowings from the general layout of Minoan architecture, if somewhat less grand and graceful and far more fortress-like than its exemplar. The language of the Mycenaeans was an early form of Greek, as became clear once the written code called Linear B was cracked, revealing a pictographic-syllabic set of markings, a language of accounting derived from Linear A but full of Greek roots and proper names. This writing system would be lost to the Mycenaeans after the tenth century B.C. in a "Dark Age" of Greece we know little about. (Eventually, the Greeks would require a new form of writing that could sustain not only commercial but literary needs.)

But in the culture of protohistoric Mycenae, as in other parts of Greece, invader and native were coming together, "language mixing with language side-by-side," as Homer puts it in the *Odyssey*. So much so that when the curtain rises on the historic period, there is no longer any way of separating these influences, for by 800 B.C. Greece, once a patchwork of conflicting identities (only a few of which we can identify today), emerges from its prehistoric shadows as a diverse but unified world.

I
THE
WARRIOR
HOW TO FIGHT

Zeus, who controlled rain and clouds and held in his hand the awful thunderbolt, was Lord of the Sky and greatest of the gods, but not the oldest. He and the eleven other Olympians—the gods and goddesses who dwelt in the heaven at the top of Mount Olympus, Greece's highest mountain—had been preceded in their reign by the elder gods, the Titans, whom they had overthrown. The Titans had been formed by Father Heaven and Mother Earth, which had existed before any of the gods, having emerged from the primordial Chaos, whose children, Darkness and Death, had given birth to Light and Love (for Night is the mother of Day), which made possible the appearance of Heaven and Earth.

Zeus, son of the deposed Titan Cronus, was perpetually falling in love, wooing and usually raping beautiful women, both immortal and mortal, who would then give birth to gods and demigods, complicating considerably family relations on Olympus. Hera, Zeus's wife and sister, was perpetually jealous, scheming to best one rival after another with cruel retribution. But all the goddesses, even the virginal ones, were prone to jealousy; and it was this fault that helped bring on the Trojan War—which began, like Eve's temptation in Eden, with an apple.

There was one goddess, Eris, not an Olympian, whom the gods were inclined to leave out of their wonderful celebrations, for she was the Spirit of Discord. True to her nature, when she found she had not been invited to the wedding of King Peleus with the sea nymph Thetis, she hurled into the Olympic banqueting hall a single golden apple with two words on it, tēi kallistēi (to the fairest). All the goddesses wanted to claim it, but the three most powerful were finally left to fight over *it: the cow-eyed goddess Hera, the battle goddess Athena—the child of Zeus who had sprung from his head—and Aphrodite, whom the Romans called Venus, the laughing, irresistible goddess of Love, born from the foam of the sea.*

Zeus wisely declined to be judge of this beauty contest but recommended Paris, prince of Troy, who had been exiled as a shepherd to Mount Ida because his father, King Priam, had received an oracle that his son would one day be the ruin of Troy. Paris, Zeus averred, was known as a judge of female beauty (and of little else, he might have added). The three goddesses lost no time appearing to the astounded shepherd-prince and offering their bribes, Hera promising to make him Lord of Eurasia, Athena to make him victorious in battle against the Greeks, Aphrodite to give him the world's most beautiful woman. He found for Aphrodite, who gave him Helen, daughter of Zeus and the mortal Leda.

There was one small complication: Helen was married to Menelaus, king of Sparta and brother of Agamemnon of Mycenae, Greece's most powerful king. But with Aphrodite's help, Paris was able in Menelaus's absence to spirit Helen away from her home and bring her to Troy. When Menelaus returned and found out what had happened, he called on all the Greek chieftains, who had previously sworn an oath to uphold Menelaus's rights as husband should just such a thing as this occur. Only two were reluctant—shrewd, realistic Odysseus, king of Ithaca, who so loved his home and family that he had to be tricked into signing up for the adventure; and Greece's greatest warrior, Achilles, whose mother, the sea nymph Thetis, knew he would die if he went to Troy but who joined the Greek forces in the end because he was fated to prefer glorious victory in battle to a long life shorn of pride. Thus did the many ships of the Greek kings, each vessel bearing more than fifty men, set sail for Troy in pursuit of a human face, Helen's—in Marlowe's mighty line, "the face that launched a thousand ships."

HOW DIFFERENT in feeling the Judgment of Paris from the Sorrows of Demeter. If the earlier story is genuine myth, dramatizing recurrent, inexorable tragedy at the level of cosmic nightmare, the later seems a sort of old-fashioned drawing room melodrama about the characteristic foibles of male and female, in which matters spin monstrously out of control and end in tragic farce. If Demeter takes us back to an agricultural way of life that imagined Earth and its manifestations as aspects of maternal nurturing, the strident gods of Olympus, challenging and overthrowing one another, males always primed for battle and sexual conquest, females seizing control only by wheedling indirection, are projections of a warrior culture that set victory in armed combat above all other goals—or at least *seemed* to, for there are always, deep within any society, dreams that run in another, even in a contrary, direction from its articulated purposes. But first let's examine the obvious: the visible surfaces of this bellicose society of gleaming metals and rattling weapons.

The Mycenaean world that Schliemann discovered was the world of Agamemnon and his predecessors, the world sung by Homer in his two great epics, the *Iliad* and the *Odyssey*, set, so far as we can judge, in Aegean Greece of the twelfth century B.C., an age I have called "protohistoric" because a cumbersome form of writing, Linear B, was then in existence, though usable only for accountants' ledgers. The stories of this age, however, were preserved as oral poetry by wandering bards and written down only much later when a far more flexible form of writing came into currency that permitted the recording of epics of massive length and graceful subtlety.

The *Iliad* begins not with the apple and the goddesses but with a far more earthly contest—between Agamemnon, leader of the Greek forces, and Achilles, the preeminent Greek champion. The Greek fleet has been long since beached on the Trojan shore and the army of the Greek chieftains is wearily besieging the well-fortified city, which has been able to withstand its assaults for nine years. But brilliant, unbeatable Achilles—whom Homer immediately calls *dios* or "noble," a word whose Indo-European root means "godlike" or "shining like the divine stars"—has left the field of battle in outrage at his treatment by haughty Agamemnon. For Agamemnon has commandeered Achilles's concubine, a girl Achilles won as war booty. Agamemnon feels justified in taking Achilles's concubine because he has had to accede to the unthinkable and give up *his* battle-won concubine. Her father, Chryses, priest at a nearby shrine of Apollo, called down his god's wrath upon the Greeks—whom Homer calls "Achaeans," "Argives," or "Danaans," depending on the needs of his meter. Homer's audience would already have known the details of the story, so they would not have been the least disoriented as he begins thus, summarizing the conflict between the two men, a conflict with fatal consequences for Greeks and Trojans alike:

> Rage—Goddess, sing the rage of Peleus' son Achilles,
> murderous, doomed, that cost the Achaeans countless losses,
> hurling down to the House of Death so many sturdy souls,
> great fighters' souls, but made their bodies carrion,
> feasts for the dogs and birds,
> and the will of Zeus was moving toward its end.

Begin, Muse, when the two first broke and clashed,
Agamemnon lord of men and brilliant Achilles.

What god drove them to fight with such a fury?
Apollo the son of Zeus and Leto. Incensed at the king
he swept a fatal plague through the army—men were dying
and all because Agamemnon spurned Apollo's priest.
Yes, Chryses approached the Achaeans' fast ships
to win his daughter back, bringing a priceless ransom
and bearing high in hand, wound on a golden staff,
the wreaths of the god, the distant deadly Archer.
He begged the whole Achaean army but most of all
the two supreme commanders, Atreus' two sons,
"Agamemnon, Menelaus—all Argives geared for war!
May the gods who hold the halls of Olympus give you
Priam's city to plunder, then safe passage home.
Just set my daughter free, my dear one . . . here,
accept these gifts, this ransom. Honor the god
who strikes from worlds away—the son of Zeus, Apollo!"

And all ranks of Achaeans cried out their assent:
"Respect the priest, accept the shining ransom!"
But it brought no joy to the heart of Agamemnon.
The king dismissed the priest with a brutal order
ringing in his ears: "Never again, old man,
let me catch sight of you by the hollow ships!
Not loitering now, not slinking back tomorrow.
The staff and the wreaths of god will never save you then.
The girl—I won't give up the girl. Long before that,
old age will overtake her in *my* house, in Argos,
far from her fatherland, slaving back and forth
at the loom, forced to share my bed!

Now go,
don't tempt my wrath—and you may depart alive."

The old man was terrified. He obeyed the order,
turning, trailing away in silence down the shore
where the battle lines of breakers crash and drag.
And moving off to a safe distance, over and over
the old priest prayed to the son of sleek-haired Leto,
lord Apollo, "Hear me, Apollo! God of the silver bow
who strides the walls of Chryse and Cilla sacrosanct—
lord in power of Tenedos—Smintheus, god of the plague!
If I ever roofed a shrine to please your heart,
ever burned the long rich bones of bulls and goats
on your holy altar, now, now bring my prayer to pass.
Pay the Danaans back—your arrows for my tears!"

His prayer went up and Phoebus Apollo heard him.
Down he strode from Olympus' peaks, storming at heart
with his bow and hooded quiver slung across his shoulders.
The arrows clanged at his back as the god quaked with rage,
the god himself on the march and down he came like night.
Over against the ships he dropped to a knee, let fly a shaft
and a terrifying clash rang out from the great silver bow.
First he went for the mules and circling dogs but then,
launching a piercing shaft at the men themselves,
he cut them down in droves—
and the corpse-fires burned on, night and day, no end in sight.

I have set out this generous quotation to remind you of
Homer's splendor. If I could, I would now proceed to quote
the whole poem before going further—it is so glorious, the
foundation masterpiece of Western literature—in this immacu-

lately forged new translation by Robert Fagles, which gives us much of Homer's precision, resurrecting the terrible beauty of Greece's Bronze Age in language as swift as Apollo's arrows—note the overwhelming inevitability of the half line "and down he came like night"—yet enclosing a gorgeous strength capable of burnishing each detail to brilliance.

The upshot of Apollo's plague is that all the Greeks come to realize the cause of their misfortune and that the priest's daughter needs to be returned to her father if the plague is to leave them. Their leader Agamemnon, forced to assent to their consensus, takes as his consolation prize Achilles's concubine, thus precipitating Achilles's withdrawal from the war. For most of the poem's twenty-four books Achilles sits in his tent in a rage, deliberating whether to remain on the sidelines or to abandon the Greeks altogether, raise his sails, and push off for home, along with the fellow countrymen who are under his command.

What a strange world this is, so far from our own. The theme of the poem, as Homer tells us in his very first word, is a hero's rage—"wrath" in the older translations—but rage and wrath seem to be everywhere: in Achilles, Agamemnon, Chryses, and Apollo, in every character to whom we are introduced in the course of the first fifty lines. Homer begins with a prayer of invocation—to the Muse of epic poetry—but within a few lines we hear a second prayer: from the priest to his many-named god, the consummately graceful but "deadly Archer" Apollo. And a third god is invoked: Zeus, to whom Achilles and Apollo are both "dear" and who, it is implied, is the hidden force behind the story, somehow pulling the strings of the action, for, as Homer tells us in an arresting phrase, "the will of Zeus was moving toward its end."

Homer has little time for comment on his characters. They

reveal themselves in word and action, not in the poet's commentary. But we feel from the outset that the human characters are caught like strong swimmers in an undertow that is much stronger than their most strenuous strivings, an undertow that will take them where it will, despite their efforts. At the same time, this undertow is not entirely a substance apart: it is rather the sum of all the characters, both gods and men, for both gods and men are driven by their need for honor. Hera and Athena's dishonor at the hands of Aphrodite and Menelaus's subsequent dishonor at the hands of Paris have made the war inevitable; Apollo is dishonored by the dishonor shown his suppliant, Chryses; Agamemnon's need to appear as supreme commander clashes with Achilles's need to be honored as supreme warrior.

Somehow, we feel, these motivations—and others' yet to be revealed—are propelling the action of the poem toward its inevitable conclusion. As the seer Calchas says in his fear of Agamemnon's rage:

> A mighty king,
> raging against an inferior, is too strong.
> Even if he can swallow down his wrath today,
> still he will nurse the burning in his chest
> until, sooner or later, he sends it bursting forth.

That's just the way of mighty kings; there's nothing to be done about it. But it's not as if Agamemnon can in his rage own the field. His rage must contend with the rage and will of others. When he taunts Achilles that he will come personally to take away Achilles's concubine—"so you can learn just how much greater I am than you"—Homer shows us Achilles's heart pounding "in his rugged chest," torn between alternatives:

Should he draw the long sharp sword slung at his hip,
thrust through the ranks and kill Agamemnon now?—
or check his rage and beat his fury down?

Only the intervention of Hera "of the white arms," who "loved both men and cared for both alike," prevents Achilles's wrath from finding its target. She speeds down to earth the battle goddess Athena, who, unseen by all but Achilles, constrains him, seizing his "fiery hair"; and Achilles submits, though, as he says, "his heart breaks with fury," so dearly would he love to see Agamemnon's "black blood gush and spurt around my spear!" But "if a man obeys the gods, they're quick to hear his prayer."

These conflicting forces—all the rages and outrages of gods and men—seemingly balanced in an endless seesaw, will in the end produce a result, the fall of Troy. In the view of the ancients, however, to which Homer is here giving expression, this result is but another swing of the seesaw, which will eventually be balanced in its turn by an opposite result. This view of the ancients, then, is a true worldview, that is, an attempt to see the reality of human experience as a totality, both psychological (in its assessment of human motivations) and theological (in its assumption that heaven intervenes in human affairs). The results of human motivations and heavenly interventions make for preordained results, but preordained only in a way so complicated and with so many conflicting strands that no one but a seer or prophet could sort it all out beforehand and identify in the present the seeds of future results. This means that human beings—and even to some extent the gods themselves—are caught, like figures in a tapestry who cannot undo their thread, playing out their assigned roles of hero or king, loving mother or sexual prize, divine patron of this or that person or city, with

only flickering insight into what result their character and needs
will have upon the whole of the human enterprise.

From time to time, an omen announces a future outcome. Once
the Greek armada had been assembled many years before and while
the Greek forces were offering their sacrifices "under a spreading
plane tree" at Aulis prior to setting sail for Troy, just such an omen
appeared, as Odysseus reminds the troops in their despair:

> "A snake, and his back streaked red with blood,
> a thing of terror! Olympian Zeus himself
> had launched him into the clean light of day . . .
> He slid from under the altar, glided up the tree
> and there the brood of a sparrow, helpless young ones,
> teetered high on the topmost branch-tips, cowering
> under the leaves there, eight they were all told
> and the mother made the ninth, she'd borne them all—
> chirping to break the heart but the snake gulped them down
> and the mother cried out for her babies, fluttering over him . . .
> he coiled, struck, fanging her wing—a high thin shriek!
> But once he'd swallowed down the sparrow with her brood,
> the son of crooked Cronus who sent the serpent forth
> turned him into a sign, a monument clear to see—
> Zeus struck him to stone! And we stood by,
> amazed that such a marvel came to light.
>   So then,
> when those terrible, monstrous omens burst in
> on the victims we were offering to the gods,
> Calchas swiftly revealed the will of Zeus:
> 'Why struck dumb now, my long-haired Achaeans?
> Zeus who rules the world has shown us an awesome sign,
> an event long in the future, late to come to birth
> but the fame of that great work will never die.

As the snake devoured the sparrow with her brood,
eight and the mother made the ninth, she'd borne them all,
so we will fight in Troy that many years and then,
then in the tenth we'll take her broad streets.' "

It may be hard—from the point of view of a twenty-first-century Westerner—to imagine what comfort such an omen could give the Greek troops. Indeed, Homer calls its symbols "terrible, monstrous" and, by his repetition of the phrase "she'd borne them all," hints at his sympathy for the Trojans in their coming demise, as well as for the sparrows "chirping to break the heart." Such omens were of but fitful comfort not only because of their obscurity—as Odysseus says, "Courage, my friends, hold out a little longer. / Till we see if Calchas divined the truth or not"—but because they lack detail. All right, perhaps the Greeks will win, but the omen does not count the cost either to the army or to individuals.

Despite the limited insights that an individual can gain into his (or another's) fate, there is also a way in which the vast interaction of the Trojan War can be plotted with almost mathematical precision, as if it were an extremely complex and elusive algebraic formula in game theory. It is this formula that Homer means to reveal to us, a deliriously elaborate three-dimensional portrayal of human affairs, which can show us just how each rounded figure has played his or her part and how each one's part has interacted with the others' parts to make the story that we have. Homer, therefore, intends to offer us prognostication in reverse, insight after the fact. Eleven centuries after Homer, the Greek Sophist Philostratus will articulate a creed on prognostication that shows us how long the Greeks believed the same thing: "Gods perceive future events, mortals present ones, whereas the wise sense those that are imminent."

Though not all are equally far-seeing, there *is* a pattern to be discerned, and Homer will unveil it for us.

To do this, he relies on a seemingly divine ability—aided, no doubt, by the Muse he regularly invokes—to give us living portraits in a few deft strokes. He must handle three immense casts of characters—the gods, the Greeks, and the Trojans—each replete with quirks and characteristics of its own. Yet he manages to give to each a concrete realm that lends it vivid reality. It is perhaps not so surprising that the self-defeating struggles within the Greek army are given with characterization, force, and familial details (a sense of the place each champion hails from, what kind of people he left behind), details that evoked recognition and emotion from Homer's proudly Greek audiences. Nor do we, so many centuries since anyone prayed to a Greek god, find it so very unlikely that the gods can still thrill us with their size and speed, their combination of divine generosity and supernal fury, their everlasting banquets and their spite. They are, after all, the eternal superheroes of human imagination.

Surely astonishing, though, is the presentation of the Trojans, who, though the sworn enemies of Homer's Greeks, are given full humanity. The legendary *New York Times* war correspondent Chris Hedges has written that war normally creates a cruel dynamic: "We demonize the enemy so that our opponent is no longer human. . . . In most mythic wars this is the case. Each side reduces the other to objects—eventually in the form of corpses." Though no one in history has greater claim to Greek nationality than Homer, nor is there a war more mythic than the Trojan War, amazing Homer never fails to make his Trojans at least as sympathetic as his Greeks. Homer in his generosity toward the Trojan enemy serves as the exception that proves Hedges's rule.

Thus do the unassailable towers and ramparts of "holy Troy"

rise once more for each of Homer's readers, its mighty Scaean Gates, its plain intersected by the flowing Scamander and ending at the Ocean's edge where the thousand hollow ships are beached, its "deep-breasted women" standing on the battlements "trailing their long robes." Even the Trojan fighting style is distinctive, hysterical in comparison with the Greek:

> Now with the squadrons marshalled, captains leading each,
> the Trojans came with cries and the din of war like wildfowl
> when the long hoarse cries of cranes sweep on against the sky
> and the great formations flee from winter's grim ungodly storms,
> flying in force, shrieking south to the Ocean gulfs, speeding
> blood and death to the Pygmy$^{\alpha}$
> warriors, launching at daybreak
> savage battle down upon their heads.
> But Achaea's armies
> came on strong in silence, breathing
> combat-fury,
> hearts ablaze to defend each other to
> the death.

The characters on the Trojan side are distinct and individual. Helen, the cause of the war, has few moments in this drama, but they are unforgettable. We find that she spends her time creating an autobiographical work of art on the implications of her abduction, a sort of "My Life and Times":

> weaving a growing web, a dark red
> folding robe,

α *Pygmy* is a Greek word indicating the length of a man's arm from elbow to knuckles and was used also for a race of midgets of similar length who were thought to live in Ethiopia and to be preyed on by cranes in summer. There is a story that the Pygmies attempted to subdue Hercules, two whole armies of them pinning him down while he slept—an image that Jonathan Swift borrowed for *Gulliver's Travels*. When in the late nineteenth century European explorers discovered a dwarfish people in equatorial Africa (and, later, similarly small peoples in parts of Asia), these were with some reason designated "pygmies," since their discovery seemed to confirm that the Greek legend had some basis in fact.

working into the weft the endless bloody struggles
stallion-breaking Trojans and Argives armed in bronze
had suffered all for her at the god of battle's hands.

Hearing that Paris and Menelaus, "her husband long ago," are
to fight it out in single combat, while the two sides look on,
her heart is filled "with yearning warm and deep/for her husband long ago, her city and her parents." Helen is a sincere
woman, and the robe she works is not a form of egotistical self-
praise but an expression of her condition as a woven figure who
cannot undo her thread, a pawn in the game of gods and men.

"Quickly cloaking herself in shimmering linen," "live tears
welling," Helen rushes to the walls of Troy, where she is observed by "the old men of the realm," whom Homer compares
to grasshoppers or, in Fagles's translation, "cicadas"—

settled on treetops, lifting their voices through the forest,
rising softly, falling, dying away . . . So they waited,
the old chiefs of Troy, as they sat aloft the tower.
And catching sight of Helen moving along the ramparts,
they murmured one to another, gentle, winged words:
"Who on earth could blame them? Ah, no wonder
the men of Troy and Argives under arms have suffered
years of agony all for her, for such a woman."

Thus, as we are at last allowed to glimpse the fabled Helen
through the old men's eyes, does Homer heighten our appreciation of her beauty.

While the old men murmur on, hoping that Helen, despite
her resemblance to "a deathless goddess," will "go home in the
long ships," for she has been "down the years an irresistible sorrow," King Priam receives her with exquisite kindness:

"Come over here, dear child. Sit in front of me,
so you can see your husband of long ago,
your kinsmen and your people.
I don't blame you. I hold the gods to blame. . . .
                                    Here, come closer,
tell me the name of that tremendous fighter."

And Helen speaks, revealing her conflicted state of mind:

"I revere you so, dear father, dread you too—
if only death had pleased me then, grim death,
that day I followed your son to Troy, forsaking
my marriage bed, my kinsmen and my child,
my favorite, now full-grown,
and the lovely comradeship of women my own age.
Death never came, so now I can only waste away in tears.
But about your question—yes, I have the answer.
That man is Atreus' son Agamemnon, lord of empires,
both a mighty king and a strong spearman too,
and he used to be my kinsman, whore that I am!
There was a world . . . or was it all a dream?"

In a later speech, she will ring a change on her self-description—
"bitch that I am"—then once again "whore that I am," a woman
whipped by conscience, if enslaved by passion.

Meanwhile, down on the field of battle, Paris, her abductor,
a sort of matinee idol with little staying power, is about to lose
his life in the hand-to-hand combat with Menelaus, who is by
far the better fighter. But Paris's great patron Aphrodite intervenes, wraps her protégé in "swirls of mist," and snatches him
away, setting him down "in his bedroom filled with scent."
Then the goddess lures Helen to the bed where Paris lies, "glis-

tening in all his beauty." Though Helen at first protests with spirit, she in the end succumbs to the goddess and to Paris's invitation to "lose ourselves in love," while Homer shows us Menelaus stalking "like a wild beast, up and down the lines," trying to discover where Paris has hidden himself.

After nine years of interminable war, both sides are battle-weary. Homer lets us overhear their exhausted attempts to find an ending: the Greeks hold a kind of soldierly town meeting and consider sailing home, their objective unachieved, while not a few Trojans are ready to surrender Helen—only Paris will not have it, and Paris, prince of Troy, can have his way. The hand-to-hand combat between Paris and Menelaus seemed for a moment to portend a solution—whoever won, it was agreed by both sides, would win the woman and end the war—but Paris's magical disappearance means that the wholesale butchery must continue:

At last the armies clashed at one strategic point,
they slammed their shields together, pike scraped pike
with the grappling strength of fighters armed in bronze
and their round shields pounded, boss on wielded boss,
and the sound of struggle roared and rocked the earth.
Screams of men and cries of triumph breaking in one breath,
fighters killing, fighters killed, and the ground streamed blood.

As we come to know more and more of the warriors on each side, their families and rearing, their present fears and future hopes, Homer's unblinking descriptions of battle wear us down and, like the fighters themselves, we begin to dread the coming of day, which can lead only to more gore, as in the sequence in which Greek Diomedes, under the protection of Athena, brings down Trojan Pandarus:

With that he hurled and Athena drove the shaft
and it split the archer's nose between the eyes—
it cracked his glistening teeth, the tough bronze
cut off his tongue at the roots, smashed his jaw
and the point came ripping out beneath his chin.

The *Iliad* contains hundreds of similar descriptions: the body
of a man we have come to know is ripped open, his entrails
spilling out, as he goes down, clawing the dust in "black waves
of pain," "and the dark comes swirling thick across his eyes." But
though Homer may intend these passages to impress on us the
cost of war, he never means merely to disgust. War may be hell,
but it is glorious hell, the height of human suffering, the pith of
human virtue, the acme of human achievement, combining the
ultimate tragedy of death with the lasting grace of the great
deed—the greatest of all deeds, courage in combat. Because of
this, Homer can admire Menelaus "crazed for sweet human
blood," an example of what the dauntless Ajax, second in valor
only to Achilles on the Greek side, calls "the joy of war."

"The skin of the coward changes all the time," avers the
immensely self-possessed Cretan captain Idomeneus, who will
live to return home (and become the subject of Mozart's
pageant-like early opera *Idomeneo*):

"he can't get a grip on himself, he can't sit still,
he squats and rocks, shifting his weight from foot to foot,
his heart racing, pounding inside the fellow's ribs,
his teeth chattering—he dreads some grisly death.
But the skin of the brave soldier never blanches.
He's all control. Tense but no great fear.
The moment he joins his comrades packed in ambush
he prays to wade in carnage, cut-and-thrust at once."

On seeing such a warrior as charging Idomeneus "fierce as fire," comments Homer with admiration,

> Only a veteran steeled at heart could watch that struggle
> and still thrill with joy and never feel the terror.

Or as George C. Scott, in his unforgettable portrayal of the battle-hardened General George S. Patton, admits as he surveys a battlefield littered with the wounded and the dead, "I love it. God help me, I do love it so. I love it more than my life."

ACHILLES MAY BE the incomparable Greek champion, but because he spends most of the poem offstage nursing a grudge in his tent, he is not the ultimate hero of the *Iliad* (which, after all, means a work about Ilium, the ancient name for Troy). That position is reserved for the Trojan champion Hector "breaker of horses," son of King Priam and and Queen Hecuba, Paris's brother, the man who almost singlehandedly animates the Trojan troops with fighting spirit while never doubting that his fate is to die on the plain of Troy, leaving his beloved wife Andromache and their son Astyanax to the mercies of the Greeks. We have no trouble finding Achilles in his massive strength simple and credible, as well as so many of the other heroes that Homer describes for us. But Homer's Hector, though "a stallion full-fed at the manager" and a lion "claw-mad for battle," is a far more complicated cat than any of his principal adversaries, beneath his bellicose facade a man "of gentle temper," as Helen calls him, and, in the end, no match for Achilles.

Like the other heroes, he is wedded to what he calls "the lovely give-and-take of war." But he is also wedded to Andromache in a male-female soul friendship. He takes time out from battle to have what he senses may be his last meeting with "my own dear wife and my baby son." Homer, though he comments little on the action of his characters, allows himself in this meeting a verbal tenderness seldom found in his poem, calling Andromache Hector's "warm, generous wife" and the daughter of a "gallant-hearted" father, naming Astyanax "the darling of [Hector's] eyes and radiant as a star," and showing Hector "the great man of war breaking into a broad smile, his gaze fixed on his son, in silence." The silence is important, for Hector is not an effusive man.

Andromache begs him to withdraw from the battle, for she has already lost her entire family—"the great godlike runner Achilles butchered them all." "You, Hector," she pleads,

"you are my father now, my noble mother,
a brother too, and you are my husband, young and warm and
     strong!
Pity me, please! Take your stand on the rampart here,
before you orphan your son and make your wife a widow."

But Hector cannot remain safe within the unassailable walls of Troy. His reply is considered and sad:

"All this weighs on my mind too, dear woman.
But I would die of shame to face the men of Troy
and the Trojan women trailing their long robes
if I would shrink from battle now, a coward.
Nor does the spirit urge me on that way.
I've learned it all too well. To stand up bravely,
always to fight in the front ranks of Trojan soldiers,
winning my father great glory, glory for myself.
For in my heart and soul I also know this well:
the day will come when sacred Troy must die,

Priam must die and all his people with him,
Priam who hurls the strong ash spear . . .

                                        Even so,
it is less the pain of the Trojans still to come
that weighs me down, not even of Hecuba herself
or King Priam, or the thought that my own brothers
in all their numbers, all their gallant courage,
may tumble in the dust, crushed by enemies—
That is nothing, nothing beside your agony
when some brazen Argive hales you off in tears,
wrenching away your day of light and freedom!
Then far off in the land of Argos you must live,
laboring at a loom, at another woman's beck and call,
fetching water at some spring, Messeis or Hyperia,
resisting it all the way—
the rough yoke of necessity at your neck.
And a man may say, who sees you streaming tears,
'There is the wife of Hector, the bravest fighter
they could field, those stallion-breaking Trojans,
long ago when the men fought for Troy.' So he will say
and the fresh grief will swell your heart once more,
widowed, robbed of the one man strong enough
to fight off your day of slavery."

Then, Homer tells us, Hector "in the same breath" reaches
down for his son, but the child screams out "at the sight of his
own father,"

terrified by the flashing bronze, the horsehair crest,
the great ridge of the helmet nodding, bristling terror—
so it struck his eyes. And his loving father laughed,

and his mother laughed as well, and glorious Hector,
quickly lifting the helmet from his head,
set it down on the ground, fiery in the sunlight,
and raising his son he kissed him, tossed him in his arms,
lifting a prayer to Zeus and the other deathless gods:
"Zeus, all you immortals! Grant this boy, my son,
may be like me, first in glory among the Trojans,
strong and brave like me, and rule all Troy in power
and one day let them say, 'He is a better man than his father!'—
when he comes home from battle bearing the bloody gear
of the mortal enemy he has killed in war—
a joy to his mother's heart."

                                                So Hector prayed
and placed his son in the arms of his loving wife.
Andromache pressed the child to her scented breast,
smiling through her tears. Her husband noticed,
and filled with pity now, Hector stroked her gently,
trying to reassure her, repeating her name: "Andromache,
dear one, why so desperate? Why so much grief for me?
No man will hurl me down to Death, against my fate.
And fate? No one alive has ever escaped it,
neither brave man nor coward, I tell you—
it's born with us the day that we are born."

A few more words, and they are parted—as we know, forever—Hector "aflash in arms," Andromache "weeping live
warm tears," turning to face the separate fates Hector has fore-
seen for them.

    This scene is unique in the *Iliad*, an oasis of familial tender-
ness amid the gore of war. But it is also unique in world
literature, the first time an ancient author (whether Meso-

potamian, Egyptian, Hebrew, or Greek) attempts to portray the unbreakable bond of affection between a married couple, the first time a family is shown as a loving unit.β Andromache is bound to Hector not merely by the dutiful bond one might expect in a time of arranged marriages. There is more than duty here, so much so that it is not too extravagant to call it romantic love, a phenomenon commonly thought to have entered human relationships only with the arrival nineteen centuries later of the Courtly Love tradition.

Similarly, the couple's affectionate laughter at the infant's needless fear and Hector's easy willingness to doff his terrifying helmet to assuage the child suggest that both parents understand that childhood is a time apart, with special claims and needs that adults must bend to—a consciousness usually thought to have found expression no earlier than Rousseau's *Émile*, which would trace its beginnings to the eighteenth century of our era. More striking even than the couple's understanding of childhood is Hector's touching humility in the face of a new generation, expressed in his prayer that his son will prove an even "better man than his father." Not a few fathers, even of supposedly more enlightened societies, have proved incapable of such selflessness.

This singular scene of Hector and his family on the walls of Troy gives us assurance that at least some people were

β There are much earlier examples of love poetry—fragments from Mesopotamia dating to as early as the second millennium B.C. and considerable collections from Egypt of similarly ancient dates—but these are all set not as part of a story but as ritualized dialogues or monologues and are normally put in the mouth(s) of a god and/or goddess. Many may have been intended for use in sacred orgies—in which a king would represent the god, a sacred prostitute the goddess—which were certainly commonplace in Mesopotamia. At any rate, these poems tend to be sexually provocative and there is never any suggestion that the lovers are *married*, in fact quite the opposite. The first (and only) Hebrew example of the genre is the Song of Songs, probably post-Exilic and therefore unlikely to be earlier than the fifth century B.C.

"human" in our way of looking at things—that is, tenderly familial—long, long before scholars have been comfortable
acknowledging.[γ] And it is just this depth of feeling among
these three that renders the events to come so irremediably
tragic.

Achilles continues to brood in his tent even as Hector's forces
push the Greeks back against their ships, almost to the sea, and
proceed to set the ships on fire. In response to the alarming proximity of a final Greek defeat, Achilles allows his inseparable boon
companion, Patroclus, to take the field in his stead, even wearing
Achilles's armor and borne onto the plain in Achilles's chariot,
drawn by his own immortal steeds. Hector kills Patroclus, pro-
voking in Achilles an unquenchable grief
and impelling his return to the field (once
he has been given back his concubine—
untouched, as that desperate "dog-face"
Agamemnon assures him). Achilles, un-
stoppable as a tyrannosaur, rages forth
and—in the saddest scene in all of ancient
literature[δ]—cuts down Hector, whose
soul "wing[s] down to the House of
Death." But Achilles is not done. Shouting "Die, die!" over the dead Trojan
prince, he strips the body of its armor and
invites the other Greeks to dishonor the
corpse,

> all of them gazing wonder-struck
> at the build and marvelous, lithe beauty
>   of Hector.
> And not a man came forward who did
>   not stab his body,

[γ] There are vast literatures
on what scholars conceive
to be the late Western origins of romantic love and
the extremely slow evolu-
tion of the idea of childhood. See, for instance,
Denis de Rougement's *Love
in the Western World* and
Philippe Aries's *Centuries of
Childhood*.

[δ] The death of Hector on
the plain of Troy was considered throughout the classical world to be the acme
of the tragic experience in
literature, and the passage
continued to be held in the
same esteem well into the
medieval period. An Irish
scribe of post-Roman
times, having copied out an
account of a Latin retelling
of Hector's death, wrote a
personal note in the manuscript's margin: "I am
greatly grieved at the
above-mentioned death."

glancing toward a comrade, laughing: "Ah, look here—
how much softer he is to handle now, this Hector,
than when he gutted our ships with roaring fire!"

Though Achilles holds funeral games in honor of Patroclus,
builds a funeral pyre to incinerate his body, and buries the remains in a specially constructed tomb, he can no longer sleep
and spends his days and nights driving around the tomb,
Hector's lashed corpse dragging behind his chariot. At length,
another mourner, Hector's father, Priam, who can bear this dis-
honoring no longer, comes to Achilles by night as a suppliant
and begs the return of his son's body. Priam's inconsolable ancient visage, fouled by days and nights of mourning, and his
desperate courage in crossing the battle lines at last reach
Achilles's spirit and he responds with human sympathy to the
old king's cry:

"Revere the gods, Achilles! Pity me in my own right,
remember your own father! I deserve more pity . . .
I have endured what no one on earth has ever done before—
I put to my lips the hands of the man who killed my son."

Those words stirred within Achilles a deep desire
to grieve for his own father. Taking the old man's hand
he gently moved him back.[e] And over-
    powered by memory
both men gave way to grief. Priam wept
    freely
for man-killing Hector, throbbing,
    crouching
before Achilles' feet as Achilles wept
    himself,

---

e The posture a suppliant had to assume was to kneel before the man to be suppli-cated, one hand on his knee, the other holding his bearded chin. Needless to say, it was difficult to effect this posture if the potential grantor was bent on avoid-ing you; and the posture was in itself the nadir of servility.

now for his father, now for Patroclus once again,
and their sobbing rose and fell throughout the house.

Zeus's detached exclamation a little earlier in the story, after
the death of Patroclus, can serve as epitaph for this scene, too:

"There is nothing alive more agonized than man
of all that breathe and crawl across the earth."

But the last line of Homer's long poem belongs not to a god,
nor to a king, nor to a living champion, but to Hector. His
body, now reclaimed, is burned upon a pyre, his white bones
collected in a golden chest, shrouded "round and round with
soft purple cloths," and buried beneath a barrow of "huge
stones" on the storied, soon to be uninhabited, plain of Troy.

And once they'd heaped the mound
they turned back home to Troy, and gathering once again
they shared a splendid funeral feast in Hector's honor,
held in the house of Priam, king by will of Zeus.

And so the Trojans buried Hector breaker of horses.

IN HOMER'S EPIC every age since his has found relevance
to its own time. For us, Achilles may resemble nothing so
much as a pouting adolescent whose extraordinary physical maturity has far outstripped his judgment. The contemporary military historian Victor Davis Hanson has even compared
Homer's descriptions of his heroes' exploits to rap lyrics that
"glorify rival gangs who shoot and maim each other for prestige, women, booty, and turf." Surely the audiences for both

forms of entertainment have much in common, especially a need to be flattered about their aggressive attitudes. Homer's patrons, after all, were down on their luck and had been for many generations: they were eighth-century aristocrats living in a transitional time—at the end of the Dark Age but revering memories of heroic ancestors who had lived in a better age, the heroic age of Agamemnon, Menelaus, and the other chieftains who had won everlasting glory in legendary battle.

Because Homer's subject is a siege five centuries old, his battlefield is full of military incongruities. He and his audience remembered, for instance, that the chieftains fought in chariots; but because men of the late eighth century had no idea how such warfare might have been conducted, Homer has his charioteers drop the heroes off on the battlefield where they dismount and then fight, often in close formation. The chariots, dimly recalled as essential equipage for aristocratic warfare, have little use in Homer beyond the aura of antiquity they lend to the proceedings. Once the heroes have dismounted, they appear to be much closer in technique and dress to the hoplite infantrymen of Homer's own day, who wore heavy armor— helmet, shield, breastplate, greaves, sword, spear, and other bodily defenses that may have come to seventy pounds—fought in tight formation, and engaged the enemy at close quarters. They did not fling javelins from chariots as their ancestors had once done in a less populous world where warfare more closely resembled a game of chicken or a gang rumble than the massing of two trained armies on a field.

This peculiar combination of the experienced and the imagined distances the action, setting it off from us (and from all its previous audiences) and giving it a slow-motion timelessness that is also part of its universal appeal. We know, for instance, that warriors have never had the opportunity to deliver elegantly wrought speeches to one another before fighting to the death—as happens repeatedly in the *Iliad*. But neither could Shakespeare's Macbeth have taken the time, just before his last duel, to inform his challenger, Macduff, of his assurance by witches that he cannot be slain by "one of woman born," nor could Macduff have taken the time to respond in four carved lines of iambic pentameter that he "was from his mother's womb / Untimely ripp'd." Both Homer and Shakespeare lift their warriors to the level of tableau and urn, where we can see them as their essential selves, caught for all time in characteristic poses.

But we should not let the balletic and the anachronistic elements of Homer's narrative conceal from us his basic realism: here is war as it was fought in Homer's day, not in the time of Agamemnon. In legend, Homer was thought to have been a wandering blind bard (who sees more deeply because of his blindness), but this is almost certainly due to Homer's description of a blind bard who performs in the *Odyssey*, later taken to be a self-description of the poet. Whatever the case, he must have been sighted, at least earlier in life, for there is too much in the *Iliad* of gritty reportage for us to think that the poet never saw battle. It would, in fact, be most unlikely if Homer did not serve as a soldier. The early tragedian Aeschylus fought at Marathon; his younger contemporary Sophocles was a general in the Athenian conquest of Samos; the philosophic gadfly Socrates was lauded for his heroism in three separate battles— Potidaea, Amphipolis, and Delium; the historian Thucydides was the admiral who failed the Athenians at Amphipolis; Xenophon's military history, the *Anabasis*, was an account of his own wartime experience, the March of the Ten Thousand; the orator Demosthenes fought at Chaeronea and then organized Athens's last defenses against Alexander the Great. There is scarcely a Greek figure of any consequence who did not serve in the military as a young man or did not afterwards take a keen interest in warfare. "War," said the early philosopher Heraclitus, "is the father of all, the king of all." And for Plato, greatest of all philosophers, war remains a necessity, "always existing by nature."

As we inspect more closely the battlefield that the poet presents to us, we can discern most of the elements of subsequent Western warfare, all of them innovative departures from the antiquated techniques of the Mycenaean chieftains. Despite the many descriptions of confrontations between two opponents, warfare is largely conducted as an affair of massed charges of armored infantry, moving slowly in their serried ranks, row upon row, attired not in aristocratic capes that sweep dramatically behind them as the wind streams over their dashing chariots but caparisoned like beetles, protected cap-à-pie in heavy bronze, chinking and clunking forward on foot like an unwieldy but inexorable machine:

> tight as a mason packs a good stone wall,
> blocks on granite blocks for a storied house
> that fights the ripping winds—crammed so close
> the crested helmets, the war-shields bulging, jutting,
> buckler-to-buckler, helm-to-helm, man-to-man massed tight
> and the horsehair crests on glittering helmet horns brushed
> as they tossed their heads, the battalions bulked so dense.

Within three centuries, such terrifying displays as this inventive phalanx (a Greek word) will be supplemented by siege engines, counterfortifications, cranes, levers, and artillery, and military organization and division by rank will continue to evolve—but

already in Homer's day warfare had been essentially transformed.

The Greek audience was moved by the personal valor of
Homer's soldiers. The world wept at Hector's bravery, as it
would weep so many centuries later over the words of the
tragic cavalier poet Richard Lovelace when he left Lucasta's
"chaste breast" to fly "to war and arms": "I could not love thee,
dear, so much, / Loved I not honor more." Such heroic senti-
ments must be voiced emphatically, memorably, repeatedly if
the home front is to lend unstinting support to the men dying
in the field. But the historic Greek army can be spotted—amid
all the expressions of heroism—as the brutal innovation it actually was: a mass of men no longer individuals but subject to an
iron discipline, technologically superior to their opponents,
their generals having learned that wars must be managed art-
fully, each battle planned and played out in the mind before the
armies are engaged, and that, insofar as possible, the time, the
place, and the conditions of battle are to be chosen beforehand
to enhance one's own position and put the enemy at a disad-
vantage. From this moment in the late eighth century, the
Western war machine is operational, its objective to field a
force so lethal as to inspire abject terror in all opponents; and
Western soldiers march through history no longer exemplars of
aristocratic valor but as the component parts they actually are.

"Western warfare," writes Hanson, "is terrifying—both relatively and absolutely. The march of European armies has been
both reckless and murderous, ultimately smashing anything that
has raised its head over two millennia of organized military opposition. Other belligerent traditions in China, the Americas,
India, and the Pacific islands also boast a continuous military
culture of great duration. But they cannot claim a practice of

similar effectiveness and flexibility, or a warring capability so accomplished in its devastation, as Alexander's decade-long swath to the Ganges, Caesar's 'pacification' of Gaul, the six-year spoliation of Europe in the Second World War, or the single-day atomization of Hiroshima and Nagasaki attest."

Hanson's interpretations of ancient military history are much in favor among those, such as Dick Cheney, who are influential with George W. Bush. These advisers have signed on to the Greek view of war as "terrible but innate to civilization—and not always unjust or amoral if it is waged for good causes to destroy evil and save the innocent," as Hanson puts it in *An Autumn of War*. Robert D. Kaplan, another contemporary commentator lionized by American militarists, has even urged in *Warrior Politics: Why Leadership Demands a Pagan Ethos* that American foreign policy not allow itself to be constrained by Judeo-Christian morality and that "progress often comes from hurting others." If we are to maintain our global preeminence, we must, in Kaplan's view, return wholeheartedly and unashamedly to our pagan Greek roots.

So much of our current military approach—and often even our vocabulary—can be traced back to the transformations that were taking place on the Greek battlefields of Homer's time in the late eighth and early seventh centuries. Overwhelming military force, for instance, the doctrine put forward most notably in recent years by General Colin Powell at the outset of the First Gulf War, has proven far more decisive in diverse confrontations throughout Western history than the bravery of individual soldiers. Cold calculation and rational planning, not heroic rhetoric or mystical faith, have served as the principal weapons of the Western military machine. Through these means, the conquistadors, for instance, were able to subdue the populations of Mexico and the Caribbean and their haughty but brittle traditions within three decades. Whereas the Spaniards quickly took the measure of Aztec society, its strengths and weaknesses, by a combination of cool observation and inductive logic, the Aztecs, as Hanson puts it, "for weeks after the entry of the Castilians were still baffled as to whether they were up against men or demigods, centaurs or horses, ships or floating mountains, foreign or domestic deities, thunder or guns, emissaries or enemies."

Of course, we occasionally overshoot. From Thermopylae to Little Big Horn to Vietnam, there stand out those historical exceptions that managed, at least for the moment, to overturn the machine of Western military dominance. And it has yet to be seen what the final outcome will be in the unending global "war" against terrorism, a war in which the enemy has no territory to defend and cannot be met on any known battlefield, a war in which all initiative lies with the enemy and every shadow may conceal a hideous surprise. Is it possible that international terrorism in the age of technological globalization represents an innovation for which we have yet to find an adequate military antidote (and is it possible that a *military* antidote is not what is needed)? Or is it more likely that our current arsenal of techniques will suffice to preserve our hegemony? Certainly, it is worth asking if the Western tradition of militarism, which can now boast nearly three millennia of success, is reaching the end of its usefulness, even if any attempt to answer this question definitively would be premature.

Such a question, however distasteful to closed minds, is very Greek in spirit. Thinking the unthinkable, posing the impossible, considering all options: such habits of discourse can flourish only in free discussion among unfettered minds. A component of Greek militarism that we have yet to consider is that it was rooted in nascent notions of citizenship and popular participation. Homer understood that the societies of Agamemnon and Priam were tribal agglomerations, where all decisions of peace and war were made by powerful chieftains who could lead their followers into whatever dangers their whims might prompt them to. Thus are two societies brought to the brink of destruction by what should have been an ephemeral love affair. But Homer also tucked into his narrative examples of freewheeling discussion conducted by the Greek troops on everything from Agamemnon's personal limitations to alternative tactics for tomorrow's clashes. These level-headed, wide-ranging, open-ended discussions belong to the military culture of Homer's day and later, not to twelfth-century Mycenae, and they seem in their specificity to spring from Homer's own experience of a sort of campground town hall in which Greek troops took an intense interest in the enterprise they were engaged in and made lively contributions to the logistics of battle. It was the general invitation to discuss strategy beforehand—*strategy* being another Greek word, formed from *stratos*, Greek for "army," *stratēgos* for "general"—coupled with a commitment to subsequent group discipline, that helped create the unrivaled killing machine of Greek warfare.

One may well wish to ask how such a combination arose that came to affect the whole of subsequent history in the West and in the world. In the past, a great many commentators, whether classicists, politicians, or common readers, were tempted to put a racist spin on this business: we in the West are mentally and spiritually superior to other civilizations; this is why we have conquered. But the pendulum of popular conviction may now have swung the other way; and meditation on the twentieth century, steeped in blood that must, at least in part, be attributed to the Western war machine, has encouraged commentators to a kind of reverse racism: the West is now commonly seen as more savage than other supposedly more pacific, more noble cultures. Both approaches are flawed and fantastic because neither is supported by evidence. In point of fact, the Persians and other peoples conquered by the Greeks would dearly have loved to be the conquerors and would have spared no effort, however bloody, to become so. Such combativeness has been the norm for virtually all those vanquished in the wars of the West, so there is little point to be made in touting the moral superiority of the losers.

Nor can we legitimately trace some single simple element—say, the way microbes worked in our favor or our strategic geographical position—as giving the West its superiority. Hanson takes to task the popular biohistorian Jared Diamond (*Guns, Germs, and Steel*) on just this point: "The efforts of those who seek to reduce history to biology and geography deprecate the power and mystery of culture, and so often turn desperate. . . . Land, climate, weather, natural resources, fate, luck, a few rare individuals of brilliance, natural disaster, and more—all these play their role in the formation of a distinct culture, but *it is impossible to determine exactly whether man, nature, or chance is the initial catalyst for the origins of Western civilization* [emphasis mine]."

To inquire into the ways in which an unpredictable historical combination—in this case, the combination of dogged military practicality with unprecedented citizen responsibility—may generate a new cultural force that has tremendous impact on the world over many centuries brings us as close as we are likely to come to the deep mysteries of the historical process. It may be best simply to acknowledge the success of this virtually unbeatable combination and to say, with Dr. Seuss, that it just "happened to happen."

II
THE
WANDERER

HOW TO FEEL

It is Odysseus, hero of the Odyssey, who dreams up the way to end the Trojan War in Greece's favor—by sending the Greek fleet from the shore as if it had sailed for home and leaving on the now-empty battlefield outside Troy's unassailable walls the parting "gift" of an immense Wooden Horse. Once it is within the gates, the horse proves to be hollow and lined with warriors, who descend in the night, open the gates to their concealed fellows, destroy the city, and take the women captive. Astyanax, the infant son of Hector and Andromache, is hurled from the walls, and the Greeks, outrageous in victory, commit many atrocities. By this time, many famous warriors on the Greek side have fallen in battle. Achilles has fallen to Paris, of all people, who (it would be claimed in later times) shot an arrow into Achilles's heel, his only patch of physical vulnerability. Paris himself has also fallen; and Helen, who had been given to one of his brothers, is returned at last to Menelaus.

The war done, it takes Odysseus ten years of wandering to return home because he has become the enemy of the sea god Poseidon, who keeps him from reaching his destination. One of his many fabulous adventures is a visit to Hades, the Greek underworld (named for its ruler, who is also called Pluto), in order to consult the famous seer Teiresias. There the souls of the dead lead a vague, insubstantial existence, and there Odysseus meets many of those he knew in life. As Odysseus relates it:

"But now there came the ghosts of Peleus' son Achilles,
Patroclus, fearless Antilochus—and Great Ajax too,
the first in stature, first in build and bearing

of all the Argives after Peleus' matchless son.
The ghost of the splendid runner knew me at once
and hailed me with a flight of mournful questions:
'Royal son of Laertes, Odysseus, man of tactics,
reckless friend, what next?
What greater feat can that cunning head contrive?
What daring brought you down to the House of Death?—
where the senseless, burnt-out wraiths of mortals make their home.'

    The voice of his spirit paused, and I was quick to answer:
'Achilles, son of Peleus, greatest of the Achaeans,
I had to consult Teiresias, driven here by hopes
he would help me journey home to rocky Ithaca.
Never yet have I neared Achaea, never once
set foot on native ground . . .
my life is endless trouble.
                   But you, Achilles,
there's not a man in the world more blest than you—
there never has been, never will be one.
Time was, when you were alive, we Argives
honored you as a god, and now down here, I see,
you lord it over the dead in all your power.
So grieve no more at dying, great Achilles.'

    I reassured the ghost, but he broke out protesting,
'No winning words about death to me, shining Odysseus!
By god, I'd rather slave on earth for another man—
some dirt-poor tenant farmer who scrapes to keep alive—
than rule down here over all the breathless dead.' "

W E TEND TO associate the freewheeling public discussion of the Greeks with their institution of democracy. But the soldierly town meetings of the *Iliad* preceded democracy by two centuries. The political innovation the Greeks called "democracy" began to take shape only in the last decade of the sixth century in one particular city, Athens. Homer, however, gives ample evidence that, long before, Greeks in general were comfortable with a freedom of discussion unknown in other nations. But this freedom progressed virtually in tandem with another innovation of the late eighth century, the alphabet, which in its turn triggered the possibility of widespread literacy.

Early writing systems—in Mesopotamia, Egypt, China, and later in Mesoamerica—were pictographic at the outset, employing a picture per word or, in some cases, combining two or more pictures to represent more complex words. These symbols were not related to a particular language and its sounds but might be usable by another language, just as today's universal road and toilet signs may be comprehensible whether one speaks English, Arabic, or Korean. This was true, also, of the earliest symbols employed in the systems we call Linear A and Linear B.

But though pictographs may be drafted to represent nouns and fairly low numerals (and were therefore admirably suited to the work of ancient accountants, who could confine themselves to counting the number of chariots and javelins in the armory and the number of horses in the stables), they are less serviceable in representing the multiple forms of a verb and begin to disintegrate altogether under the weight of such linguistic complications as subordinate clauses. So these ancient systems soon added other, more arbitrary signs to represent more accurately the actual labyrinth of language, eventually introducing even symbols that represented some of the syllabic sounds of a specific language. The final network of symbols was a combination of pictographs, considerably stylized and simplified by generations of scribes, and other complicated signs and syllabaries. These hundreds, sometimes thousands, of separate symbols could be mastered only by those who had years to devote to the study. Such cumbersome writing systems became the fuel on which their civilizations ran—the oil of the ancient world. If you participated in ownership, you had it made in the shade. Otherwise, according to Claude Lévi-Strauss, the main function of such systems was "to facilitate the enslavement of other human beings"—literacy as oppression.

Though we don't know who thought of it, we know where the *idea* of an alphabet came from: the Levant, that small corridor of coast running from Syria to the Sinai and encompassing Lebanon and Israel-Palestine. The first alphabet was, in the main, a borrowing from the underutilized syllabaries hidden away in the vast network of Egyptian hieroglyphs. Like most inventions, this one probably evolved in several stages and was helped along by more than one inventor. But by the middle of the second millennium B.C., we find a language being written on stones in the Sinai that is neither pictographic nor strictly syllabic, the alphabetic precursor of written Phoenician-Canaanite-Hebrew. This primitive alphabet came to the Greeks probably by way of Phoenician merchants, whose welcome ships, loaded with metals and such exotic materials as the precious red-purple cloth of Phoenicia, plied the whole of the Mediterranean littoral.

The Greeks added vowels to the Semitic consonants and set this list of pronunciation symbols in an unvarying order, giving us the alphabet (*alpha* and *beta* being the first two letters), on which the Romans would subsequently make their own revision—and so bestow on us the very symbols in which the book you hold in your hands was printed. For a long time the Semitic (or, as we would now call it, Hebrew) alphabet and the Greek were written sometimes left to right, other times right to left, oftentimes in a column, circle, or spiral, or as boustrophedon—that is, "turning like an ox plowing a field" in lines alternating right-to-left and left-to-right. It took a long time before the levels of uniformity that we are used to were introduced and became at last unvarying. For all this, it remains true that the Levantine Semites are the inventors of the world's only alphabet, an alphabet improved by the Greeks and then with only slight variations imposed (very nearly) worldwide by Roman centurions and their successors.^α

Almost as interesting as the invention itself are the uses to which the Greeks swiftly put their writing. If the pictographic systems, in their early incarnations, served simply as accountants' tools

α The oldest examples of an alphabet-in-the-making were found in the Sinai at Serabit el-Khadim, a honeycomb of ancient copper and turquoise mines, once worked by Semitic slaves and their Egyptian overseers. Though there is no reason to suppose that the idea of the alphabet first arose at this particular site (just that it offers our oldest extant evidence), there is good reason to think that the Sinai lies on the route of cultural transmission that takes us from Egyptian hieroglyphs to the fully articulated Semitic alphabet. Is it only coincidence that Moses, the greatest of all Hebrew figures and the one to whom the earliest Hebrew writings are credited, was known to have had an upper-class Egyptian education (and therefore to have been literate in hieroglyphs) and to have led Semitic slaves through the Sinai sometime toward the middle of the second millennium? Is it possible that the legend of Moses's authorship of the ancient Torah possesses a kernel of historical truth—that he invented alphabetic writing or, more likely, that he found the first truly literary use for this invention by committing the Commandments of the Hebrew god to stone tablets?

and if the Semitic consonant alphabets were, to begin with, employed to similar purposes—or, in the Sinai, used perhaps to record short prayers—the Greek alphabet, from the first, takes off in a delightfully unserious direction. The earliest inscription we have is scratched on an Athenian wine jug of Homer's time, proclaiming playfully that

> The dancer of consummate grace
> will take this vase as his prize.

Not a glint of the green eyeshade of the accountant or a hint of the furrowed brow of the believer. And even when a god is mentioned, as in the three lines of verse inscribed on a drinking cup almost as old as the Athenian jug, found in the Bay of Naples at Ischia, the oldest of Greece's many colonies, we could hardly ascribe high seriousness to the poet:

> Who am I? None other than the luscious
> drinking cup of Nestor. Drink me quickly—
> and be seized in lust by golden Aphrodite.

Unlike earlier writing systems, forged to count wealth, to ensure control, to invoke the patronage of a deity, the ancient Greek alphabet announces a civilization of leisure. To hell with your ponderous obsessions; let's have some wine, women, and song.

It has long been understood that a fully articulated alphabet served as the medium for the gradual democratizing of the ancient societies in which it was introduced and took hold. The desert amphictyony of the Israelites—memorialized in the Torah's scenes of Moses in earnest conversation with his people—is the earliest indication in mankind's historical record of a tribal assembly that welcomed debate. If it seems far from modern democracy, it possessed nonetheless many democratic features we might still long to emulate: spontaneity, face-to-face questioning and counter-questioning, the possibility that even the least participant might have a contribution to make, even to the point of taking seriously what might emerge from "the mouths of infants and sucklings."

A writing system of some twenty-odd characters meant that anyone might learn to read, even a child, a woman, or a slave. What empowerment this implied!—especially when considered against earlier systems. But the Hebrew alphabet, because of its lack of vowels, still retained a certain mystery, a soupçon at least of the mumbo-jumbo that had been the stock-in-trade of the scribes and *seigneurs* of Egypt and Mesopotamia. One needed to know Hebrew well in order to read it confidently. If Hebrew was not your mother tongue, you would always be guessing which vowel sounds to supply between the consonants. But written Greek, because of the addition of vowels, required no subjective judgment or interpretation. It was completely objective, completely *out there*, completely distinct from the reader. Just as the simplicity of alphabetical writing made possible general access to literacy, which in its turn encouraged democratic give-and-take, the utter objectivity of the Greek alphabet encouraged the demystification of the world.

One of the most certain byproducts of demystification is irreverence, which made its first recorded appearance in this world of ours on the rim of the Ischian drinking cup of 700 B.C. (or thereabouts), recommending to its imbiber lascivious inebriation under the tutelage of laughing Aphrodite—or, more simply, how about a little fun, huh? Of the many prehistoric influences on the shaping of Greek culture, none is more catalytic than the Semitic, giving Greece its alphabet and, perhaps simultaneously, its appreciation of the liberating value of public discussion. But the Greeks took these extraordinary gifts as if they were nature's own bounty and, marinating them in characteristically Aegean seasonings and omitting the lard of Semitic seriousness, prepared a dish that was both lighter and more piquant than what they had been offered.

Many cultural commentators have theorized that oral society—that is, society in which writing is unknown—is far more communal and visionary than society in which human thought is objectified by writing and that written language encourages the reader in his separateness to individualism (uncommunity) and by its sequential format to sequential, rational analysis (unvision). Though there is probably much truth in such theories, it may also be true that the *type* of literacy a given society enshrines may work greater wonders than the *fact* of literacy itself. A type of literacy that can be grasped easily by almost anyone will tend to spread some kind of proto-democratic consciousness far and wide, even if this is accomplished only in small steps over a very long period of time. (In contrast, if our laws had been written in cuneiform instead of the alphabet, isn't it almost inevitable that slavery would still be legal?) A type of literacy that demystifies the act of reading, erasing for all time the aura of an unapproachable Sacred Brotherhood of scribes, wisemen, and potentates, will by its very nature tend to demystify additional realms of human experience.

AMONG SCHOLARS it is an open question whether Homer was literate or not. But the best evidence—that is, the texts themselves—leads us to posit that the *Iliad* and the *Odyssey* are hybrids: literate works that are profoundly influenced by many previous generations of oral transmission. Let us suppose that both works began as stories of real people at the end of the Mycenaean Age. These stories—of Achilles and the Trojan War, of the Greek captain Odysseus's almost superhuman attempts to return to his island home of Ithaca after the war was over—were told and retold, molded and remolded, over many generations by wandering bards till one of them, a man known to us by his name but by no other solid biographical facts, gave them at last a highly selective and definitive treatment in two epic renderings in the very period that alphabetical writing was spreading across the Greek world.

Did he write his renderings down? To my eye and ear, the Homeric epics could never have been expressed with Homer's beautifully concealed artfulness had they been committed only to memory. Peoples of oral cultures are famous for prodigious feats of memory, feats impossible to the literate, but they do not produce artifacts of such elegant refinement as the *Iliad* and the *Odyssey*, stories so leanly structured that nothing is repeated without purpose, few strings remain untied, and so much is left unsaid—left, in other words, to reverberate and extend itself in the imaginations of individual members of the audience. From a vast epic cycle of oral stories (most of them now forgotten or known to us only in later summaries), Homer made severe choices, leaving out most of the stories (or leaving them *in* only by delicate allusion), giving us in the *Iliad* but a few crucial weeks in a ten-year war and setting these entirely—with almost claustrophobic intensity—on the Trojan coast. The *Odyssey* gives us—by cinematic flashbacks—ten years of Odysseus's adventures but narrates directly just the small number of days that lead to the hero's return to Ithaca and the revenge he takes there.

These are works that one artist had the leisure to write and rewrite, to double back over, to shorten and extend as he saw fit. Though he relied on the long tradition of oral conventions that the illiterate bards had employed—especially their use of metrical tag lines ("godlike Achilles," "the Achaeans' fast ships," the "deep-breasted women" of Troy)—he made something essentially new, two epics, each divided into twenty-four books, each book designated by one of the twenty-four letters of the Greek alphabet, starting with Alpha and ending with Omega. No one can now affirm absolutely that Homer himself, whose very existence we are reduced to speculating about, made the twenty-four divisions. But these episodes are the work of a skilled artist, each with its own internal unity—a beginning, a middle, an end—and an organic relationship to the greater whole of the poem of which it is part. Was Homer literate? I would bet on it.

A few decades ago it was fashionable to assert that these poems were merely collections of oral folktales, stitched together by performing rhapsodes (literally "stitchers of song"), that they did not have a common author, and that "Homer" was simply a convenient designation of the ancient world. Now the tide has turned; a slight majority of contemporary scholars tends toward the likelihood of one author who, if not literate, at least dictated his poetry to others. Only a few tin-eared commentators continue to insist that the poems are oral compilations; those who still insist on two Homers point to differences in the language in the two poems, to differences in outlook between them, and to an undeniable falling off in the power of the poetry at the end of the *Odyssey*, which almost all would acknowledge to be a later composition than the *Iliad*. But the theory that best answers these objections is that the *Iliad* is a young man's poem, that Homer's worldview underwent transition and even transformation as he aged, and that he may have died before he could quite finish the second poem, which was then finished off by a disciple.

For all that the *Iliad* has enjoyed primacy through most of literary history—and was certainly held by the Greeks (and all subsequent warrior societies almost up to our own day) to be the greater of Homer's two works—it offers us the conventional wisdom of the ancient world: in this fated universe, ruled by passions human and divine, violence is inevitable, whether the violence of the gods or the violence of man against woman or of man against man. "It is a law established for all time among all men," Xenophon would write, echoing much of the *Iliad*'s wisdom, "that when a city is taken in war, the persons and the property of its inhabitants belong to the captors." No Geneva conventions to be observed here, as we look forward to Andromache's life of concubinage and endless servitude; and much of the *Iliad* conforms to this dreary fatefulness about human prospects. Someone, alas, will always be angry and violent, if not Agamemnon, Achilles, if not Hera, Zeus. The great gods of the Greeks are neither the Titans nor the Olympians but Might and Luck; and war is the relentless engine of Homer's *Iliad*.

And yet, even in the *Iliad*, Ares, the god of war, is the most hated of all the gods. When Thetis gives her son Achilles new heavenly armor made for him by the crippled smith god Hephaestus,^β Homer devotes more than a hundred lines to a

β Hephaestus the Cripple—in one of the great fakeouts of Greek myth—is married to (surprise!) Aphrodite. When she and Ares bed down together, artful Hephaestus exposes their adultery by a cunning ruse that holds them up (literally) to public ridicule by the other gods. A "gossamer-fine" net wrought by Hephaestus scoops up the lovers in flagrante delicto, as Hephaestus calls the other gods to witness the humiliation of the lovers, naked and writhing for all to see. "A bad day for adultery!" quip the laughing gods. The story is recounted in Book 8 of the *Odyssey* by the bard Demodocus as "The Love of Ares and Aphrodite Crowned with Flowers."

description of the great shield whereon Hephaestus forges "two noble cities filled/with mortal men." One city is at war, surrounded by "Strife and Havoc . . . and violent Death"; the other, filled with "weddings and wedding feasts" and courts that dispense only justice, is not merely a city at peace but the City of Peace, surrounded by "broad rich plowland" and harvesters reaping ripe grain. There is a vineyard "loaded with clusters":

And there among them a young boy plucked his lyre,
so clear it could break the heart with longing . . .
And the crippled Smith brought all his art to bear
on a dancing circle, broad as the circle Daedalus
once laid out on Cnossos' spacious fields
for Ariadne the girl with lustrous hair.
Here young boys and girls, beauties courted
with costly gifts of oxen, danced and danced,
linking their arms and gripping each other's wrists.
And the girls wore robes of linen light and flowing,
the boys wore finespun tunics rubbed with a gloss of oil,
the girls were crowned with a bloom of fresh garlands,
the boys swung golden daggers hung on silver belts.
And now they would run in rings on their skilled feet,
nimbly, quick as a crouching potter spins his wheel,
palming it smoothly, giving it practice twirls
to see it run, and now they would run in rows,
in rows crisscrossing rows—rapturous dancing.
A breathless crowd stood round them struck with joy
and through them a pair of tumblers dashed and sprang,
whirling in leaping handsprings, leading on the dance.

Peace may be only an impossible ideal in the *Iliad*, but we cannot doubt which city Homer would prefer. He loved and longed for the leisure and playfulness that peace makes possible. He stood with the historian Herodotus, who would one day write: "No one is so foolish as to prefer war to peace: in peace children bury their fathers, while in war fathers bury their children."

THE GLORIES OF WAR have faded considerably by the time Odysseus, the hero of the *Odyssey*, tries to make his way home from Troy. The hero of Homer's second poem is no shining demigod but a man using all his wiles and wits to get himself out of one fix after another. Odysseus is *polytropos* (a man of twists and turns), *polymetis* (versatile), *polytlas* (long-enduring), and *polymechanos* (a great tactician)—all those *poly*s (meaning "very," "much," or "many") crediting him as the pinnacle of canny resourcefulness. He doesn't so much attack his enemies head-on with brute strength as find a clever way around the many monsters he encounters. Whether he faces the land of the Lotus-eaters (whose drug makes men forget their homes), the hideous giants called cyclopes, Aeolus king of the winds, the cannibal Laestrygonians, the witch Circe, the Sirens whose enchantments lure all sailors to their deaths, or the impossibility of steering a safe course between the jagged rock of Scylla and the gigantic whirlpool of Charybdis,^γ he defeats all challenges with cunning, occasionally with the bold lies that human speech makes possible. He manages to survive even a visit to Hades, the Greek

γ "Between Scylla and Charybdis" is one of the most useful metaphors of world literature. The monstrous alternatives were real enough to ancient sailors who, navigating the narrow Straits of Messina between Italy and Sicily, often came to grief. Scylla was imagined to be a monster with six heads, each bristling with six rows of sharp teeth, who sat on her perilous rock. Charybdis, who lived under an immense fig tree, swallowed the waters of the sea three times each day, throwing them up again from her great throat.

underworld. In the ancient world, Odysseus the dissembler was thought contemptible, a second-rate hero when placed against the noble Achilles. To the modern reader, Odysseus is a far greater hero than a petulant boy who leaves the playground with his toys.

The character of Odysseus is so subtle that this second work of Homer could not be understood much before the modern period. Only in the early eighteenth century did the distinguished Cambridge classicist Richard Bentley, naming the poems by their Greek titles, begin the process of redeeming Odysseus's story from the reproaches leveled against it: "Take my word for it, poor Homer . . . wrote a sequel of songs, to be sung by himself for small earnings and good cheer, at festivals and other days of merriment; the *Ilias* he made for the men, and the *Odysseis* for the other sex." Though Bentley was quite right about the circumstances of performance in Homer's day, he was probably a little off about the audience for the *Odyssey*, which was almost certainly performed for both sexes. Still, there is a delicious bit of truth in his remarks, for in the *Odyssey* Homer found the subject of his old age, female sensibility—not an outright rejection but certainly an epic-long negation of the strutting male militarism of the *Iliad*.

In the *Iliad*, the worst opprobrium that one hero can hurl at another is to call him "a woman." In the *Odyssey*, Odysseus and his men are overcome repeatedly by "tides of sorrow" as they recall their lost homes, "consumed with grief and weeping live warm tears"—just the words Homer used in the *Iliad* to describe Andromache on the verge of losing her man. Yes, in the *Iliad* Achilles and Priam weep together once—at the climax of the poem—but the *Odyssey* contains an inexhaustible torrent of tears. Odysseus, stranded on Calypso's island, weeps for his lost home. He weeps again at the performance of a harping bard who sings a song entitled "The Strife Between Odysseus and Achilles," an allusion to a piece of the prehistoric epic cycle otherwise unknown to us:

> but Odysseus, clutching his flaring sea-blue cape
> in both powerful hands, drew it over his head
> and buried his handsome face,
> ashamed his hosts might see him shedding tears.

But later, when the same bard, blind Demodocus, "the faithful bard the Muse adored above all others"—no wonder the self-praising Greeks thought Homer was here referring to himself—sings the story of the Greeks' treacherous Wooden Horse that brought Troy down, Odysseus comes apart, no longer shielding his sorrow from public view:

> but great Odysseus melted into tears,
> running down from his eyes to wet his cheeks . . .
> as a woman weeps, her arms flung round her darling husband,
> a man who fell in battle, fighting for town and townsmen,
> trying to beat the day of doom from home and children.
> Seeing the man go down, dying, gasping for breath,
> she clings for dear life, screams and shrills—
> but the victors, just behind her,
> digging spear-butts into her back and shoulders,
> drag her off in bondage, yoked to hard labor, pain,
> and the most heartbreaking torment wastes her cheeks.
> So from Odysseus' eyes ran tears of heartbreak now.

In his sympathetic response, Odysseus has surpassed even Hector, the most humane male figure of the *Iliad*. The unthinkable has come to pass: Odysseus has become Andromache.

When, in Book 16 of the poem, Odysseus and his son, Telemachus, recognize each other at last, their mutual tears know no limits:

> "No, I am not a god,"
> the long-enduring, great Odysseus returned.
> "Why confuse me with one who never dies?
> No, I am your father—the Odysseus you wept for all your days,
> you bore a world of pain, the cruel abuse of men."
>
> And with those words Odysseus kissed his son
> and the tears streamed down his cheeks and wet the ground,
> though before he'd always reined his emotions back. . . .
> Odysseus sat down again, and Telemachus threw his arms
> around his great father, sobbing uncontrollably
> as the deep desire for tears welled up in both.
> They cried out, shrilling cries, pulsing sharper
> than birds of prey—eagles, vultures with hooked claws—
> when farmers plunder their nest of young too young to fly.
> Both men so filled with compassion, eyes streaming tears,
> that now the sunlight would have set upon their cries
> if Telemachus had not asked his father, all at once,
> "What sort of ship, dear father, brought you here?—
> Ithaca, at last."

Likewise in the eighteenth century, the first century capable, I believe, of appreciating what Homer was up to in the *Odyssey*, the percipient Samuel Johnson remarked, "To be happy at home is the ultimate result of all ambition, the end to which every enterprise and labour tends, and of which every desire prompts the prosecution." Such a sentiment was seldom, if ever, expressed with such conviction by any commentator before the eighteenth century, except the mysteriously godlike Homer, so refreshingly unpartisan, so unideological, and so confoundingly secular in his old age. Johnson's "end" is not anyone's end in the *Iliad*, but it is Odysseus's homely purpose, which would only have earned him the contempt of Achilles and the whole procession of heroes. All Odysseus wants to do is make it back to his wife, son, and home. Another towering figure of the English eighteenth century, Jonathan Swift, himself a clergyman, ridiculed the hair-splitting theological divisions of Christianity that had led to the bloody wars of religion in the previous century. So much needless bloodshed over such paltry prizes had at last alerted the most penetrating observers to the smothering dreariness, the insurmountable fecklessness of war.

In the nineteenth century, as passionate theological commitments began to ebb in Europe, Odysseus really began to come into his own as a figure of further poetic inspiration. Alfred Tennyson in "Ulysses" (the Latin form of Odysseus's name) saw him in his never-say-die posture as the quintessential modern hero ("To strive, to seek, to find, and not to yield") for whom experience itself is the ultimate object:

> 'Tis not too late to seek a newer world.
> Push off, and sitting well in order smite
> The sounding furrows, for my purpose holds
> To sail beyond the sunset, and the baths
> Of all the western stars, until I die.
> It may be that the gulfs will wash us down;
> It may be we shall touch the Happy Isles,
> And see the great Achilles, whom we knew.

Ignoring Homer's longing to end with the hero at rest at home, the far more upbeat Tennyson sends him off adventuring again;

and for Tennyson, as for Greeks many centuries after Homer, the shadowy realms of Hades have been transformed into the Happy Isles—the Elysian Fields of later Greek mythology, where the great and the good are spared the dark near nonexistence of Hades.

In the twentieth century, Constantine Cavafy, a native of Alexandria who wrote in modern Greek, saw the *Odyssey* as a metaphor for the journey of life, the end of the journey being not nearly as important as the journey itself. In his much-quoted poem "Ithaca," he advises the reader:

> Hope the way is long.
> May there be many summer mornings when,
> with what pleasure, with what joy,
> you shall enter first-seen harbors . . .
> Keep Ithaca always in your mind.
> Arriving there is what has been ordained for you.
> But do not hurry the journey at all.
> Better if it lasts many years;
> and you dock an old man on the island,
> rich with all that you've gained on the way,
> not expecting Ithaca to give you wealth.
>
> Ithaca gave you the beautiful journey.
> Without her you would not have set out.
> She has nothing more to give you.

For James Joyce, Odysseus served as the archetype around which he built the character of Leopold Bloom, Dublin's "wandering Jew" in *Ulysses*, the twentieth century's most characteristic masterpiece. Bloom, the perpetual outsider, must best the many monsters of modern life, using only his wits. His adventures, which take place not over the course of ten years but within the compass of one day, are the ordinary adventures of an ordinary life and have mythological reverberations in the mind of Bloom, who experiences them. His "journey to Hades," for instance, paralleling that of Homer's original, holds none of the outsized epic terrors that faced Odysseus but is only a visit to a Dublin cemetery, prompting Bloom to reflect on the various, once prominent Dubliners buried there—Joyce's equivalents of Homer's legendary heroes—and to think (in the haphazard, pedestrian way human beings actually think about such things) about the mystery of death: "Plenty to see and hear and feel yet. Feel live warm beings near you. Let them sleep in their maggoty beds. They are not going to get me this innings." Circe's cave in Homer becomes Bella Cohen's whorehouse in Joyce. The faithful Penelope becomes the more realistic Molly—Bloom's "home" and the object of all his striving—dreamy and unfaithful, if faithful in her fashion.

Each of these interpretations can find some justification in Homer. Odysseus, who asks to be strapped to the mast so that he can hear the irresistible song of the Sirens as his ship passes their island, does not let his ears be stopped with wax, as do his crew. Though he knows he cannot allow himself to be drawn by the song, he knows, unlike his men, that he must allow himself to *hear* it. The premium Homer's Odysseus thus places on experience is used to appropriate effect by Tennyson and Cavafy—even if each poet knowingly contradicts a central Homeric theme, Tennyson by suggesting that his hero became bored after he got home and yearned for further adventures, Cavafy by giving all material value to the adventures and none but formal value to the homecoming. Joyce's insight is deeper, appreciative of the unexpectedly, even shockingly antiheroic nature of Homer's second text and its status as the world's first comic novel—and first romantic comedy—albeit a comedy that dramatizes "a world of pain."

Surely no modern author has reconfigured the adventure of Odysseus/Ulysses more appositely than did W. H. Auden in "The Wanderer," which is a short summation in a modern idiom of much of the emotional content of Homer's second poem:

Doom is dark and deeper than any sea-dingle.
Upon what man it fall
In spring, day-wishing flowers appearing,
Avalanche sliding, white snow from rock-face,
That he should leave his house,
No cloud-soft hand can hold him, restraint by women;
But ever that man goes
Through place-keepers, through forest trees,
A stranger to strangers over undried sea,
Houses for fishes, suffocating water,
Or lonely on fell as chat,
By pot-holed becks
A bird stone-haunting, an unquiet bird.

There head falls forward, fatigued at evening,
And dreams of home,
Waving from window, spread of welcome,
Kissing of wife under single sheet;
But waking sees
Bird-flocks nameless to him, through doorway voices
Of new men making another love.

Save him from hostile capture,
From sudden tiger's leap at corner;
Protect his house,

His anxious house where days are counted
From thunderbolt protect,
From gradual ruin spreading like a stain;
Converting number from vague to certain,
Bring joy, bring day of his returning,
Lucky with day approaching, with leaning dawn.

Odysseus makes it home in the end, is reunited with his son, clears his home of interlopers,[δ] and once more sleeps with his faithful wife Penelope in the great rooted bed. ("Warm beds," muses Leopold Bloom, "warm fullblooded life.")

Penelope is herself a fascinating character, utterly different from all the Homeric prima donnas and self-dramatizing primo divos we have been in the presence of up to now. Though he scarcely awards her an aria of her own, Homer constantly shifts his description of her, as if to underscore her many facets. She is "reserved," "discreet," "cautious," "wary," "poised," "alert," "guarded," "composed," "well aware," "self-possessed," "warm, generous," of "great wisdom," "the soul of loyalty." She, too, weeps in private, draws a veil across her face in public. She is the female equivalent of her husband, secretly strategic, full of wiles, keeping the overbearing suitors at bay for years with one deception after another. Odysseus, who in his years of travel has lived with the nymph Calypso and slept with the enchantress Circe—and would hardly have been expected to do otherwise by Homer, Penelope, or anyone else—remains in

δ The interlopers are the suitors of Penelope, who wants none of them but cannot drive them out, despite the fact that they are depleting her resources. Odysseus kills them all (in concert with his son Telemachus) in what can only be called a comic, even a ghoulishly humorous, episode. Such rough comedy, not quite to our taste, is nonetheless not far from the comic violence of Saturday morning cartoons and movies made for teenage boys. It may be violence, but it's zany violence, full of physical unlikelihoods and impossibilities, alerting us to the fact that we are not to take it too seriously, just enjoy the revenge to our hearts' content.

Penelope's eyes "always the most understanding man alive." *Her* most important virtue, more important even than her considerable discernment and fortitude, is her faithfulness.

Unsure if it is at long last her husband who stands before her, she tests him, asking her maid to move their bed, a bed no one has ever seen but the woman who sleeps in it, her loyal maid-servants, and her husband, who carved its posts out of a branching olive tree rooted in the midst of their house. The bed is unmovable; and Odysseus's fury at hearing her ask that it be moved ("Woman—your words, they cut me to the core! / Who could move my bed?"), tells her that her husband is home at last.

Theirs is the ultimate result of all ambition, the end to which all labors tend, the "great rooted place," in Yeats's words, that Odysseus in Book 6 of the poem wished for Nausicaa, the beautiful young princess he met on the Phaeacian shore:ᵉ

> "And may the good gods give you all your heart desires:
> husband, and house, and lasting harmony too.
> No finer, greater gift in the world than that . . .
> when man and woman possess their home, two minds,
> two hearts that work as one. Despair to their enemies,
> joy to all their friends. Their own
> best claim to glory."

ᵉ In Odysseus's nude encounter with Nausicaa—she and her maids having just had a swim, he, ship-wrecked, having been tossed up naked on their beach—he attempts to shield his private parts with an olive branch and figure out whether, in such extremities, he can assume the posture of a suppliant and "clasp her knees." The whole business could almost be silent cinema slapstick.

We may leave them now, Odysseus and Penelope, bidding farewell in the words with which Homer sees them off, the words that end with line 296 of Book 23:

> So husband and wife confided in
> each other

while nurse and Eurynome, under the flaring brands,
were making up the bed with coverings deep and soft.
And working briskly, soon as they'd made it snug,
back to her room the old nurse went to sleep
as Eurynome, their attendant, torch in hand,
lighted the royal couple's way to bed and,
leading them to their chamber, slipped away.
Rejoicing in each other, they returned to their bed,
the old familiar place they loved so well.

These may be the last lines Homer wrote before he died, leaving the remainder of his poem to be finished by a disciple. At the outset of Book 1, "sparkling-eyed" Athena delivered to Telemachus the extraordinary news "I tell you great Odysseus is not dead." Not dead after twenty years away. Not dead after 2,700 years. Did Homer understand that his comic, weeping, warm Odysseus would at some time in the distant future seem more alive than all his bully-boy heroes and their moribund military traditions? Was an ancient song entitled (in Fagles's translation) "The Strife Between Odysseus and Achilles" known to the audiences of Homer's day or is it a fictional construct of Homer's, sounded in the *Odyssey* to reverberate in listeners' minds, a whisper of the conflict in Homer himself between war as a way of life—really, death to others as a way of life—and a life of connection to other human beings, a life that draws on all the resources of mind and heart? We look back over the great arc of Homer's art that takes us from the rage of Achilles amid the clanging of battle on the Trojan shore to the modest domestic peace with which the *Odyssey* closes and ask ourselves: Is there any way to characterize Homer's intent over the lifetime of his evolving art? Perhaps there is. For, in the end, the rage of Achilles is stilled only in the bed of Penelope.

III
THE
POET
HOW TO PARTY

Let us begin our singing from the Heliconian Muses
who possess the great and holy mountain of Helicon
and dance there on soft feet by the dark blue water
of the spring, and by the altar of the powerful son of Cronus;
who wash their tender bodies in the waters of Permessus
or Hippocrene, spring of the Horse, or holy Olmeus,
and on the high places of Helicon have ordered their dances
which are handsome and beguiling, and light are the feet they
   move on. . . .
And it was they who once taught Hesiod his splendid singing
as he was shepherding his lambs on holy Helicon,
and these were the first words of all the goddesses spoke to me,
the Muses of Olympia, daughters of Zeus of the aegis:
"You shepherds of the wilderness, poor fools, nothing but bellies,
we know how to say many false things that seem like true sayings,
but we know also how to speak the truth when we wish to."
   So they spoke, these mistresses of words, daughters of great Zeus,
and they broke off and handed me a staff of strong-growing
olive shoot, a wonderful thing; they breathed a voice into me,
and power to sing the story of things of the future, and things past.
They told me to sing the race of the blessed gods everlasting,
but always to put themselves at the beginning and end of my singing.

So begins Hesiod's Theogony with his call from the Muses to be a
poet and to sing the genealogy of the gods. Hesiod's poetry, which lacks
the sweeping drama and unforgettable characterizations of Homer, is exceedingly useful to us because it catalogues so much mythological infor-

mation. Hesiod, a struggling farmer in Boeotia and younger contemporary of Homer (and something of a regional chauvinist), discovers the Muses dancing on Mount Helicon in his own neighborhood, though their traditional home was on the slopes of Mount Olympus.

The Muses were the nine goddesses of song and poetry or, perhaps better, sung poetry, since the Greeks did not distinguish one from the other. Their name is the root of the word music. *In early times, all public utterances were chanted, so that the voice of the speaker—who, needless to say, had no microphone—could reach as far as possible. This is the origin of chanting by priests at religious services, though the sung poems of the Greeks were often chanted not by single performers but by dancing choruses.*

The Muses could be capricious in awarding their favors and vindictive in withholding them. Thus Homer's need to placate his Muse regularly, lest she withdraw his gift of inspiration. Inspiration and truth were two different things, however. The success of a poetic performance lay in the emotional transformation it wrought on its audience. The Muses didn't care whether what they inspired was true or false as long as it grabbed the listeners. Each Muse came to have her specialty: Calliope inspired epic poetry, Clio historical narrative, Euterpe aulos playing, Erato poetry sung to the lyre, Terpsichore dance, Melpomene tragedy, Thalia comedy, Polyhymnia prayers and ritual, Urania astronomical demonstrations or perhaps pageants under the stars.

IN THE PREVIOUS CHAPTER, wishing to distinguish Homer's two great poems, I underscored how different are their approaches to both militarism and what might best be called personal feeling—that is, the ability to sympathize, to mourn, and to cherish familial relationships, an ability which, in the ancient world, was almost exclusively the domain of women. Though I call the military traditions of the Greeks "moribund," I am well aware that they have much life left in them. Simone Weil, whose insight into Greek culture was profound, wrote in 1939: "Those who had dreamed that force, thanks to progress, now belonged to the past, have seen the [*Iliad*] as a historical document; those who can see that force, today as in the past, is at the center of all human history, find in the *Iliad* its most beautiful, its purest mirror." These words, from an essay written for *Nouvelle Revue Française*, were never published there, for before the issue could be printed Paris had fallen to the Nazis. Little more than half a century after that event, I can hardly claim that the Greek military spirit is dead; it is still, as it was in Weil's day, "at the center of all human history." At most, one could hope that more human beings than in the past have come to love peace more deeply than they wish for war, that the sensibility of Odysseus continues to gain adherents.

To name this realm of personal feeling "the sensibility of Odysseus" is, of course, to write paradoxically and in a kind of symbolic shorthand. For Odysseus, though he may afterward have wept over the consequences (and may therefore stand as

Homer's literary exemplar of an evolved sensibility), was the Greek who designed the treacherous ruse that brought Troy to ruin, steeped in the blood of so many innocents, the man distrusted as too clever by half—distrusted not only by his fellow Greeks but, later, by the Romans as well. In the last decades of the pre-Christian era, just before the birth of Jesus, the great Roman poet Virgil worked in declining health on a massive epic, the *Aeneid*, about the founding of the city of Rome at the pristine bend in the River Tiber by Aeneas, a Trojan prince who escaped as Troy burned. Virgil modeled large parts of his long poem quite consciously on the *Iliad*. There was, after all, no alternative: if a Roman poet wished to summon his fellow countrymen to greatness by recalling the feats of their glorious ancestors, the Homeric epic was the only pattern available to him. But if he had no recourse but to employ a Greek literary model, Virgil exhibited typical Roman ambivalence toward the Greeks themselves by bringing before us Odysseus's Wooden Horse and putting in the mouth of a truth-telling Trojan the famous line "I am wary of Greeks even when they bring gifts." The ancient world seethed with ethnic caricatures, none more constant than the warning against gift-bearing Greeks, this people too subtle to be trusted.

If Virgil views Odysseus as the embodiment of Greek shiftiness, it is also true that the Roman poet makes explicit a somewhat hidden strand of Homer's narrative: Troy in the *Iliad* functions as a kind of utopia. It is a doomed utopia—doomed, it must be pointed out, by Odysseus's preternatural stealth, for otherwise its walls had proved impregnable. Troy is a place of greater justice and harmony than Greek society, the place the Romans would rather think of themselves as hailing from. Like the City of Peace on the miraculous shield of Achilles, Troy is an ideal, not the begrimed, imperfect world of the Greeks, not a world of give-and-take, of compromise and equivocation, but the uncompromised paradise of lost nobility—of brave, loving Hector and generous-hearted, compassionate Priam—where we would all rather claim our origin.

Here in Homer is the first faint note of a dream that will become ever more present to the Greeks, who, despite their unswerving realism and proud practicality—or perhaps *because* of their unblinking understanding of things as they truly are— yearn, however unrealistically, however impractically, for a great, good place beyond the unsatisfying ambiguities of the world we must actually live in. (Odysseus and Penelope's Ithaca was, by the time the *Odyssey* was known, a second lost ideal, a utopia of aristocratic virtue where, as Yeats would have it, "innocence and beauty" are born "in custom and in ceremony.") This striking combination of seemingly opposite qualities—of practicality and grounded realism united to a longing for a state of being beyond anything one has ever known (and, beyond the longing, an ability to *imagine* what such a state might be like)—fostered the germination of the first nontraditional, nonconservative society in world history, the first culture that did not give as its knee-jerk response to every challenge "This is the way we've always done things."

Like Tennyson's Ulysses seeking "a newer world," like the adventurous Greek sailors whose graceful, elongated vessels plied ever farther—from the Aegean to the Adriatic to the Mediterranean to the far Atlantic—Greece quickly morphed from the usual custom-ruled society into a civilization characterized by open questioning and experimentation. In the words of the contemporary British classicist Oliver Taplin, "The poems [of Homer] seem to emerge . . . as a kind of opener of discussion, an invitation to think about and scrutinize the structures and allocations of power and of respect. Thus, while everyone within the poems agrees that honour . . . should be given where honour is due, they do not agree on the criteria for its allocation. So while Homer does not positively advocate any particular kind of political change, this is surely not the poetry of political conservatism or retrenchment either. It is part and parcel of an era of radically widening horizons; and it is a catalyst to change."

The questioning and experimentation, though centered on political matters, will eventually spin far beyond the political sphere—to such an extent that the Greek world will continue in almost constant cultural revolution from the time of Homer to the day Rome brings Greece to its knees in the second century B.C. This period—more than half a millennium of conscious change—marks the longest trajectory of fluid development in any society known to history.

G REEK LITERATURE begins with Homer and soon finds its way to every corner of the Greek mainland, the peninsulas, the islands, and the far-flung settlements and colonies. Though the poems of Homer and his successors were recorded, there will be no Greek reading public till we reach the fifth century B.C. To begin with, literary works were scratched onto sheets of lead or, in the case of especially valued monumental inscriptions, impressed in gold or bronze or carved in stone. Wooden tablets coated with wax and prepared animal skins also provided writing surfaces, but none of these methods encouraged the broadcast sale of "books" or the establishment of libraries, such as would become possible in later centuries. Carting home what would have been, in Homer's case, pounds of poetry was hardly feasible; and it would be a long time before imported sheets of lightweight Egyptian papyrus would be available in sufficient quantities to allow longer literary works to become readily transportable. There was, instead, a *hearing* public that formed responsive audiences at festivals and contests.

The rhapsodes (or "stitchers of song"), whom we have already met, were wandering performers who traveled from occasion to occasion, hoping for payments in kind and, once coinage became general in the sixth century, monetary rewards. As the courts of the old aristocracy, which could lavish hospitality on bards and rhapsodes, gradually sank beneath the waves of societal change, their role as patrons of poets was assumed by large assemblies, gathered for religious occasions. These festivals—some local, others, like the Olympics, Panhellenic[α]—though originating as religious holidays, were held on vast, circus-like fairgrounds near sanctuaries dedicated to particular gods throughout Greece and drew the devout and the curious, the sharp-eyed and the mercenary, the raucous and the rascally.

At these events, there were, of course, religious ceremonies to honor the god—usually featuring a chorus of maidens or boys or men—as well as contests of athletes and poets. There were also merchants' booths, fluttering their brightly colored canvas

[α] In their own language, the Greeks are called "Hellenes." *Pan* is Greek for "all"; thus *Panhellenic* refers to all of Greece. Despite the popularity of these festivals, which proved such a draw to poets, the customs of court poetry did not die out entirely, since there were always new political leaders in need of poetical praise. In the late sixth century B.C., Pindar, who wrote most of his poems to order (almost all of them for winning athletes, making his poetry the *Sports Illustrated* of its day), wrote a choral ode to Hieron I, the newly minted tyrant of Syracuse, a Greek colony on the southern coast of Sicily. Hieron had won the Olympic horse racing *kudos* (a much-abused Greek *singular* meaning "the glory of victory"). Hieron's capacity for receiving praise was nearly infinite, but Pindar must have chafed under his assignment and got his own back in the last lines of his ode to Hieron:

The highest peak can only crown itself,
and there's no need to look for higher peaks.
So may your highness loom without surcease—
Like me, who keeps only winners for friends,
Me, the greatest poet in all Greece.

awnings, their proprietors hawking small statues of patronal gods and goddesses, religious amulets, food and drink, and other goods and services. As late as the first century A.D., we find New Testament references to merchants like Paul, Priscilla, and Aquila, who traveled from one Greek festival to another, setting up shop to sell their skills at making and mending tents and similar shelters that shaded fairgoers from the Greek sun, brighter, fiercer than in any other European sky. Competition was in the blood of the Greeks, and everywhere at these festivals contestants vied for the attention of the crowds. Dour, anxious Hesiod writes about the daily round of farming and the effects of the seasons on rural life but also speaks in his *Works and Days* about the value of festal competitions with "potter against potter, carpenter against carpenter . . . poet against poet."

The liturgical choruses needed poets to write the verses they sang; top athletes paid for poems in their own praise; and funerals of great men were additional occasions that required the presence of poets who, like the athletes, competed in funeral games. Both the rhapsodes, who performed the poems of others, and original poets showed up at all these—and many smaller, more intimate—occasions to sell their wares of words. Nor were words all they had to sell. Performers sang their poetry while accompanying themselves on stringed lyres or were accompanied by pipers, who blew into reeds called *auloi*, instruments pierced by holes along their length, enabling a musician to change the pitch of a note by stopping one or more holes with his fingers. Though *aulos*[β] is usually translated as "flute," the instrument's timbre was closer to an oboe and sounded, according to the Greeks, like the buzzing of wasps and, at its high end, like the honking of geese.

β The Greek masculine singular regularly takes the ending *-os*, the masculine plural *-oi*, corresponding to the Latin endings *-us* and *-i*.

But what, on the whole, did Greek music sound like? We would love to know for sure, though the few scraps we still possess of ancient musical notation belong to later periods and are of uncertain interpretation. From fragments of evidence, however, we can approach an answer. There is no suggestion in the evidence that the singers, even when singing in chorus, sang in harmony. Though lyres and sets of pipes must have been capable of simple harmonies, the music seems to have been centered on melody, rhythm, and—something less familiar to us—mode. In our Western music we still know the modes "major" and "minor." The Greeks had five modes, known to us by their names—Ionian, Aeolian, Lydian, Dorian, and Phrygian—which referred also to ethnic groupings within Greece. Each of these modes, each of which had submodes, was easily recognized by listeners, and each created a characteristic mood, just as we might say, "That sounded like a Scottish ballad. This sounds like a Spanish dance." Each Greek mode was constructed from an invariable sequence of relationships between the notes that no other mode possessed, more distinct than E flat major is from C minor, perhaps at times more akin to Asian music with its larger intervals and quarter tones. The Dorian was martial, the Phrygian engendered contentment, the Mixolydian (one of the submodes) was plaintive, the Ionian softly alluring, apparently making seduction easier. In all, Greek music probably sounded something like the late medieval music of Europe with its emphases on catchy, easily singable melodies, exaggerated rhythms, and humble instrumental accompaniment—Gregorian chant gone wild in the streets.

Greece has been, in fact, through all of its history a land of music and dance. "Let me not live without music," sings the dancing chorus in Euripides's play *Heracles*. To be without music was, for the ancient Greeks, to be already dead, as Sophocles describes it in *Oedipus at Colonnus*, his meditation on death: "without wedding song, lyreless, chorusless, death at the end." Though there were, as we have seen, professional performers, there is evidence that every Greek, whether king or serf, looked forward to the many opportunities for singing and dancing. Even our tattered and incomplete records yield at least two hundred terms for different kinds of dance. The most hard-assed soldier was expected to strum the lyre to regain his composure, as Homer shows Achilles doing in his tent in Book 9 of the *Iliad*. Women of substantial estate, like Penelope, arranged musical evenings in their private quarters. Shepherds piped to their flocks, sailors used their oars to beat time to their sea chanties, teachers, as a bounden duty, taught musical skills to their charges. Though professional entertainers regaled well-heeled revelers at banquets, each of the revelers was expected to contribute his own party piece to the evening's festivities— and it seldom took long before the revelers rose from their couches to dance through the night, locking their arms together and pounding the earth, for all the world like Kazantzakis's Zorba, who danced as if "there was a soul struggling to carry away [his] flesh and cast itself like a meteor into the darkness."

The fishmonger sang of his fish, the militia marched to martial rhythms, the laundress sang the blues, while others sang songs of different colors. It was said that after the disastrous Sicilian Expedition in 413 B.C. Athenian soldiers, held captive in the horrible quarries outside Syracuse, won their freedom by singing and dancing choruses from the plays of Euripides, whose songs the Sicilians were mad about. Daily life could sometimes seem a sort of amateur contest, an eternal audition with a host of hopeful voices—primeval Paul Simons and Judy

Collinses, Tom Waitses and Ani diFrancos—competing for attention. Ancient Greece was a culture of song.

To be unmusical, as sly Sappho informs us in a short poem to a deceased woman who had shown talent neither for performance nor for appreciation, was a fate worse than death. You might as well never have lived:

When you were living, never did you smell
the roses by Olympus, where the Muses dwell.
Now that you're dead, your faded ghost in hell
is unremembered here on earth. You ring no bell.

This poem, constructed like a well-aimed body blow, is the work of a woman the Greeks called "the tenth Muse," the greatest poet after Homer, born in the late seventh century on the large Greek island of Lesbos, celebrated for the sweetness of its wine and the tartness of its verse. Unfortunately, much of post-Homeric poetry—called lyric poetry because it was usually sung to a lyre—was lost in the upheavals of subsequent centuries, especially in the depredations and decay that would follow the barbarian incursions into the Greco-Roman world in the fifth century A.D. In Sappho we have been particularly unlucky, for her work survives mostly in small clusters of words, though sometimes in longer fragments, like exotic petals and branches cut from a mysterious tree whose fullness we can never know.

These fragments suggest that Sappho ran a sort of finishing school for wellborn young ladies, a school at which they were trained (no doubt among other refinements) to sing in choruses at festivals, especially at weddings. These choral performances, which featured individual students as soloists, may have served the girls as their social debut, the hope being that they would

attract a suitable suitor and, soon thereafter, make an advanta-
geous marriage. Several of Sappho's most (seemingly) characteristic poems are *epithalamia*, bridal songs.ᵞ Others have been
interpreted as laments for girls who are gone, perhaps to marriage, and whose absence is a suffering to Sappho. Here is one
of the more complete examples:

Some say cavalry, others infantry,
still others say a navy is
black earth's most beautiful thing.
But I say it's whatever,
whatever you may love.

An easy thing to understand.
For Helen, whose beauty surpassed us all,
walked out on him one day,
her high-class husband,

sailed for Troy,
and not to child nor doting parents
did she give a thought,
led to earth's end [by longing].

So does [my soul] fly up,
remembering Anaktoria,
[gliding] lightly, [lightly,]
now she's gone.

I'd rather study her graceful step
and the way light moved across her face
than look on Lydian chariots
or ranks of bristling hoplites.

ᵞ One *epithalamion* begins with the bracing line "Raise high the roofbeam, carpenters!" encouraging workmen in their construction of a bridal bower—while at the same time encouraging the bridegroom to raise his own "beam" to the height of physical ardor. J. D. Salinger used the line as the title of one of his novellas about the Glass family.

[   ] what cannot happen.

[   ] human [   ] to pray for part

[   ]

[   ]

[   ]

[   ]

[   ]

[   ] toward [   ]

[   ]

[   ]

[   ]

[   ] surprise.

Is Anaktoria on her honeymoon or is she dead? Was she real or just a literary fiction? Is this a solo number or a memorial chorus for a dead student? What might be the surprise with which the poem ends? How we are tempted to fill those empty brackets with words. (The lines that fall within the empty brackets are completely unreadable in the manuscript fragments we still possess; the words within brackets are educated guesses based on partly damaged text.)

The consensus of current scholarship is that the Greek lyric poets, though formerly presumed to be writing personal poetry such as we might read in a volume from a contemporary poet, were all writing for performance—their own or that of another performer or chorus—and that the "I" of Greek lyric poetry is no more personal than the "I" of modern popular songs, as in "I got a right to sing the blues." When a singer delivers such words to us in a darkened nightclub, we take them as representative of a particular human feeling, understood by all and shared by all at one time or another, but we do not mistake

them for an expression of what the singer herself may be feeling at this particular moment, nor do we feel any obligation to
commiserate with her personally. We understand she is acting a
part, as are we, vicariously sympathizing but—at some level—
savoring her pretended misery.

The Anaktoria fragment could certainly fit such a pattern.
But there are other Sapphic fragments that are harder to wedge
into this thesis:

> If you still love me, you will take
> a younger bedmate. I'm not up to sleeping with you
> now that I am old.

Could this ever have been just another song? And, finally, there
is a complementary fragment—or, as I suspect, a complete poem:

> The moon has set
> and the Pleiades:
> it is the middle of the night,
> and time passes, time passes—
> and I lie alone.

This, it seems to me, is personal poetry, an authentic "I" that
somehow slipped through the impersonal masks of Greek song
culture. In recent years, scholars have questioned whether these
last lines should even be attributed to Sappho. Well, they have
been so attributed since ancient times, and they sound like
Sappho, an elegant beauty who taught feminine graces to so
many girls, now observing the irreversible process of aging, resolved to be honest with herself without large helpings of self-
pity, Sappho at her most nakedly personal. Such forthrightness
is exceedingly rare—and not only in Greek lyric poetry.

By and large, Greek lyric poets present themselves in disguise, personae for the moment; and not a few write, as did W. B. Yeats and T. S. Eliot, poems in the voices of the decrepit elderly though they themselves are still young. But these efforts can have a conventional ring, even when, like Sappho, the poet relies on the metaphorical storehouse of nature. Sappho's moon and stars and her "black earth" are staples of Greek lyric poetry, as are kingfishers, halcyons, and waves of the wine-dark sea. Alcman, active in Sparta in the second half of the seventh century, composed a responsorial poem during which—in this fragment—a solo singer, masked as an old man, engages a girls' chorus:

> O honey-voiced maidens singing divinely,
> my limbs can carry me no more.
> Would a kingfisher I could be,
> who flies with halcyons over the wave bloom,
> fearless, sea-purple springtime bird.

Alcman lacks Sappho's spare honesty; he seems to beg our pity. This is no spontaneous folk idiom but self-consciously constructed poetry. It has been said that Greek lyricism celebrates the literary springtime of the ancient world. When a poet like Alcman speaks, it can seem a somewhat manufactured spring, a bit predictable. When Sappho sings with Dickinsonian frugality, we can almost feel the warmth of the ancient sun, even if we are aware, as in the myth of Demeter, that the spring breeze always carries a slight scent of decay:

> I love what is delicate,
> luminous, brave—
> what belongs to the sunlight.

> That's what I crave.

About Sappho's craving: the word she uses is *eros*, sexual desire. Like the standard nature metaphors, *eros* returns repeatedly in the lyric poets, whether as erotic craving or as Eros himself, the divine personification of Love. By Sappho's day the segregation of women had become more definite than it is in Homer's poems, where women, though hardly prominent, show no sign of being forbidden social intercourse with men. Sappho might almost be running a seraglio, so indistinct are men in her poems, none of them having the physical nearness of a girl like Anaktoria, whose perfume we can almost smell. Such division of the sexes— whether in harems, brothels, convents and other sexually segregated religious residences, single-sex boarding schools, prisons, mercenary armies, or ships long at sea— inevitably triggers a rise in homoerotic relationships.δ Though there are no references in Homer to homosexuality, such references are notable in lyric poetry from the late seventh century onward; and by the sixth century these are commonplace—so much so that Greeks of a later day read the relationship of Achilles and Patroclus as homoerotic, even though Homer offers no evidence for such an interpretation, all of his heroes appearing to be aggressively heterosexual.

There were other female lyric poets, but Sappho is the only one whose fragments are extensive enough for us to sketch a provisional picture of her and her circumstances. The fragments of the male lyric poets, however, provide abundant evidence of homoerotic attraction, espe-

δ In subgroups that are exclusively homosocial, there is always a greater incidence of homoerotic activity than in the larger society that surrounds them. The New York Jesuits, who had missions in the Caroline and Marshall Islands, used to joke among themselves that in the indigenous language of the islands there was no word for homosexual till the Jesuits established a boys' boarding school. But it is also possible for whole societies to encourage a rise in homoerotic relations by the vigilant social division of the sexes. This was true—well into the nineteenth century—of Samurai culture in Japan, where upper-class males invariably preferred other males as sexual partners, and it tends to be true today of the puritanical Islamist societies of the Middle East.

cially of adult men for pubescent boys. Some of this evidence is ambiguous, as when Sappho's Lesbian contemporary Alcaeus urges:

> Drink, get drunk and drunker, even tread
> The path of rage. For Myrsilus is dead.

But there can be no mistaking the meaning of Anacreon, a poet of the sixth century who because of political upheavals lived in many different parts of Greece (and whose bitchy allusion to goings-on in Sappho's Lesbos gave us the present meaning of *lesbian*):

> O boy of the virginal eyes,
> I crave you, though you stand apart,
> so heedless and so unaware,
> thou charioteer of my heart.

Nor can we mistake what Anacreon has in mind in this address:

> Bring water, boy, and bring us wine,
> bring each of us a flowering crown.
> Sit next to me upon this couch—
> where I will wrestle Eros down.

Perhaps the boy with the virginal eyes has finally taken notice of Anacreon and is about to allow himself to be seduced. But, more likely, these entreaties are addressed to different boys, the first a noble of Anacreon's own class who must be wooed with great care and significant gifts, the second a well-regarded servant in Anacreon's home, who is allowed to mix the wine with water and then to serve his master's pleasure in the course of a banquet for intimate friends.

The banquets of the Homeric age seemed to grow out of dim religious obligations, such as the need to appease a god by blood sacrifice or the need to hold an elaborate, weeklong funeral observance to ensure that the shade of the deceased may cross the River Styx to reach Hades and not be condemned to eternal wandering. In such cases, generously carved portions of sacrificial meat—of beef cattle, sheep, goat, or pig—were distributed among the participants for their consumption. We might get the impression from Homer's descriptions that this was how the Greeks always ate. Far from it: their usual dishes were endless variations on bread and fish ͤ —the secular food of everyday life, the medium of friendship and conviviality, unconnected to propitiation of the gods. Besides bread and fish, there might be mouth-watering artichokes deep-fried in olive oil, the occasional spitted fowl, fresh greens, fat Sicilian cheeses (if you were very lucky), fruit, nuts, and of course considerable cups of wine—which the Greeks mixed with water, the better to swill it:

> I'd say *wine* is the thing—and not tears,
> which cannot heal wound or cure curse.
> With dry eyes I'll party all night—
> it sure can't make anything worse.

Thus Archilochus, the earliest of the lyric poets, a tough, much wounded veteran, whose humorous lyrics are full

ͤ As in their similar approaches to deliberative assemblies and alphabetical writing, the currents of Greek and Hebrew life continued to run in rough parallel: these ingredients are not so far from the "loaves and fishes" of the New Testament, the everyday food of the ancient Jews, who like the Greeks reserved meat for religious occasions. But whereas the Jews limited themselves to fish with fins and scales, the Greeks welcomed the fruit of the sea in all its variety. A floor mosaic by Sosos of Pergamon, titled *The Unswept Hall* (or, rather, a Roman copy of Sosos's work), gives us a wonderfully complete picture of the comestibles offered at a typical symposium: scattered evenly along the floor, in *trompe l'oeil* fashion, are wishbones and claws, fruit and vegetables, and the discarded bones and bits of just about every sea creature that swims the Mediterranean.

of mockery and world-weariness. He is reputed to have loved one woman intensely but been denied by her father. Father and daughter then became the subjects of Archilochus's widely repeated satirical verses, so cutting that both subjects were forced to suicide. After this, the poet seems to have sunk, like Swift in old age, into a kind of mordant despair, his poetry specializing in the pornographic humiliation of women. In this one, Alcman's immortal kingfisher is put to novel use:

> She flipped and she flopped round his cock
> As a kingfisher flaps on a rock.
> She stooped, slurped him up—oh my dear!—
> like a Phrygian drinking his beer
> through a straw, then presented her rear.

No doubt this sort of thing, which occupies a good deal of Archilochus's surviving fragments, got a big reception from his friends.

Banquets of like-minded friends were called *symposia*. (The singular, *symposium*—the Greek original is *symposion*[ζ]—means "a drinking together," that is, a drinking party.) These banquets took place in private homes in a room called the *andron*, literally "men's room," but the sense is closer to "men's club." At such gatherings upper-class males arranged themselves on comfortable couches ample enough for two or three guests to recline together, wore floral crowns, ate from low food-laden tables, and were regaled with music and served bowls of wine by servants—usually teenage male servants or females who were professional *hetairai*, literally "companions," actually on the order of accom-

ζ The *-ion* ending, like the Latin *-ium*, is neuter singular. The plural ending is *-a* in both languages. Later in this same paragraph, *hetairai* is a feminine plural form; the singular is *hetaira*; the masculine plural *hetairoi* becomes *hetairos* in the singular.

plished geishas or call girls. Interestingly, the male guests were called *hetairoi*, the same word Homer uses for companions-in-arms. So they all got together—the *hetairoi*, the *hetairai*, and the *paides* (boys)[η]—for a rousing evening. Early in the banquet, libations were poured to Dionysus, god of wine, and a dithyramb, a song-and-dance to the inebriating god, was beaten out. You may, if you like, label this prayer, but it was from our perspective a lot closer to a conga line, as doughty old Archilochus informs us:

> I lead the dancing to the dithyramb,
> the hymn to Dionysus, lord divine.
> I'm *good* at it, I'm even quite the ham—
> Provided that my brains are braised in wine.

There was plenty of tension in Greek life, since the Greeks, however many parties they threw, became as time went on even more bellicose than they had been in Homer's day. These symposia may have been, as much as anything, occasions to release the pent-up anxieties of a society always at war—"the father of all, the king of all," "always existing by nature," as the Greek philosophers expressed it. Enough wine and one could forget about the war of the moment or, if not forget, reduce its importance at least temporarily. Thus this ditty attributed to Theognis, an early-sixth-century songwriter of airy facility who believed in good breeding, great parties, and lively romance between men and boys, the Cole Porter of ancient Greece:

[η] Girls were kept carefully apart, at least if they were from better-off families, to learn—under the watchful tutelage of women like Sappho—the arts that would stand them in good stead in married life.

> Strike the sacred strings and let us drink,
> and so disport ourselves 'mid sounding
>   reeds

that our libations gratify the gods—
and who gives a shit about war with the Medes?

But as tends to be the case when drunkenness substitutes for thoughtfulness, the hilarity often ended badly. In this fragment from a fourth-century comedy by Eubulus, an already wobbly Dionysus boasts of how the typical symposium progressed:

Who but Dionysus pours the flowing
    wine
and mixes water in the streaming bowls
    tonight?
One bowl for ruddy health, then one
    for getting off;
the third brings sleep—and wise men
    leave before they're tight.
For after that the bowls no more belong
    to us:
the fourth's for *hubris* and the fifth for
    lots of noise,
the sixth for mindless fucking, followed
    by black eyes,
the eighth brings the police, the ninth's
    for throwing up,
the tenth for trashing everything before
    we stop.[θ]

There's sadness beneath the merriment. It is as if, no matter how much these revelers sing, dance, howl, recite their jokes, and screw one another, a constant, authoritative note of pes-

θ While it is dangerous to take any society's comedy as a literal description of its mores, the humor would make no sense at all if it did not refer to recognizable behavior. There are other comedic passages in which excess is derided as a vice typical of foreigners rather than of Greeks. In *Acharnians*, produced in the midst of the bloody Peloponnesian War between Athens and Sparta and the earliest of several antiwar plays by Aristophanes, the comic genius of Athens, there is an exchange between the main character, Good Citizen, and a decadent ambassador, who lauds the banquets of the barbarians because the barbarians "esteem as men of importance only those who eat and drink in enormous quantities." "While we [Greeks]," replies Good Citizen, "esteem them as cocksuckers and buttboys"—one of a number of generous hints in Aristophanes that homosexual relations were not everywhere applauded.

simistic pain sounds beyond all their frantic attempts not to hear it. Even Archilochus, a sensational athlete in his time and a master of the revels if ever there was one, cannot deny that none of these nighttime activities makes good sense. In his most thoughtful lines, he seems to remove the mask, denuding himself of his gruff and rollicking persona, and to counsel himself in the clear light of day not to excess but to sobriety—to balance, modesty, and even resignation:

> O heart, my heart, no public leaping when you win;
> no solitude nor weeping when you fail to prove.
> Rejoice at simple things; and be but vexed by sin
> and evil slightly. Know the tides through which we move.

The last sentence is quietly ominous. The tides through which we move—the highs and the lows, the peaks and the troughs—tell us repeatedly that nothing lasts and that all life ends in death. Let us temper our excitement and agitation, whether for the ecstasy of battle or the ecstasy of sex, whether over great achievement or great loss, and admit to ourselves that all things have their moment and are gone. If we live according to this sober knowledge, we will live as well as we can.

IV
THE
POLITICIAN
AND THE
PLAYWRIGHT
HOW TO RULE

Menelaus, king of Sparta, proves an exception. After the war he returns home with the errant but repentant Helen to rule a harmonious kingdom. Most of his fellow chieftains, however, have already been slain at Troy or, like Odysseus, meet with impossible obstacles on the home-going voyage or find crippling troubles awaiting them on their return to Greece. These stories of the oral tradition, which are probably traceable to the twelfth century B.C., may be symbolic of the mysterious and precipitate decline of Mycenaean culture that archaeologists have discovered at the end of the Greek Bronze Age. One story particularly struck the Greeks—that of Menelaus's brother, haughty Agamemnon, king of Mycenae and leader of the Greek forces at Troy. Though Agamemnon is its central figure, the story begins before his time and continues after him and is usually given the title "The Fall of the House of Atreus," after Agamemnon and Menelaus's father, Atreus, who was believed to have founded the Mycenaean kingship.

Atreus and his successors were under a curse because Atreus had— at what had been billed as a banquet of reconciliation—fed his unwitting brother Thyestes the flesh of his own sons, Atreus's nephews. Atreus was himself killed by Thyestes and Aegisthus, Thyestes's last surviving son; and Atreus was succeeded by Agamemnon. During Agamemnon's long absence at Troy, Aegisthus moved in and became the lover of Agamemnon's wife, Clytemnestra, who had it in for Agamemnon anyway, since just prior to the Trojan War he had offered their daughter Iphigenia as a human sacrifice to the goddess Artemis. (Artemis, angry at the Greeks, had to be assuaged because she had sent contrary winds that prevented their fleet from sailing out of the port of Aulis for Troy.)

Agamemnon returned from Troy with his new concubine, Cassandra, daughter of Priam and Hecuba and sister of Hector and Paris. Cassandra had from Apollo the gift of predicting the future but labored under the burden that no one believed her. Earlier, she had prophesied the fall of Troy to her disbelieving fellow Trojans. Now, hysterically, she foresees what Clytemnestra has in store, but to no avail. Agamemnon, who is wheedled into taking Clytemnestra's elaborate welcome as his due, is murdered in his bath by his hate-filled wife in a scene worthy of Alfred Hitchcock:

> great sprays of blood, and the murderous shower
> wounds me, dyes me black and I, I revel
> like the Earth when the spring rains come down,
> the blessed gifts of god, and the new green spear
> splits the sheath and rips to birth in glory!

—as Clytemnestra exultantly relates her deed to the horror-struck citizens of Mycenae. Cassandra also falls to her hostess's avenging wrath.

But the vengeance creates a new generation of avengers, the children of Agamemnon and Clytemnestra: Electra and her younger brother, Orestes, who are bound to avenge their father. After the mild-mannered Orestes, thrust forward by his more bloodthirsty sibling, murders his mother and her lover, he is pursued by the Furies, terrifying goddesses of avenging conscience who never allow the guilty any peace. Orestes, the mother-murderer, takes refuge in Athena's temple on the Acropolis at Athens, where he pleads for justice. A trial is arranged with Orestes as defendant, the Furies as prosecutors, and a jury of Athenian citizens, including Athena herself. Their votes turn out to be divided equally between conviction and acquittal. Athena then declares that, for all time, when there is a hung jury the defendant is to be acquitted.

The Furies, primeval, unrelenting spirits of Earth, are furious but *are encouraged by wise Athena to become more beneficent and to take a new name, the Eumenides, or Kindly Ones. They are given a temple at the base of the Acropolis, where they are to transform themselves into patron-protectors of the Athenians, in Athena's words "these upright men, this breed fought free of grief," whom they are to love "as a gardener loves his plants."*

This is the version of the story given by Aeschylus, the first of the great dramatists, in his trilogy of plays, the only Greek dramatic trilogy to survive intact, collectively known as the Oresteia *and produced at Athens in 458 B.C. There are many variants. In one of these, a version by Euripides,* Iphigenia in Tauris *(c. 413 B.C.), Artemis secretly saves Iphigenia and makes her a priestess in the Crimea. But in none of the versions is the House of Atreus a model family.*

For, in truth, the House of Atreus, even among the bellicose Greeks, was a synonym for savagery, for the barbarism latent within each human being and within society itself. In Aeschylus's trilogy, however, the story becomes (to use Richmond Lattimore's phrase) "a grand parable of progress," taking us from Greece's chthonic roots in prehistoric Mycenae to the wind-swept freedom of its most forward-looking city. Though Zeus, the great father-god, "lays it down as law / that we must suffer, suffer into truth" (as the chorus of Mycenaeans reminds us), this suffering into truth becomes "our rite of passage from savagery to civilization" (in the words of translator Robert Fagles), for "the Oresteia *dramatizes our growth from primitive ritual to civilized institution."*

The generations of Atreus have suffered enough; it is time to bring reason to bear on the woven patterns of unending vengeance. Tradition, fretted inextricably through human culture, is one thing, but true civilization must be another altogether, the result not of habitual taboos and unexamined impulses but of rational deliberation and conscious choice.

I N T H E T I M E of the lyric poets, the most distinguished ex-
ponent of the ancient wisdom of resignation—expounded
at the end of the last chapter by the unlikely Archilochus—
was Solon, *archon eponymos* (or chief magistrate) of Athens in the
early sixth century. Solon was a sort of Athenian Franklin D.
Roosevelt, an innovative though basically moderate statesman
who found ways to improve the economy and raise the public's
expectations of government—by, for instance, the introduction
of coinage—despite the many conflicting political interests that
constantly threatened to tear Athens apart. He was an aristocratic
reformer who understood instinctively that the aristocracy's
monopoly on power had to be loosened and some power given
to the lesser orders if social peace was to be shored up. He was
seen as a traitor to his class because he abolished such pigheaded
injustices as slavery for debt; but he favored relative justice, attempting to be fair while always aware that perfect justice was
beyond human possibility. His genius for political compromise,
which saved Athens from many disasters, stemmed from his vision that human beings must make themselves satisfied with
pieces of temporary happiness that can never be complete.

His sensible verses, not nearly so gay or extravagant as many
of the examples we considered in the last chapter, struck a deep
chord with the mass of Greeks, who thought they touched on
the truth—and with such clarity as to require no commentary:

Happy he who has his sons and hounds,
his horses and a friend far from his bounds.

Just as rich he of abundant horn
of gold and silver, fields of blackest clod,
and horse and mule; and he, though lesser born,
who eats and sleeps well and goes softly shod
and now and then enjoys a girl, a lad,
and vigor quite enough to have a go.
Here's *true* wealth, for there's no one, king or cad,
can take it with him when he goes below.
And none of us can buy escape from death
or dread disease or failing force and breath.

One cannot fail to be attracted to Solon's reconciled serenity, nor can the modern reader fail to notice to what extent
his attitude is fortified by aristocratic advantage. The "lesser
born" is imagined as enjoying the simplest pleasures of life—
food, sleep, sex—just as much as the aristocrat enjoys his
horses and hounds and the rich man his estates and treasury.
Each may find contentment in his lot. This is at base the
sentiment of a Tory, not dissimilar to the entitled voice of
Victorian England, where an enlightened churchman could
preach on the simple cotter "rejoicing over his potato," while
the churchman was doubtless looking forward to a rather
richer repast. But it is nearly impossible to find the lesser born, speaking on their own behalf, anywhere in world literature before the eighteenth cen-tury, when writers such as Robert Burns ("A Man's a Man for A' That") speak for the first time in the authentic voice of the cotter; and such voices are heard infrequently enough even to the present moment.[α] In the an-

---

α Frank McCourt's *Angela's Ashes* caused such a stir when it was published in 1996 in part because the clean elegance of its prose was married to the narra-tive of a kind of life that is seldom memorialized in lit-erature. Few who grow up in circumstances of extreme poverty have the opportu-nity to master the middle-class craft of writing.

cient world, the lesser born found voice only through the mouths of those who had the requisite skills to speak aloud.

Solon appears, in retrospect, the representative figure in a great transition. In Homer there are no cities to speak of (except for utopian Troy), just large aristocratic holdings, like those of Odysseus on Ithaca and Menelaus at Sparta, surrounded by lesser landowners, interspersed with peasant farmers, free tenants, and slaves. As these familiar clustered settlements, known to agricultural societies throughout the world, grew into cities—with demarcated streets, temples and other official buildings, marketplaces and other gathering centers, import-export warehouses, and docks where exotic cargoes and even more exotic foreigners were unloaded—power shifted somewhat from landed aristocrats to the better-placed urbanites, who controlled trade and who in the diversity of their experience began to think new thoughts. Though this process is typical of the development of city culture everywhere, the Greeks, with their well-established spirit of innovative and independent thinking, were in a position to push urbanization in directions never before dreamed of. This was especially true of Greek cities in possession of natural harbors that could be turned into thriving ports, such as Athens with its large, beautifully sheltered harbor of Piraeus, facing southeast toward the stepping-stones of the Cycladic isles and, beyond these, the coast of an Asia overflowing in desirable commodities.

In Homer's day, Greek communities were ruled by a *basileus* like Odysseus. This word, usually translated as "king," had in early times the somewhat humbler connotations of chieftain, captain, lord, leader, judge. (It will be the word put into the mouth of Jesus in the New Testament parables about God and

his *basileia*, his kingdom or dominion.) But it was a decidedly
hereditary position, one that did not fit well with city life. Since
cities were experiments in themselves, it made sense to the
Greeks to experiment with modes of urban government. As the
day of the landed gentry began to fade, Greek cities adopted, or
sometimes had forced upon them, the new office of *tyrannos*.
Though *tyrannos* gives us our word *tyrant,* the initial difference
between the *basileus* and the *tyrannos* was that the *tyrannos* was
a nonhereditary king, one who had obtained his position by
sheer excellence. It was only as the *tyrannos* turned (as often as
not) into a dictator unconcerned for the wishes of his people
that the designation acquired a pejorative connotation.

Though tyrants would continue to rule many Greek cities
for much of their history, Athens in the early sixth century was
already experimenting with a system based on the consensus of
its citizens. Solon came to be *eponymos* of Athens neither by
heredity nor by force but by election; and his rule was limited
to one year. By this point, Athenian government had evolved
from monarchy to aristocracy, that is, rule by a consortium of
archons (of whom the *archon eponymos* was chief), supplied by
Athens's leading families. Aristocratic Solon, however, used his
year to enlarge the political and economic power of all freeborn
male citizens.

The city's existing law code, drawn up in 621 by one Draco,
was so harsh that it has given us the word *Draconian,* though
Draco's code did remove from individual families the right to
pursue vengeance on their own—the Hatfield-McCoy premise
on which Orestes and Electra pursued their father's murderers.
Solon labored intensively to give every citizen a stake in
Athenian society. Henceforth, every male born at Athens to a
citizen father—very nearly the only way one could become a
citizen—would have the right to prosecute a crime, even if he

were not the direct victim. Solon fashioned this innovation to impress on all their unrelinquishable obligation to the commonweal. Every citizen now had the further right to appeal unfavorable decisions of the magistrates to the great Assembly of citizens, in effect a jury of their peers. By abolishing the universal Greek custom of enslaving debtors who defaulted on their bond, Solon encouraged the security of small landowners; and he divided the citizenry into four classes, based on their holdings.

Each class now possessed specific legal rights and honors, and each was taxed accordingly. Though the wealthiest class— the *pentakosiomedimnoi*, whose holdings yielded five hundred bushel measures or more of grain, wine, or oil—bore by far the largest tax burdens, these were linked to their eligibility for the highest public offices and their status as financial sponsors of the great festivals, both of which conferred such public honor that no one would attempt to evade his obligations. In making this change, Solon tied the office of archon to wealth rather than birth and thus broke the stranglehold that the wellborn had previously exercised over politics. The two middle classes—the *hippeis* (riders of horses) and the *zeugitae* (keepers of oxen)—were also eligible to hold public office, though not at the exalted levels of the five-hundred-bushel chaps.

The upshot was that every citizen felt empowered, all assured a say in something; and even the lowest class of citizens— the *thetes* (tenant farmers and those whose tiny plots produced fewer than two hundred bushels)—had new dignity as members of the Assembly, which had the final say in most matters. Though the big winners in this new system were the smaller landowners, who gained unprecedented new rights and at last achieved defined political status, Solon carefully left many of the hereditary privileges of the aristocratic families intact.

Without the goodwill and public beneficence of the aristocracy, nothing could be accomplished; and Solon's goal was never perfect justice but the emergence of a secure and balanced society that could remain viable from one generation to the next.

But rival aristocratic clans—the Coastmen, the Plainsmen, and the Hillsmen—continued their brawling attempts to eliminate one another. Solon, who spent his retirement traveling through foreign lands to broaden his knowledge of other cultures, returned to find his beloved Athens so rent by discord that it had become impossible to elect new archons. *Anarchia*—anarchy, that is, a city without archons, ruled by nobody—swiftly followed. Solon, now past eighty, lived just long enough to see the rise of his cousin Pisistratus, a political grandstander of the vilest variety, a mine owner's son who presented himself as a populist speaking on behalf of the Hillsmen, the poorest of the Athenian parties.

Pisistratus staged an attempt on his own life and in the ensuing chaos pushed the Assembly into voting him a bodyguard, which he then used—just after Solon's death—to seize the Acropolis, the lofty citadel that loomed over the city. Declaring himself tyrant, Pisistratus was subsequently driven out by a temporary alliance of Coastmen and Plainsmen, an alliance that frayed soon enough, plunging Athens into tumult once more. Here was Pisistratus's opportunity. He made a sensational return in a golden chariot accompanied by an extraordinarily tall and beautiful young woman dressed in full battle armor, who he announced was the goddess Athena come to restore order to her city. Simple people knelt along Pisistratus's parade, raised their arms, and gave thanks in the streets. Though only the most credulous members of the Assembly could be counted on to swallow such nonsense, there were, as there often are, quite enough of them to ensure initial political victory to an unscrupulous liar who piously invoked the powers of heaven. Only later, when the damage is done, do such dodos of democracy regret allowing themselves to be so easily taken in.

Athens would be saddled with Pisistratus and his progeny for a generation and would reestablish its Solonian ideals only in the last decade of the sixth century after expelling the last Pisistratid. The citizens then began the long process of changing the nature of their Acropolis (or "city height") from a threatening fortress to an airy civic promontory. Over the course of the next fifty years, the peak was flattened to a plateau, and lofty temples and sanctuaries, dignified memorials and promenades were constructed, none more august than the Parthenon, the Temple of the Virgin, dedicated to the city's patronal goddess. By the mid-fifth century, the master sculptor Phidias set upon the promontory a towering statue of *Athēnē Promachos,* Athena Who Leads the Charge, her bronze helmet and spear tip gleaming in the sun and visible to sailors as far away as the Cape of Sounion. No one would again mistake a mere mortal for the awesome thirty-three-foot-high goddess who now stood on the Acropolis, protecting her city.

Solon's laws were displayed along the promenades on wooden tablets, and his moderating, sententious verses were learned by heart. Often enough in the nearly two centuries that followed the establishment of Athenian democracy—a political experiment that would end only with the coming of Alexander the Great in the final decades of the fourth century—Athens lived in the spirit of Solon's ideals, its citizens acting toward one another in *eunomia,* the harmony, good order, restraint to which he had counseled them. By and large, they illustrated in their dealings with one another Solon's characteristically Greek combination of practicality and wisdom, the political path he had opened to them. For, as the wooden tablets reminded them, "Men preserve agreements that profit no one to violate."

Though American democracy is often compared to its supposed Athenian model, the American experiment—as well as other modern examples of democracy—derives not directly from Greece but from the European Enlightenment of the seventeenth and eighteenth centuries of our era. The rediscovery of Athenian political ideals by the humanists of the Renaissance certainly acted as a catalyst to Enlightenment thought, but as one surveys the actual terrain of Athenian democracy, one is more likely to be struck by the vast historical and cultural divide that separates the burgeoning of Athenian democracy from the seething North American colonies of Massachusetts, Virginia, and New York in A.D. 1765, the year the Stamp Act Congress dared to pass its Declaration of Rights and Liberties.

There are, of course, interesting similarities, such as the close association of citizenship and property. Life spans were notably shorter in both Athens and North America than they are today—mid-forties on average for men, mid-thirties for women (for whom pregnancy and childbirth presented major health risks)—but an exemplary diet and regular physical exercise gave both Greek citizens and American colonials considerable advantage over the many cultures of scarcity that subsisted around them. In both societies, the economic gap between rich and poor citizens was not nearly so dramatic as it is in our contemporary Western world. The five-hundred-bushelers, for instance, were on average five, at most ten, times as rich as the *thetes*, the lowest grade of citizen. Five times as rich would have seemed a whole lot in fifth-century Athens, where tunics were mostly interchangeable, domestic buildings and even public ones were modest in size, and the only form conspicuous consumption could take was sponsoring a public festival or throwing a memorable party for your friends. Today, the gap between, say, a municipal bus driver and a Fortune 500 CEO approaches infinity.

Populations were much smaller in ancient Athens and in colonial America than they are today. At their height, Athenians probably numbered no more than a quarter million, of which as many as 100,000 may have been slaves—another similarity between democratic Athens and early democratic America. Women and children, both Greek and foreign, were commonly enslaved by the victors in war, after their husbands and fathers had been put to the sword; and though it was possible to win one's freedom, most slaves were born to their condition and remained so to their deaths, passing on their status to their children. Slaves had virtually no rights and could be bought and sold at will; and, though both male and female slaves were completely at the disposal of their masters' whims, women slaves were especially ill-used because they could become pregnant and often died in childbirth. It was a precept of Athenian law that female slaves had to be tortured before giving evidence in court cases; and if a slave owner showed himself reluctant to offer his female slaves to the torturers, he fell immediately under suspicion. Worse than torture and death was to find yourself a slave in the privately administered silver mines of Laurion southeast of Athens, source of much of Athens's prosperity, where miners were routinely starved, savagely beaten, and, seldom seeing daylight, worked to death.

It is possible that slaves made up as much as forty percent of the population of Athens and its outlying farms and that *metics*—resident aliens, nonvoting freemen engaged in trade—made up close to another forty percent. This would leave a citizen population of little more than twenty percent, which would have included males who had not reached their majority as well as females. Such a society, based economically on the slavery of others, has actually been rare in recorded history: Athens, central Roman Italy, the American South, the Caribbean, and Brazil provide our only known examples. In other "slave" economies, such as ancient Mesopotamia and Israel, the so-called slave was not viewed as mere chattel and, more like a medieval serf, possessed a number of rights, nor was the proportion of serfs to freemen in such societies as high as it was in genuine slave economies.

However similar Athens and colonial America may appear in these respects, the differences remain glaring and decisive. For one thing, Athens was a city, not a country; and the Greeks never thought to unite all Greek speakers in one political union. Because each Greek gloried in his singular excellence— and each Greek clan gloried similarly—it was hard enough to unite a city. Each city or *polis*—from which come our words *politics, politician, metropolis*—thought itself unrivaled in some essential quality and reveled in its reputation. Corinth, for instance, situated strategically between two seas on the isthmus that joined northern Greece to the Peloponnesian peninsula, was the unbeatable merchant city, principal trade route between north and south and between east and west. Crossroads of desirable refinements, Corinth became in time a byword for sybaritic self-indulgence.

β Our word *xenophobia* is formed from two Greek nouns, *xenos* (stranger) and *phobos* (panic flight or panic fear). *Phobos* is used in English in many Greek-inspired combination words, such as *acrophobia* (fear of heights), *agoraphobia* (fear of open spaces).

Landlocked Sparta, not many miles south on the Peloponnese, ruled by its *gerousia*, or council of old men, was an airless, artless nightmare of xenophobic[β] military preparedness, the North Korea of its day. A Spartan boy was taken from home at age seven and thereafter raised in barracks, directed by an older boy with whom he was encouraged to develop a permanent and ardent relationship. He could neither leave the barracks nor marry till the age of thirty, by which time he had become a brutal army grunt; and he could not leave the army and settle in a house of his own till the age of sixty. Black broth and much-diluted wine were his daily fare through all this time; his occasional baths were cold. Girls hardly fared better, since theirs was a similar single-sex regimen, shortened only by Sparta's need to produce children. With such a regimen, it is not surprising that the city's population declined, a perilous precipitation for Sparta, which depended on an abysmally servile population of *helots*, fellow Greeks who lived under permanent military occupation in the neighboring countryside and who tended the land while Sparta's citizenry, who despised farming, trained for war. These state-owned serfs—there were seven of them for every citizen—led comfortless lives and were perennially on the verge of revolt. Each year the newly elected *ephors* (Sparta's five chief magistrates) declared ritual war on the helots and every potential leader among them was assassinated. Sparta's teenage citizens were encouraged to roam in bands through the helots' territory, ruining their pitiable compounds and spreading abject terror. Sparta needed a constant show of armed power by sufficiently massive forces just to keep its serfs in check. It was the helots who truly knew what *Spartan* meant.

Each of the principal Greek cities had a highly distinctive personality that set it off from its sisters. Athens was the home of thoughtfulness, democracy, and art. Its Solonian political establishment and its open culture, which put a higher premium on individual accomplishment—political, cultural, intellectual—than any human settlement prior to the European Renaissance, spread far and wide as its uniquely attractive qualities were imitated by its hundred fifty or so colonies throughout Eurasia. Athenian democracy was different from the much later American form, not only because it was the expression of a single city-state but because it was a direct, rather than a representative, democracy. To us, looking backwards, it may seem imprudent to invite all citizens to vote on all major initiatives, but Solon was right to appreciate that no Athenian freeman could allow himself to be left out of *anything*.

The continual buzz of conversation, the orotund sounds of the orators, the shrill shouts from the symposia—this steady drumbeat of opinion, controversy, and conflict could everywhere be heard. The *agora* (marketplace) was not just a daily display of fish and farm goods; it was an everyday market of ideas, the place citizens used as if it were their daily newspaper, complete with salacious headlines, breaking news, columns, and editorials. For more formal occasions, there nestled beside the Acropolis the hill of the Pnyx, where thousands of citizens voted in their Assembly. They faced the *bēma* (speaker's platform) and, behind the speaker, the ever-changing backdrop of Athens itself. Though there were wooden benches, set into the steps of the hill, participants were too taken up by the proceedings to bother to sit down. The word the Athenians used for their Assembly was *Ekklēsia*, the same word used in the New Testament for *Church* (and it is the greatest philological irony in all of Western history that this word, which connoted equal participation in all deliberations by all members, came to designate a kind of self-perpetuating, self-protective Spartan *gerousia*—which would have seemed patent nonsense to Greek-speaking Christians of New Testament times, who believed themselves to be equal members of *their* Assembly).

Ten thousand men could be accommodated comfortably, fifteen thousand uncomfortably, on the Pnyx, where the Assembly convened forty times a year, each meeting lasting but a couple of hours. Six thousand citizens constituted the quorum necessary for ratification of many of the decrees. Imagine your fellow citizens—at least twenty percent of them, sometimes as many as fifty percent—squeezing forty times a year into an open-air stadium, listening to debates, noisily electing magistrates (including the ten *stratēgoi* chosen annually to conduct the city's wars), voting on decrees by a show of hands, impaneling jurors. On each of the popular courts, called *dicastēria*, 201 to 501 citizens served as both judges and jurors, the number of citizens depending on the seriousness of the matter under consideration. Once a year, the citizens voted on whether or not they should hold an ostracism. If the majority voted yes, each member of the Assembly then wrote on an *ostrakon* (potsherd) the name of the person he felt the city could best do without. Whoever turned up on the most *ostraka* was banished for ten years, after which time he could return, his property still intact. In this way, would-be tyrants—and not a few other nuisances—were eliminated. (If at first the primitiveness of this procedure shocks you, consider for a moment what benefits it could bring to *your* city.)

Athens, the world's first attempt at democracy—a Greek word meaning "rule by the people"—still stands out as the most wildly participatory government in history. Never again would such a broadly based, decidedly nonrepresentative model be attempted. And, given the compactness of Athens, the theatrical extroversion of its citizenry, and the consequent excitement of their meetings, it worked.

THE ASSEMBLY was not Athens's only arena of democracy. In Solon's old age, another kind of forum emerged, an artistic innovation as inventive as the political one. It was made possible by the air of free discussion that permeated the city, and it afforded its citizens regular opportunities to consider the profoundest issues of their political and social life. It was called *drama*; and it rose out of the musical presentations that were central to the great religious festivals. The soloist who stepped forward from the chorus often represented a storied god or hero, an assumed persona, sometimes dressed in a recognizable costume (say, the armor of Athena or the lion skin of Hercules), sometimes wearing a mask for further identification. In time, the dialogue between soloist and chorus became more elaborate, as episodes from one of the myths were reenacted on a circular dancing floor (called an *orchestra*) around a stepped altar dedicated to the festival god. The chorus, arranged around the altar, sang its commentary on the soloist's story and danced in consecrated movements, while the members of the audience, seated in a *theatron* (watching place), a semicircular terraced hillside, listened in hushed reverence to the story and supported with their own voices the musical responses of the chorus. This is the essence of what the Greeks called *leitourgia* (work of the people, public service performed without recompense, liturgy).

Out of liturgy, then, rose the world's first drama, as it would rise a second time out of liturgy—in the eleventh century when a soloist, in this case portraying an angel, stepped forward from the monastic chorus, portraying the women at the tomb of Jesus, and asked, "*Quem quaeritis?*" ("Whom seek ye?") From pagan Greek liturgy came all of ancient drama; from medieval Latin liturgy came all of modern drama. That drama has always risen out of liturgy suggests that even the most secular theater is caught up in some aspects of communal religious experience: a large, hushed arena of spectators, who laugh, cry, applaud (and perhaps even sing) together and are therefore conscious of their fleeting bonds of community—their communion with the personae brought to life by the actors, their communion with one another as witnesses to a symbolic story that is, at least in some archetypal sense, a mirror of their own lives and the lives of their families and friends. It is this (usually) unspoken religious dimension that can give theater such depth, even at times such mystical resonance.

A legendary figure called Thespis (whence *thespian*) is credited with developing the soloist into a genuine stage character, partly by his invention of a larger-than-life mask, which enabled a character to be identified even by the lowest orders of society occupying the back rows of the theatron and enabled a young man to play a woman or an old man and, by careful training and by virtue of the megaphone built into the mouth of the mask, to project his voice as far as the last row. High, thick-soled shoes called *buskins* increased the actor's stature. Despite its hushed attention, the Athenian audience was an impatient one, hoping to be seized by emotion but poised to taunt a bumbling actor or an indifferent script. Even beloved theatrical figures could receive rough treatment. The famous tragic actor Hegelochus was hooted off the stage when (in Euripides's *Orestes*) he slipped up on a tongue twister—"The calm that comes when storms are past again I see"—and uttered with consummate dignity something on the order of "The comb that calms when palms are stashed again I pee."

In the fifth century, Aeschylus, the first of the great playwrights, added a second actor to the dramatic ensemble and made his actors the principal players, concomitantly reducing the role of the chorus, who nonetheless retained a role in the unfolding of the plot. His plays contain no cliffhangers, no surprises. Drawing, rather, on stories known to all—such as "The Fall of the House of Atreus," with which this chapter began—Aeschylus presents us with august, slow-moving pageants of times past. His characters give poetic speeches and employ exalted language. The simplicity of Aeschylus's cycles of plays has much in common with the simplicity of the medieval mystery cycles: this is this, and that is that. Their beauty lies not in complexity of metaphor nor subtlety of concept; they exemplify the clarity of orthodox religious thought—the lesson that god is god and cannot be hoodwinked by men. In Aeschylus's case, the god is Zeus, whose justice falls on those whose *hubris* (insolence) has tempted them to defy the right order of the world. Guilt, like wealth, can be inherited, falling in a never-ending chain reaction on the children of the guilty, then on their children, then on theirs. Only the creation of a finer, more just human system—which in Aeschylus's *Eumenides*, the third play of the *Oresteia*, turns out to be Athenian democracy—can arrest this downward spiral and transform even ancient goddesses of unending vengeance into public-spirited presences, watching, like all divinities, over the blessed fate of Athens.

Aeschylus used ancient legend to speak to a contemporary issue, namely, opposition by aristocrats to their loss of power under the democratic reforms. The playwright's final message: heaven wills a better way, so your objections, like those of the aboriginally terrifying Furies, are beside the point; though we must fear you and take you into account, you will no longer control all outcomes. Thus was the sacred pattern set for Aeschylus and the dramatists who followed him: a consecrated, apodictic story, its truth beyond contest, its roots sunk deep in Greek consciousness, but shaped now by the playwright to speak to the *polis* in its present moment. The chorus came in many plays to represent the common man, the audience, amazed by the outsized nature of the action, mouthing simple verities and coming to new insight in the course of the drama.

The second great tragedian was Sophocles, Aeschylus's younger contemporary, who introduced a third actor in his dramas, a practice gladly imitated by Aeschylus in his later plays. This paucity of actors on the stage reflects the liturgical roots of Greek theater, which continued to stick close to its religious origins. Authentic liturgy is always steeped in tradition and, eschewing novelty, changes slowly lest it lose its essence. But gradually, other improvements were introduced: a raised platform at the back of the orchestra, forerunner of our modern stage, from which the actors delivered their lines; the *skēnē* (whence our *scene*), the facade of a building that served as backdrop for the stage and concealed the actors' dressing rooms. On its roof certain actions could be played, such as the setting for the palace watchman at the outset of *Agamemnon*, the first play in the *Oresteia*. Its wide central doorway could be opened to reveal a tableau, such as bloody Clytemnestra standing over the savaged bodies of Agamemnon and Cassandra. For such a display, the actors were wheeled through the double doors on a platform, called an *ekkyklēma* (roller). Another machine, called a *mēchanē*, was a sort of crane that swung an actor playing a god over the parapet of the *skēnē* and out above the stage (thus the Latin phrase *deus ex machina* for a solution from nowhere, an unforeseen answer to prayers).

Though the Greeks found it unnatural to avoid innovation entirely, in their theater they limited themselves to what seemed necessary enhancements to the drama itself. The roller, for instance, was necessary because the actual violence of murder could not be depicted as part of religious ritual; only its consequences could be displayed. As with a Christian crucifix, some distancing, some framing, some symbolization was required; one could not bring the actuality into liturgy. But certain elements—the altar in the open-air circle, the stepped hillside for seating—remained constant throughout the history of Greek theater, which spread eventually from Athens to en-

thusiastic audiences as far away as Italy and Gaul, Arabia and
Persia.

In Sophocles we reach Greek theater at its most exquisitely
political; and never in theatrical history has there been a more
political play than Sophocles's *Oedipus Tyrannos* (called often by
its Latin title, *Oedipus Rex*). Young Oedipus traveled to the city
of Thebes while it was being terrorized by a monster called the
Sphinx, who ate all those who could not answer the riddle she
posed: What walks on four legs in the morning, two at noon,
and three at evening? The answer: a man, who crawls in in-
fancy and uses a stick in old age. Oedipus solved the riddle,
whereupon the Sphinx committed suicide and the newcomer
was welcomed as *tyrannos* of Thebes. He married the desirable
Jocasta, widow of the recently murdered king, Laius, and sired
two sons and two daughters by her.

This is the proximate background to the play, which opens
on a Thebes newly beset, this time by plague, a curse inflicted,
as we know from the *Iliad*, by the god Apollo. "Death / so
many deaths, numberless deaths on deaths, no end— / Thebes
is dying," sings the chorus. Oedipus, typical politician, delivers
a speech to the citizen-petitioners of the chorus, gathered in
front of his palace:

> My children,
> I pity you. I see—how could I fail to see
> what longings bring you here? Well I know
> you are sick to death, all of you,
> but sick as you are, not one is sick as I.
> Your pain strikes each of you alone, each
> in the confines of himself, no other. But my spirit
> grieves for the city, for myself and all of you.
> I wasn't asleep, dreaming. You haven't wakened me—

I have wept through the nights, you must know that,
groping, laboring over many paths of thought.

He feels their pain—and vows to get to the bottom of things, to learn why Apollo has sent the plague, and to "bring it all to light myself."

But even as the chorus in their middling intelligence soon suspects, this crisis will not yield to Oedipus's heroic intelligence as did the Sphinx. Apollo's oracle at Delphi—Greece's holiest, most mystical site—pronounces that the plague has come because the blood of Laius, Thebes's murdered king, goes unavenged and that the murderer himself is the corruption harbored by the city. Oedipus, as the Greek audience would have known, is the murderer. Though he does not know it, Laius was his father and Jocasta is his mother. Laius long ago, learning from the Delphic oracle that he would be murdered by his own son, ordered that his newborn babe be exposed^γ upon Mount Cithaeron, left to be eaten by animals or to perish in the elements, his ankles pierced together with a spike. The Theban slave to whom Jocasta gave the child, however, could not in his tenderness leave him to die and entrusted him instead to a Corinthian shepherd, who brought him to his own city, where the boy was raised as the adopted son of the childless king and queen. As a young man Oedipus himself heard at Delphi that he would murder his father and marry his mother. Unaware of his adoption, he left Corinth for good, preventing, as he thought, the prophecy from coming to pass. On his journey, princely Oedipus passed Laius and his party at a "triple crossroad," not knowing who he

γ In the ancient world, in which contraception was normally by magical means and abortion often spelled death for the woman, exposure of infants was common, giving us the common Latin surname *Expositus* (Esposito in later Italian and Spanish), which came to designate an orphan abandoned—more often on a doorstep than in the wild.

was. When the haughty old king attempted to push Oedipus off the road, Oedipus killed him, then journeyed on to Thebes, saved the city, became its king, and married the widowed queen.

All this Oedipus, in his determination to "bring it all to light myself," will learn step by step. Toward the play's end, just after the final revelation, Jocasta hangs herself. Oedipus, discovering her, "eased her down / in a slow embrace," then tore from her body

> the long gold pins
> holding her robes—and lifting them high,
> looking straight up into the points,
> he digs them down the sockets of his eyes, crying, "You,
> you'll see no more the pain I suffered, all the pain I caused!
> Too long you looked on the ones you never should have seen,
> blind to the ones you longed to see, to know! Blind
> from this hour on! Blind in the darkness—blind!"
> His voice like a dirge, rising, over and over
> raising the pins, raking them down his eyes.
> And at each stroke blood spurts from the roots,
> splashing his beard, a swirl of it, nerves and clots—
> black hail of blood pulsing, gushing down.

For the original spectators, the turns of the screw that Sophocles administered throughout this play must have been received with sharp pain, not because they did not know the story but because these cocky, princely, Oedipal Greeks were being made to feel acutely the limitations of human society— in which no political leader, no matter how gifted or courageous, can remain a savior forever, in which every man must come to know that he is no hero but essentially a flawed and luckless figure and that "the pains we inflict upon ourselves hurt most of all." As blind Oedipus is led away by his daughters to the wretched, vagrant life that faces them, the chorus speaks the play's last, comfortless words:

> People of Thebes, my countrymen, look on Oedipus.
> He solved the famous riddle with his brilliance,
> he rose to power, a man beyond all power.
> Who could behold his greatness without envy?
> Now what a black sea of terror has overwhelmed him.
> Now as we keep our watch and wait the final day,
> count no man happy till he dies, free of pain at last.

Aeschylus's trilogy on the House of Atreus begins at Mycenae and ends at Athens. The action of Sophocles's *Oedipus* begins and ends in a single day at Thebes, all its scenes taking place on the steps of the palace of the *tyrannos*, its matter the straightforward inquiry by Oedipus into the source of the city's pollution, an inquiry that begins and ends with him. For the fourth-century Athenian philosopher Aristotle, *Oedipus* was the perfect tragedy, observing the unities of time, place, and action, presenting as its central character a model human being, whose *hamartia* brings him down. This *hamartia* (tragic flaw, the same word that early Christians will use for "sin," especially for original sin, the sin we are born with, the sin beyond any human being's control) is not incidental to Oedipus but is, rather, essential to his admirable character. He is strong, courageous, self-possessed, taking charge and striding boldly where others fear to go—the very qualities that foretell his undoing. Our vicarious involvement in the lives of the principal characters elicits our pity for them and our fear for ourselves—lest something similar should happen to us. The *peripeteia*, the fall of people better than ourselves, and their *anagnōrisis*, their recognition of their true situation—Jocasta in her suicide, Oedipus in his self-mutilation—finally engenders in us, the audience, a *catharsis*, a purging of our distraught emotions on their behalf and our behalf.

We remember in the final moments of the drama, said Aristotle, that this is not life but *mimēsis*, a mimicking of life, an imitation. The actors leave the stage and the central doors are shut for the last time. It is as if we have been playing with dolls, imitation humans that we have now put back in their box. We leave the theater warned by what we have witnessed but purged of negative emotions. We are pleasantly exhausted now, as if we had recently expelled a poison from our body. We are at peace, exalted by our encounter with this pageant of truth, just as a medieval pilgrim would have felt after looking on a sequence of brightly colored windows depicting the passion of Jesus. I am restored by this vicarious brush with destruction and death. I didn't die. I am still alive—and can face tomorrow with a certain placid wisdom.

Aristotle's analysis—though, much later, it would lead the French playwrights of the seventeenth century to bind themselves by rigid rules—has never been improved upon. Freud's "Oedipus complex" may be an insightful treatment of the Oedipus myth for modern psychological purposes, but it sheds little light on this play. Aristotle's aesthetic, however, which is laid out in his treatise the *Poetics*,[δ] enables us to penetrate the emotional (and even the religious) temper of classical Athens.

The Greeks were strivers far more than they were individualists, men who all felt in their heart of hearts that they should be in charge like Oedipus, women who all saw themselves as gracious but sharp-eyed queens

---

δ *Aesthetic* and *poetics* are derived from Greek, as are our many words ending in *-ic* and *-ics*.

like Jocasta. If we could save but one word from Greek civilization, it would have to be *aretē*, excellence. The aristocrats gave themselves their name, the *aristoi* (the best). It is an open question whether anyone considered himself a member of the *kakoi* (the worst, the craven, the dumb shits), though this put-down prances everywhere in the surviving literature. But there can be no question that *aristoi* striving for *aretē* don't kill their fathers or sleep with their mothers and that shame—the paralyzing fear of being numbered among the *kakoi*—is the hidden engine that ran Greek life.

These were people who thought very well of themselves, as the not-so-humble Aristotle happily informs us himself:

> Europeans, as well as peoples who live in cold climates generally, are full of spirit but somewhat lacking in intelligence and skill; and because of these deficiencies, though they live in comparative freedom, they lack political organization and the ability to rule others. Asians, on the other hand, though intelligent and skilled by nature, lack spirit and so are always subject to defeat and slavery. The race of the Greeks, however, which occupies the center of the earth, shares the best attributes of West and East, being both spirited and intelligent. Thus does this race enjoy both freedom and stable political institutions and continue to be capable of ruling all humanity.

The Greeks, as their playwrights if not their philosophers knew, were in desperate need of the admonition—the vicarious comeuppance—that a play such as *Oedipus* could provide.

You will not be surprised to learn that, like so much else in Greek life, playwriting turned into a contest. At the springtime Dionysia, the Athenian festival in honor of Dionysus, three days of tragedies, chosen in advance, were performed almost in the manner of a modern film festival, though with significant differences. The festival began with a solemn religious procession of leading citizens, distinguished visitors, and all the choruses, garlanded and colorfully costumed for the plays they would appear in, led by officials who carried the great *phalloi*, enormous sculptures of erect penises, symbols of the god, to his temple, where the ten *stratēgoi*, the generals of the Athenian armies, poured libations and offered animal sacrifices. After this grand opening, thirty thousand festival-goers—twice as many participants as ever showed up for the Assembly—crowded into the vast open-air theater in the hollow on the southern slope of the Acropolis to watch the new productions.

Aeschylus, who wrote more than eighty plays (of which only seven have come down to us), won thirteen first-place victories. Since tragedies were presented in trilogy, this actually meant that thirty-nine of his plays were winners. His younger contemporary Sophocles, who lived to be ninety and never stopped writing, was even more successful. He had begun his theatrical career as a beautiful chorus boy and went on to hold several public offices, twice elected general by the Athenian Assembly, much helped by his temperate nature and general likability. He wrote more than 120 plays (of which we have but seven) and won twenty-four first-place victories—for the majority of his trilogies. All the rest of his plays won second place.

Euripides, the third great dramatist, was not so fortunate. A decade or so younger than Sophocles, he died just before him in 406 B.C. At the Dionysia that year, the generous, fair-minded Sophocles commemorated his colleague's death by presenting his chorus in mourning, ungarlanded. But Euripides, a loner with few friends, won in his lifetime only four victories at the Dionysia, though he wrote more than ninety plays (of which, by chance, nineteen have survived).

Far more decisive than his personality, Euripides's penchant for naturalism deprived him of recognition during his lifetime. Aristotle tells us that "Sophocles said he drew men as they ought to be, and Euripides as they were." Euripides had no patience for elevated language or the chimeras of nobility. His characters, even if they were *aristoi*, might find themselves in rags or be overheard to utter shockingly foul thoughts; and his slaves might show themselves to be truly noble. These reversals of conventional expectations were too upsetting to the audiences of Euripides's day for him ever to become the darling of Athens.

In nothing was Euripides more unexpected than his presentation of the thoughts and actions of women. In his *Medea*, for instance, the title character is a witch who already has a string of murders to her name. Having fallen in love with Jason, she used her magic to enable him to steal the Golden Fleece from her father, the king of Colchis at the eastern edge of the Black Sea. The couple then took refuge in luxurious Corinth, where Medea bore Jason two sons. But as the play opens, Jason, now well adjusted to a life of ease and tired of Medea, has deserted her and arranged a profitable new marriage for himself with the local princess, daughter of Creon, Corinth's king. Euripides's Jason is no Greek hero, hardly the swashbuckling adventurer who put out to sea with his fellow heroes, the famed Argonauts, in a story beloved by all Greeks. He is just another self-promoting, self-justifying cad, the typical cheating husband. Since the audience was full of men who cheated on their wives, who got rid of their wives once they tired of them, who had taken up with teenage chippies, men whose self-justifications were the quintessence of eloquence, it is no surprise that Euripides's *Medea* lost the competition it was entered in.

But more shocking than the playwright's daring presentation

of the typical Greek husband is his portrayal of Medea, the foreign witch who speaks the truth in her very first appearance on stage, dripping her sarcasm over the audience:

> Ladies, Corinthians, I'm here.
> Don't think ill of me. Call others proud.
> In public, in private, it's hard to get it right.
> Tread as carefully as you will,
> "She's proud," they'll say, "she won't join in."
> What human being looks fairly on another?
> They'd sooner hate than know you properly,
> even before you've done them any harm.
> And when you're a foreigner: "Be like us," they say.
> Even Greeks look down on other Greeks,
> too clever to see the good in them.
> As for me, the blow that struck me down
> and eats my heart I least expected.
> My lovely life is lost; I want to die.
> He was everything to me—and now
> he's the vilest man alive, my husband.
>
> Of all Earth's creatures that live and breathe,
> are we women not the wretchedest?
> We scratch and save, a dowry to buy a man—
> and then he lords it over us: we're his,
> our lives depend on how his lordship feels.
> For better for worse: we can't divorce him.
> However it turns out, he's ours and ours he stays.
> Women's cunning? We need all of it.
> Set down with strangers, with ways and laws
> she never knew at home, a wife must learn
> every trick she can to please the man

whose bed she shares. If he's satisfied,
if he lives content, rides not against the yoke—
Congratulations! If not, we're better dead.
A husband, tired of domesticity,
goes out, sees friends, enjoys himself—
but we must always look to him alone.
Our reward? A quiet life they promise us.
They'll grab the spears. They'll take the strain.
I'd three times sooner go to war
than suffer childbirth once.

There's not a line here that would not outrage someone's sensibility. And two lines dare to challenge divine Homer himself, whose poetry was known to all by heart. In the *Iliad*, after the death of Patroclus, Zeus delivers the famous *aperçu*:

There is nothing alive more agonized than man
of all that breathe and crawl across the earth.

"Man" is now knocked from his perch, noble "mankind" parodied by "women"! Zeus, our high god, pushed aside by this monstrous foreign hag, this Black Sea bitch, this————! The Greeks had a rich multiplicity of slurs at their command, and we can be sure they used them in this instance. *Medea* is an early play in the Euripidean canon. But the playwright would be forced to listen to the criticism that raged against him throughout his thirty-year career. By 408, he had exiled himself from Athens in bitterness and died two years later in Macedon.

At the drama's climax, Medea, having effected the excruciating death of her rival, the princess bride, murders her own children to achieve complete revenge on Jason. *Pace* Aristotle, there's no catharsis here, no wise and placid exit from the theater for all those entitled Greek males, the ones who hadn't already stormed out, the ones still quivering in their seats on the gently terraced hillside. "Of course, she was a foreign witch, not Greek at all, a depraved, unnatural woman, so what could one expect?" With such excuses they may have soothed themselves as they found their way to the exits; and violent, unbalanced Euripides gained a reputation for being unfair, especially to women. They missed the point. Euripides did not mean to expose women as more base and irrational than men. He was posing a question to his audience: what could drive a woman to such extremes that she would kill her own children? And he found the answer smack in the middle of Greek life as it was then lived.

For the strutting *aristoi* of the symposia, the nature of life was obvious: you gave it or you got it. To represent ancient Greece as a homosexual society is to miss the central lesson. It was a militarized society that saw everything in terms of active and passive, swords and wounds, *phalloi* and gashes. Aristocratic boys were courted by aristocratic men as part of a puberty ordeal, the last step before adulthood, during which the man was to act as a model and help the boy achieve bristling manhood. He could masturbate between the boy's thighs but was not allowed to come in his mouth or sodomize him. He was not, therefore, allowed to make him into a passive partner. Of course, he—and any male citizen—could do whatever he liked to anyone else, male or female, adult or child, so long as his object was not another citizen or a properly married woman. If she were divorced, as Medea was about to be, she was as fair game as anyone. The Homeric insights into longtime love between two people—Hector and Andromache, Odysseus and Penelope—are never spoken of again in Greek literature after the close of the *Odyssey*. Sappho's expressed preference for love of an individual—"black earth's most beautiful thing"—over the beautiful cavalries, infantries, and navies that entranced most Greeks remains a solitary preference, never again voiced after her death in the early sixth century. Rather, the Greeks became ever more striving, ever more competitive, ever more bellicose. Sometimes, all they seemed to be left with was fucking or getting fucked.

After Euripides died, his last trilogy of plays was presented at the Dionysia and took first place, helped no doubt by the well-regarded Sophocles's public reverence of his colleague's memory. The Athenians, who, after all, prided themselves on their openness to invention, learned soon enough to tolerate Euripidean discomfort. One of the last three plays was the *Bacchae* (*Women of Bacchus,* that is, the female celebrants of the rites of the god Bacchus, or Dionysus), and it is the most unsettling of all Greek dramas. We are back in Thebes, where King Pentheus is opposed to the introduction of the cult of Dionysus, lord of wine and wild inspiration, which the king sees only as a source of chaos. Unbeknown to him, his own mother, Agavē, has joined the cult and, inspired by the god, dances in ecstasy with her fellow *bacchae* on Mount Cithaeron. Pentheus goes to spy on them and is ripped to pieces by the *bacchae,* who, in their ecstasy, mistake him for a mountain lion. His own mother brings his head in triumph back to Thebes and only by degrees returns to herself and recognizes what she has done.

The play served as Euripides's final warning to his fellow Athenians, so sure of themselves, that there were forces in life they were militantly ignoring, forces that could undo them and their whole political and social establishment. In the nineteenth century, Friedrich Nietzsche's *The Birth of Tragedy* proposed that there were two poles in Greek civilization: daylight, intellectual clarity, mind, measure, all represented by Apollo; and darkness, emotion, inspiration, chaos, all represented by Diony-sus, the inspirer of tragedy and the more important god. But Apollo was always more important to the Greeks. Like Pentheus, they feared Dionysus and didn't quite know what to do about him. Euripides reminded them that there was a sub-terranean reality they were unaware of, a god whom, despite their festival, they had yet to acknowledge.

V
THE
PHILOSOPHER
HOW TO THINK

"Next," I said, "here's a situation which you can use as an analogy for the human condition—for our education or lack of it. Imagine people living in a cavernous cell down under the ground; at the far end of the cave, a long way off, there's an entrance open to the outside world. They've been there since childhood, with their legs and necks tied up in a way which keeps them in one place and allows them to look only straight ahead, but not to turn their heads. There's firelight burning a long way further up the cave behind them, and up the slope between the fire and the prisoners there's a road, beside which you should imagine a low wall has been built—like the partition which conjurors place between themselves and their audience and above which they show their tricks."

"All right," he said.

"Imagine also that there are people on the other side of this wall who are carrying all sorts of artifacts. These artifacts, human statuettes, and animal models carved in stone and wood and all kinds of materials stick out over the wall; and as you'd expect, some of the people talk as they carry these objects along, while others are silent."

"This is a strange picture you're painting," he said, "with strange prisoners."

"They're no different from us," I said. "I mean, in the first place, do you think they'd see anything of themselves and one another except the shadows cast by the fire on to the cave wall directly opposite them?"

"Of course not," he said. "They're forced to spend their lives without moving their heads."

"And what about the objects which were being carried along? Won't they only see their shadows as well?"

"Naturally."

"Now, suppose they were able to talk to one another: don't you think they'd assume that their words applied to what they saw passing in front of them?"

"They couldn't think otherwise."

"And what if the sound echoed off the prison wall opposite them? When any of the passersby spoke, don't you think they'd be bound to assume that the sound came from a passing shadow?"

"I'm absolutely certain of it," he said.

"All in all, then," I said, "the shadows of artifacts would constitute the only reality people in this situation would recognize."

"That's absolutely inevitable," he agreed.

E VERY GREAT PHILOSOPHY has been . . . the personal confession of its author and a kind of involuntary and unconscious memoir," exclaims Nietzsche in *Beyond Good and Evil*. No one can doubt the confessional dimension of Nietzsche's seminal first book, *The Birth of Tragedy*, published in 1872 and so disconcerting to his fellow classicists that it ruined his reputation as a scholar. But over time its thesis came to replace what had been till then the standard Enlightenment view of classical Greece as the home of "noble simplicity and silent greatness"—all those placid white statues forever maintaining their blissful dignity. Its seldom-used full title, *The Birth of Tragedy from the Spirit of Music*, hints at its grand purpose: to elevate the music of Richard Wagner as the model for a new tragic age. Nietzsche scorned both Sophocles and Euripides for, as he saw it, degrading Greek tragedy from its original Dionysian purpose by the introduction of excessive (Apollonian) rationalism. Four years later, he turned against the composer for failing to advance sufficiently into Dionysian madness; thirteen years after that about-face, the philosopher went insane and remained so till his death in 1900. Till recently, it had been universally assumed that Nietzsche's harrowing last years were the result of the effect on his brain of late-stage syphilis. But the neurologist Richard Schain has made a compelling case for "manic-depressive psychosis which gave way in time to signs of chronic schizophrenia." If so, the categories Apollonian and Dionysian may be seen as Nietzsche's attempt to name the polarity he found within himself.

But it is not necessary to buy Nietzsche's whole thesis in order to find his categories useful. Apollo, giver of sunlight and measurement, the great archer whose arrows never miss their targets, is the god of severe justice, the god in whom the sense of order is paramount, the one who cannot rest till all wrongs have been righted and all corners have been plumbed. It is Apollo who cannot bear to allow Oedipus to continue his reign and whose holy and uncanny presence is felt throughout Sophocles's play, sparking supernatural fear in all who sense his proximity. The divine model for the typical human hero, Apollo stands in stark contrast to Dionysus, dark lord from the East, giver of the vine, showing himself an alluringly effeminate youth with long, luxuriant hair, surrounded by the vines that entangle others and attended by his satyrs—boisterous creatures from the countryside, horned, betailed, goat-footed (the very images that would be adopted by Christian artists to portray devils), enormous penises erect, subhuman sex machines always at the ready. This was the god for whom the Dionysia was celebrated, whose primitive choruses—called *tragōdiai* (goat-songs)—were the origin of drama. Even in fifth-century Athens, the trilogies of the great tragedians each ended with a short satyr (or satyric) play, a coarse burlesque of mythic material connected to the preceding trilogy. It helped to set aside all that tragic seriousness and brought the day to a merry close, introducing the night of drinking that lay ahead.

That the Greeks consecrated so much time to such a god suggests they had some inkling of the dark forces that could conquer their best strivings, their quest for *aretē*, and they meant to pay these forces sufficient homage to keep them at bay. The lost utopias of cloud-bound Ithaca and lofty Troy had been replaced by a real-life ideal, a *polis* of visionary perfection, democratic Athens and its many imitators, a system in which all the inevitable political tensions were kept in balance by "agreements that profit no one to violate." The symposium and the Dionysia were two of several characteristically Greek safety valves for blowing off the social steam that might otherwise build to an explosion. But the libations, the choruses, and the processions were also pleas to the gods to leave their ideal *polis* intact, not visit it with the ills that had destroyed so many others:

> How often have whole cities had to pay
> for choosing one who can but evil do.
> On them far-seeing Zeus sends heav'nly woes—
> twinned plague and famine—till the people die.
> Their army or their walls he may cast down
> or, wreaking vengeance, sink their ships at sea.

Anxious Hesiod spoke in these lines what all Greece knew about divine justice and single rule by self-seeking tyrants. By all means, let us bow sufficiently in Dionysus's direction, but let us with fervent pleas especially implore Zeus and his divine minister of heavenly justice, Lord Apollo.

Another safety valve was the annual Lenaia, held each January in honor of Dionysus Lenaios, Dionysus of the Wine Vat. Unlike the springtime Dionysia, a magnet for spectators from all over Greece as well as for foreign tourists, the Lenaia, which took place in the month when travel was most difficult and sea voyage impossible, was a festival for Athenians, a city-wide family party in which playwrights were encouraged to speak aloud their most outrageous thoughts. Thus, the Lenaia became the principal showcase for Greece's comic poets, who took just as seriously as their tragic brethren the mandate to engage their political moment.

Aristophanes, the king of Athenian comedy, in fact went further than any tragedian dared go in criticizing his city's leading citizens and pointing out political absurdities. His comedy *Ekklēsiazousai* (*Assembly Women*), for instance, imagines the hallowed Athenian Assembly being taken over by women, who introduce economic communism—community of goods—as well as community of persons, the old and the ugly now being able to get as much sex as the young and the beautiful. A young couple are parted when three old crones assert their prior rights to the young man and leave his sweetheart in the dust. The play concludes with the chorus hurrying off to a communal dinner, where preposterously novel dishes will be served.

In *Lysistrata*, Aristophanes went even further, imagining a strike by the women of Athens, who refuse to have sex with their husbands till peace is made. They conspire with women of enemy city-states, who boycott their husbands as well, setting off a universal outbreak of priapism, as clumsy male choruses show up, attempting to sing and dance while sporting painful erections. The Athenian women secure the Acropolis and its treasury, bringing to a halt Athens's ability to wage war. A very beautiful and very naked Goddess of Peace appears, sending the men into paroxysms of pain. Peace negotiations between Athens and Sparta are quickly concluded and, as the play ends, a banquet of peace begins.

Males mocked, war mocked, Athens and its sacred institutions mercilessly satirized, while the Greeks laughed delightedly. Beyond the West, there are many parts of our contemporary world where such humor could still win you torture and execution; and even the Western world would not again see such exuberant self-confidence till two millennia had passed and the spirit of the Renaissance would issue in a new Age of Discovery. The Greeks called their spirit *to hellenikon*, the Greek Thing, a freewheeling, argy-bargy brilliance that may be easy to fault but remains relentlessly engaging and colorful, always reaching for more. As Aristophanes himself advised other dramatists through the culinary advice of the women's chorus in *Ekklēsiazousai*:

You'll come up with something brand new
if you're hoping to launch a real winner.
The banqueters won't fail to boo
if you dare serve them yesterday's dinner.

Something brand new. Beyond the social, political, and artistic innovations we have been considering, the most influential of all Greek intellectual innovations is undoubtedly the development over the course of two centuries of philosophy as a systematic study. *Philo-sophia* is a Greek word, meaning "love of wisdom"; and the first philosophers were relatively traditional sages who gradually (and probably painfully) created a new job description for themselves. These were men whose reputation as *magi* gave them at first an oracular aura, though they were actually engaged in a pursuit we might more readily call science.

They wanted to find out what made the universe work. In the Greek cities of sixth-century Ionia—the west coast of Asia from Smyrna to Miletus, which had been settled by Athenians—there rose a series of thinkers who inquired into the nature of things. Having no Book of Genesis to consult and only the sketchiest of myths about cosmic origins (in which they placed no confidence), they assumed that the world—or *kosmos* (their word, meaning "elegant order")—was, in some profound sense, eternal: it had always been there, so far as they could determine, and always would be. ("World without end," the phrase that concludes many old-fashioned Christian prayers is not a Judeo-Christian concept but a Greek one.) What faced them every day, however, was not the eternal but the mutable—all the multiplicity, diversity, motion, and change they perceived in individual beings that go from nonexistence to birth and life and, finally, to death, decay, and nonexistence. Likewise, the earth beneath their feet and even the sky above their heads presented them with panoramas of constant change. It is not possible, they reasoned, to make sense of what is mutable, what is becoming, what passes so fleetingly into existence and then is gone forever. But because there is also in our experience a quality of permanence—individuals die but humanity remains, the crops return each year, the orchards bloom once more, the zodiac comes full circle—we do not live in an arbitrary universe but a patterned one. If this is so, there must be an underlying . . . *thing* that never changes, never has changed, and never will change, the uncreated material out of which all the mutable things spring.

Thales of Miletus said this "thing"—naturally, they had trouble inventing terminology, words for elements yet to be discovered and defined—was water, a good guess, since almost everything seems to have some water in it. His Milesian successor Anaximander, the first Greek to write in prose (and, for quite some time, the only one not to avail himself of the ringing authority that meter can convey), thought this a little crude and proposed that the universal . . . um . . . *substance* was something unnameable, indeterminate, without specific qualities. His fellow Milesian Anaximenes decided the "substance" must be air.

Heraclitus of Ephesus, "the weeping philosopher" as he was afterwards remembered, said they had all got it wrong because

SPACES SACRED AND PROFANE

ABOVE: **1** The trireme, so called because on each side of the ship were three banks of oars, enabling the craft to be highly maneuverable and to travel at lightning speeds. The bow was very strong and used for ramming other ships. Each trireme had a crew of 200, 170 of whom were oarsmen, the rest soldiers, archers, and sailors. Triremes were first built at Corinth in the late seventh century B.C. By the time of the Peloponnesian War, Athens owned 300. This trireme is a modern replica, but based on exacting research. BELOW: **2** The temple of Poseidon at Paestum, Italy, is imposing but thick and a little crude when compared with more noble examples.

3 The graceful Parthenon,
temple to the Virgin (Athena),
on the Athenian Acropolis

4 The temple of Fortuna Virilis at
Rome, a fine example of a smaller
temple inspired by Greek originals
and inspiring architecture of later
ages, such as the public monuments
of Washington, D.C.

5 Early-fifth-century
B.C. fragments from
the tympanum of
the temple of Zeus
at Olympia. The
tympanum was an
elongated triangular
panel on the front
of a temple, framed
by the horizontal
cornice above the
pillars and the two sides of the slanting roof. One can still trace above the
figures the line of the left side of the roof, slanting upward (from lower left to
upper right) toward the roof's apex. It was a challenge for the artist to devise a
scene that would occupy this squished space. From the left, a hero of the Lapith
tribe struggles with a centaur, symbol of animality, who is attempting to carry
off Hippodamia, queen of the Lapiths.

6 A model of the Athenian Acropolis in the classical period

7 The theater at Epidaurus, its semicircular seating built, as was customary, into a stepped hillside

8 The Stoa of Attalus at Athens, a sheltered space for lectures, meetings, commerce, and other forms of public business

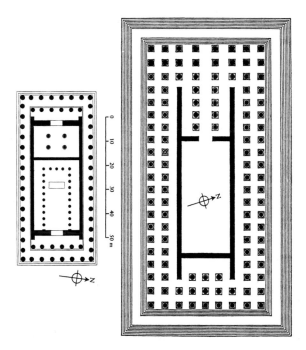

9 Beyond Athens, many cities built far grander public buildings, though seldom more delicate or satisfying to the eye. The drawings show the relative scale of the Athenian Parthenon (left) and the fourth-century B.C. temple of Artemis at Ephesus (right).

10 ABOVE: Detail from a large amphora (jug) from the time of Homer, found in a cemetery at Athens. Though geometric patterns cover most of its surface, it contains an early—exceedingly geometric—attempt at depicting human anatomy. The scene is the funeral of a hero, women seated in mourning beneath the corpse, men standing in mourning, all tearing their hair. The drawing is so elementary that the sexes are distinguishable only by their positions. A child stands to the right of the bier, perhaps attempting to touch the deceased.

11 RIGHT: A typical Egyptian figure of the archaic period. Such figures served as models for early Greek monumental statuary.

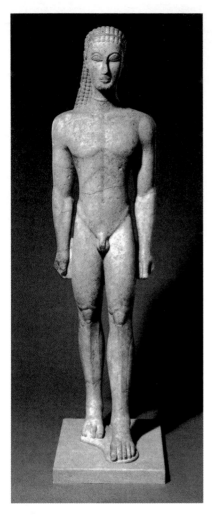

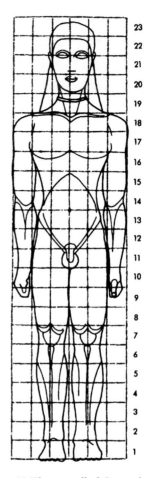

12 A typical Greek *kouros* from about 600 B.C.

13 The so-called Second Egyptian Canon, a grid system borrowed from the Egyptians and used by early Greek sculptors to plan the *kouroi*

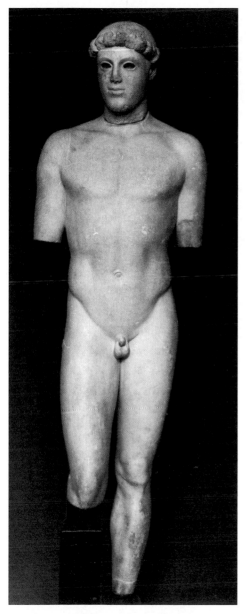

15 The "fair-haired boy," the head of a once-complete statue of the early fifth century B.C. Like the "Kritian boy," its lines are considerably softened in contrast to earlier *kouroi*. Its still-yellow hair is a reminder that Greek marble statuary was brightly painted.

14 The revolutionary "Kritian boy," early fifth century B.C.

16 The Doryphorus (spear carrier), a Roman marble copy of a bronze original made by Polyclitus about 440 B.C. Presented by the sculptor as a display of the ideal proportions for the human figure, the Doryphorus had enormous influence. The spear, once held in the left hand, is missing. The tree trunk and strut are additions made by the copyist; the hollow-cast bronze original would not have required these for balance.

17, 18 A fifth-century B.C. bronze recovered from the sea off Calabria, this warrior may be magnificently proportioned, but he's also a little scary—*brazen* is the right word for him. The whites of his flashing eyes are of ivory, his teeth silver, his eyelashes, lips, and nipples copper, and his body was once the golden brown of a man tanned by the sun.

LEFT: **19** The Discobolus (discus thrower) by Myron, fifth century B.C., in a Roman copy

RIGHT: **20** A nude very different from the Calabrian warrior, this bronze, recovered from the sea off Marathon, is of a chapleted boy engaged in light labor, probably pouring wine at a symposium.

21 Harmodius and Aristogiton by Kritios (probably also the sculptor of the "Kritian boy") and Nesiotes. Harmodius and Aristogiton were lovers who had been publicly insulted by Hipparchus, younger brother of the tyrant Hippias, after Harmodius had spurned his advances. They assassinated Hippias at a public festival and attempted to overthrow the tyranny but failed and were killed. Athenians remembered them, however, as "the Tyrannicides" and erected the bronze originals of these Roman marble copies in their memory in the *agora*.

22 Zeus, hurling his (now-vanished) thunderbolt, in an early-fifth-century B.C. bronze recovered from the sea off the Euboean coast

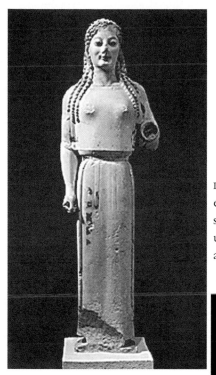

THE FEMALE

LEFT: **23** A *korē*, female equivalent of the *kouros*, of the same period as Figure 12—but unlike the male, always dressed and therefore not an ideal

RIGHT: **24** Europa (who was raped by Zeus in the form of a bull and gave birth to Minos, afterwards king of Crete), dressed as a Greek matron in typical public attire. Reconstructed from fragmented Roman marble copies of a Greek original of the late fifth century B.C.

25 A somewhat free copy from Pergamon of *Athēnē Parthenos* (Athena the Virgin), the colossal statue housed in the Parthenon at Athens. Sculpted by Phidias in the fifth century B.C., its flesh was of ivory, its dress of gold plates. Athena's left hand held her golden armor; her right palm was held outward, and on it alighted a small winged woman, a depiction of the goddess Nikē (Victory).

26 A wounded Amazon, Roman copy of a fifth-century B.C. Greek original. Amazons, who battled Greek male heroes, were not normal women but kindred to monsters—so some license could be permitted in their depiction. They were supposed to have sliced off the right breast to free their right arm for battle—a detail the sculptor has not adopted because any kind of physical deformity disgusted the Greeks and provoked them to derision. Throughout Western history there have been reported sightings of Amazons by men anxious about their prowess, most notably by conquistadors along the great river of South America, now called the Amazon.

27 Leading up to the unveiling of Aphrodite by Praxiteles, there are some fairly meek attempts [like Figure 26] to portray female nudity, but all these have the peekaboo quality of the Virgin Mary's breast—which in Romanesque art is allowed to be shown nursing the Christ Child. Here we have a scene that is probably intended to be the birth of Aphrodite from the foam of the sea, looking as if she had won a fifth-century B.C. wet T-shirt contest. The scene is flanked on the left by a modestly naked flute girl—but flute girls were all *hetairai* (female "companions" for the evening) and not usable as ideals. The relief was found at Rome but belongs to Greece, though its date is somewhat uncertain.

28 Fifth-century B.C. panel from the frieze on the little temple of Athēnē Nikē (Athena of Victory) on the Athenian Acropolis. An especially graceful example of drapery used to suggest nudity, without actually undressing, this Athena is tying up her sandal strap.

ABOVE: **29** A touching grave memorial from fifth century B.C. Paros, reminding us that, though the theme is hard to find in literature after the *Odyssey*, familial love remained part and parcel of private life. The parents of this little girl loved her very much.

RIGHT: **30** At last, Aphrodite by Praxiteles—or rather, a Roman copy of the lost marble original. The head (which comes from another copy of the same statue) should be turned a little more to the figure's left.

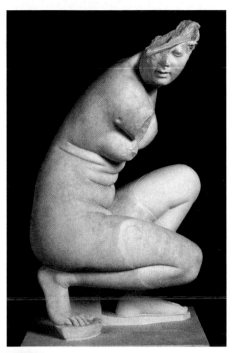

RIGHT: **31** Crouching
Aphrodite, a third-century B.C.
statue of surpassing charm

LEFT: **32** Aphrodite of
Melos, otherwise known as
the Venus de Milo, of the
late second century B.C.
and thought by many
to be the finest of all
surviving Greek female
nudes. She may have held
her drapery with her right
hand while her left rested
against a pillar, or she may
have been contemplating
her reflection in a shield.

33 A late-sixth-century B.C. herm from Siphnos. The herms are stone pillars topped by the head of the god Hermes, and they commonly sport an erect phallus. They were set at boundaries—for Hermes is the god of boundaries—and were certainly public rather than private art. I have placed the illustration here to emphasize that the herms in no way belong to the tradition of idealization. Rather, they are a survival from the distant past, and their inspiration lies in an exceedingly ancient notion common to primitive cultures: that it is possible to ward off evil and evil-wishers by a magical sign that possesses independent power. A variant of this, still with us, is the gold squiggle that some southern Italians wear around their necks to ward off *il malocchio* (the evil eye).

34 Satyrs having an orgy in a vineyard on an Attic cup of about 500 B.C. Note their brutish faces. Though their actions are homosexual—except for the satyr at right, about to bugger a (female) sphinx—this does not imply that satyrs were consistently homosexual. Rather, they were sexually omnivorous and always ready for copulation.

ABOVE: **35** *Bacchae*, also called *maenads*, possessed by the god Dionysus and thus inspired to ritual ecstasy, on an Athenian vase of about 480 B.C. Each wears a diaphanous *chiton*, the garment Greeks wore next to their skin, and though these *maenads* are sexually abandoned, they are the wives and daughters of citizens—and therefore had to be at least rudimentarily clothed. BELOW: **36** A typical scene of inebriated symposiasts on their way from one house to another on an Attic cup of the early fifth century B.C. The nude man is the leader, but the nude woman is an "entertainer" of no social standing—otherwise she wouldn't be nude. The man playing the pipes is also of the servant class: well-born Greeks avoided any physical distortion, and pipe playing, because it distorted the cheeks, could not be taken up by citizens. The lyre was their instrument.

ABOVE: **37** An orgy during the later stages of a symposium on an Attic wine goblet of about 510 B.C. It is difficult to know whether the "lucky Pierre" figure—the one getting it and giving it—is male or female, since at this period the convention was to draw men and women similarly, women distinguished only by their breasts and lack of external genitals. This figure—who is being beaten with a sandal by the man entering from behind—is probably male because its hair is less coiffed than that of the only female clearly shown. Nonetheless, the woman giving head on the right seems also to be entered from behind—and it may be that this pattern was repeated around the sides of the once-intact cup. The woman on the right is a *hetaira*, not only because she is shown naked but because she has allowed her face to become distorted—unthinkable for the citizen class.

38 An orgy in a vineyard, this time of humans rather than satyrs, on a cup from Vulci of about 530 B.C. (destroyed during the Allied bombing of Berlin in 1944). Unlike the other pottery pictured—red-figure pottery, showing human subjects with clay-red skin—this is black-figure pottery, in which the usual convention was to show men as black and women as white.

LEFT: 39 Youths courting boys on a cup from Vulci of about 500 B.C. On the reverse side, which is damaged, youths court girls—but with far more reticence and no touching.

40 Sex on an Attic cup of about 480 B.C. Rear entry, whether for anal or vaginal sex, was the preferred Greek position, interpersonal communion not being their thing. The letters descending vertically from the man's mouth form the Greek for "Hold still!"

41 A bedroom scene on the back of a Corinthian mirror of the late fourth century B.C. Eros (Cupid to the Romans) flies above.

42 Actors performing a scene from an unidentified comedy on a southern Italian *krater* (bowl) of the early fourth century B.C. They wear comic masks, comic genitals, and stuffing on their backsides.

TOWARD
REALISM

43 A late fifth- or early fourth-century B.C. bust of Pericles. The bust belongs to the era of idealization—but not many decades before portraiture turned realistic.

44 The satyr-like Socrates in a Roman marble copy of a late-fourth-century B.C. bronze by Lysippus—almost certainly an accurate likeness

45 Plato in a Roman marble copy of a late-fourth-century B.C. bronze by Silanion, probably molded from life

46 Despondent Demosthenes, who tried to warn Athenians against the threat of Macedon, in a Roman copy of a statue that was set up in the *agora* in the early third century as a silent symbol of Athenian opposition to Macedonian rule. His simple dress and considered manner are intended as a contrast to the swagger of the Macedonians.

47 The Stoic philosopher Chrysippus, reconstructed from fragments of a statue sculpted in the late third century B.C. Here is a teacher as he was in life, with no attempt at idealization. The Stoics were so called because their founder, Zeno of Citium, taught in the Stoa Poikile at Athens.

48 Alexander the Great, who probably did look this good, in a Roman copy

TOP, LEFT: **49** The Farnese Heracles (Hercules to the Romans), a Roman copy of a bronze by Lysippus. The weary hero holds behind his back the golden apples of immortality, secured in the last of his labors. Lysippus's portrayal became the standard "look" for Hercules for the rest of antiquity.

BELOW, LEFT: **50** The Apollo Belvedere, a Roman copy of a late-fourth-century B.C. bronze, was unearthed in the fifteenth century of our era. Long thought "the consummation of the best that nature, art, and the human mind can produce" (in the words of Johann Winkelmann, an early neoclassical critic), the statue has fallen somewhat from its former renown in an age that prefers less refinement.

ABOVE: **51** An armed hoplite, cast in bronze at Dodona in Epirus about 500 B.C., typical of the way Greeks looked as they entered battle

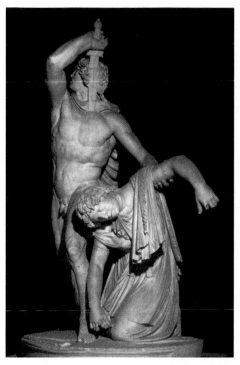

52 A Celtic chieftain committing suicide after killing his wife, in a Roman copy of a Greek bronze original of the late third century B.C. The tide of battle having turned against the Celts, the chieftain and his wife choose death—for the ancient world, the final act of courage—rather than surrender. This was part of a larger group of figures, set up as a monument in Asian Pergamon, that included the famous statue of the Dying Gaul (see *How the Irish Saved Civilization*, Volume I in this series).

53 Laocoön and his sons, which John Boardman describes "with its anguished rhetorical suffering" as "one of the finest examples of the Hellenistic high baroque." Made about 200 B.C., it was rediscovered at Rome in A.D. 1506. Michelangelo was the first artist to see it, and it had a powerful impact on him and on subsequent sculptors. More to our taste than the Apollo Belvedere [Figure 50].

LEFT: **54** The pitiable satyr Marsyas, strung from a tree by his wrists and about to be flayed alive by Apollo for challenging the god to a music contest—an example of what happens to those who in their *hubris* dare to put themselves on the level of the gods

BELOW: **55** Apollo's Scythian servant, sharpening his knife, which will be used to flay Marsyas. The Scythian's expression, whether uncomprehending, cunning, or cruel, sets him among all those who "do their duty" without a thought of the moral consequences. Both statues are late copies of Hellenistic works.

ABOVE: **56** A Hellenistic bronze original, called the "Terme boxer," a sad, brutalized figure

57 A Hellenistic marble of an old market woman, on her way to celebrate a festival, probably of Dionysus

58 A boy removing a thorn from his foot, in a marble copy of a probable bronze original of the second century B.C.

59 A drunken satyr, asleep, known as the "Barbarini faun," probably a copy of a Hellenistic work of about 200 B.C.

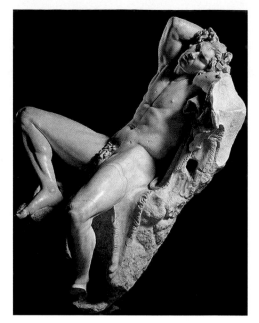

60, 61 In a Hellenistic grouping, a wide-awake satyr at the start of a revel lures a young *bacchante* (or *maenad*) to the dance.

62 Magical Dionysus, having turned pirates into dolphins, sails the wine-dark sea as his mast sprouts a vine—on the interior of a black-figure vase of the sixth century B.C. by the master potter Exekias. Not in any sense "realistic," but evidence of how Dionysus was originally portrayed.

63 Hermes with the infant Dionysus, possibly an original fourth-century B.C. marble by Praxiteles but deriving from the *kouros* tradition of the standing youth—with the innovative detail of a raised left foot

64 A satyr with the child Dionysus, a marble copy of a late-fourth-century B.C. bronze, probably by Lysippus, that seems almost an answer to the smoother Praxitelean treatment [Figure 63]. The contrast between childhood and age is similar to representations of the old year and the new year, the dying age and the age that is arriving.

65 "Dionysus is coming, Dionysus is coming!" He sure is in this pebble mosaic floor from late-fourth-century B.C. Pella.

66 A Hellenistic satyr tackling a "nymph," who is actually a hermaphrodite—as a walk around the statue will reveal

67 A phallic dancer in faience of about 200 B.C.

68 A masturbating
hunchback in bronze
of about 200 B.C.

69 The plaque carried into the universe by
NASA's *Pioneer 10* and *Pioneer 11* spacecrafts

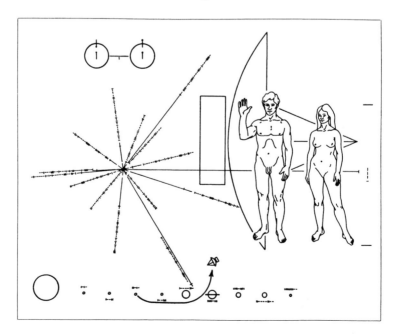

their question presumed an answer: there is no ultimate "substance"; at the heart of the universe is fire, the ultimate impermanence, always in flux. "*Panta rhei*," spoke Heraclitus oracularly. "All things flow." What you see is what you get. "You could not step twice into the same rivers; for other waters are ever flowing on to you." But because of this, "the road up and the road down is one and the same"—another gnomic way of stating that all we have is change, change that is ultimately unintelligible because there is no changeless "ultimate" to be grasped.

A little later, Parmenides of Elea (on the southwest coast of Italy), claiming Heraclitus had got it exactly backward, asserted that of course the universe had to be stable and permanent—otherwise it would make no sense at all—and that the constant changes we experience are only *accidents*, that is, appearances. Our faulty senses misperceive the true nature of things because we have no direct access to ultimate and unchangeable reality. For Heraclitus, change was the only true reality; for Parmenides, it was immutable permanence. Parmenides's long-lasting teacher, the Ionian Xenophanes of Colophon, who lived to be about a hundred and ten, though he made no contribution to these philosophical dialogues about substance and accidents, attacked belief in a multiplicity of gods, as well as Homer's presentation of the gods as having human faults and passions. God was one, said Xenophanes, eternal, effecting things by mind alone and bearing no resemblance whatsoever to flip-flopping mankind. On another front entirely, his observations of seashells in the mountains and fossil fish in the quarries of Syracuse convinced Xenophanes that the earth had once been covered in water and would be so again—since, as the Greeks assumed, reality was like a great wheel and all things return. What has been will be again.

A group of fifth-century philosophers, headed by Empedocles of Acragas in Sicily, returned to the pursuit of the eternal
substance and proposed that there were actually four basic elements out of which everything is composed in varying proportions. These elements are earth, air, fire, and water—a system
of categories that science, medicine, and psychology would
continue to rely on right into the early modern period.
Anaxagoras of Clazomenae, another Ionian, refining Empedocles's solution, proposed that everything is composed of different kinds of "seeds" and that the beings we perceive as separate
and distinct from one another are simply different kinds of
composites, all made up in differing proportions of these same
seeds. "Everything has a share in everything," proclaimed
Anaxagoras. In order to explain how this seemingly random
mixture of seeds was apportioned into the patterned universe
we behold, he reasoned that there must be a *nous* (mind), a
principle powerful enough to direct the patterning. But unlike
Xenophanes, Anaxagoras did not bother to personalize *nous* or
call it God. Like Xenophanes, Anaxagoras was also a close ob-
server of natural phenomena—in his case of the stars and plan-
ets—and came to realize that the celestial bodies rotated and
that the moon received its light from the sun, which gave firm
foundation to a theory of eclipses that weakened one of the
premises of polytheism (in which each planet, star, and satellite
was taken to be the manifestation of a different god).

Leucippus and his student Democritus, another long-lived
philosopher, took up the idea of cosmic seeds and pushed it further. What is at the heart of the universe is indeed single and
unchanging: *a-toma* (uncuttables), indivisible particles too small
to be seen. These "atoms," differentiated from each other only
by shape and size, are combined in different arrangements and
densities to form the variety of compounds in the universe,

which we misperceive as different beings. Our world or *kosmos*, they also speculated, is not unique but one of many, all of which came to be by accident and then developed by necessity. We do not need to posit the existence of gods to explain the workings of the world. Even human consciousness, thought Democritus, is an entirely physical process, as perishable as the body. He urged that men should aim at cheerfulness and wrote a treatise on the subject, *Peri euthymiēs* (*On Cheerfulness*). Cheerfulness is to be achieved by avoiding violence and disturbances of all kinds and by understanding that life is not full of impenetrable mystery, just full of atoms. He was remembered as "the laughing philosopher."

Generations before the great blossoming of Athenian philosophy under Socrates and his student Plato, these Presocratics were already sketching out the program that all Greek philosophy would subsequently follow. It was built on three assumptions: the phenomena we experience immediately possess no ultimate importance; there must be an ultimate, eternal, and (despite Heraclitus) unchanging reality; it is the task of the philosopher to . . . well . . . *attain* that reality and then direct others to the correct path. This was the strictly philosophical strand of their enterprise, which also lent the philosopher the mantle of a religious sage.

But there was also the scientific strand, which they pursued without telescopes, microscopes, or lab experiments. Such paraphernalia would never have occurred to the Ionian philosophers and their successors. Though some of them did find it useful to make simple observations of the visible world, they all believed they could *think* their way to the truth by way of what Albert Einstein would call *das Gedankenexperiment*, the thought experiment—that is, just sitting there and thinking about things. Einstein, indeed, would approach the tasks of science with a methodology strikingly similar to that of the laboratory-less Greeks. "The whole of science," he would declare in *Physics and Reality*, "is nothing more than a refinement of everyday thinking."

There are even more startling parallels between Einstein and many of the Presocratics. Like his ancient colleagues, Einstein believed in a patterned universe that made sense. "I shall never believe," he once remarked, "that God plays dice with the world." Even the way Einstein talked about the universe has a Presocratic ring to it: "The most beautiful thing we can experience is the mysterious. It is the source of all true art and science. . . . To know that what is impenetrable to us really exists, manifesting itself as the highest wisdom and the most radiant beauty, which our dull faculties can comprehend only in the most primitive forms—this knowledge, this feeling, is at the center of true religiousness. In this sense, and in this sense only, I belong to the ranks of the devoutly religious men." "Something deeply hidden," he left in a handwritten note, "had to be behind things."

Like many of the Presocratics, whose theories questioned and weakened conventional Greek religion, Einstein's sense of mystery had little in common with the orthodox beliefs and practices of the surrounding society. But his confidence that the world made sense—even if its sense eludes us ("The Lord God is subtle, but malicious he is not")—put him at odds with his younger colleague Werner Heisenberg. Heisenberg's famous "uncertainty principle"—that all our observations are unreliable because we cannot "observe nature in itself but [only] nature exposed to our method of questioning"—bears more than a little resemblance to Heraclitus's insistence on the ultimate unintelligibility of reality.

Despite these parallels, much of what the Presocratics had to say is likely to strike contemporary readers as distant from our concerns. With effort we may be able to see why they assumed that ultimate reality, in order to be intelligible, must be One and that multiplicity implies unintelligibility—this is not so far removed, after all, from Einstein's futile attempts to uncover a "grand unified theory" that would explain the universe—but our profoundest anxieties and obsessions tend to run in very different channels. So it is important to bracket the various answers of these groundbreaking philosophers and to recall that the underlying question for all of them—"What is the nature of reality?"—remains to this day a fundamental question that each of us must attempt to answer in our lives. When we recall this—and acknowledge how little progress we have made in formulating a satisfactory answer—we gain a measure of sympathy for them and the single-minded spunk with which they approached their daunting task. Because they had no guidelines to follow, they poked their noses into everything in the hopes of finding an adequate answer; and in the process they helped to invent the disciplines of philosophy, theology, the physical sciences, medicine, psychology, political science, and ethics.

Thales, for instance, is credited not only with being the first philosopher but with bringing back from a trip to North Africa the essentials of Egyptian land measurement; then, by considering this practical craft more deeply than the Egyptians had and abstracting the principles implicit in it, Thales invented *geōmetria*, geometry (literally land measurement, but actually a branch of abstract mathematics). He is also credited with predicting the exact time and place for an eclipse of the sun in the year 585 B.C. This story must have been embellished subsequently since it is scarcely possible that a sixth-century Greek had the means of predicting an eclipse at a precise geographical latitude. But Thales's ability to make some such prediction was afterwards remembered as bolstering his contention that the general workings of the *kosmos* are predictable and that therefore a principle of immutability lies at the heart of the universe. Beyond philosophy, mathematics, and astronomy, Thales certainly touched on theology. If there is a single eternal substance, reasoned Thales, it must be—of its very nature—divine, so that, concluded he, "all things are full of gods."

In company with Solon, Thales headed the list of the Seven Sages of antiquity, whose crucial sayings were inscribed on the facade of Apollo's temple at the great oracular[α] sanctuary of Delphi. "*Gnōthi sauton*," went one saying: "Know thyself." "*Mēden agan*," went the other: "Nothing in excess." The first, which has echoed down the ages, is certainly a step in the direction of psychology, but it is also meant as humbling spiritual advice: know how low your human *hamartia* places you in contrast to the powers of heaven. The second is a similar reminder to the ever-striving Greeks that excess—political, social, sexual—is the constant temptation and that Solonian balance is what we must strive for. It is certainly political advice, but medical, psychological, and ethical, too. The third and last inscription is the strangest of all, the single letter "*E*." According to the prolific Plutarch (writing in the late first and early second centuries of our era), this was meant as the second person singular, present tense, of the verb *to be*, meaning "Thou art"—a gnostic assertion attributed to the philosopher Pythagoras.

Pythagoras was a thinker of a very different stripe from all the others, more guru than philosopher. Admired for his long, lustrous hair and masculine beauty, he wrote nothing down, was reputed to possess magical powers, and was ru-

α The priestess of Apollo at Delphi was famed for her oracles. Recently, archaeologists have uncovered, under the sanctuary where she made her ambiguous pronouncements, a chasm that was known in the ancient world and from which intoxicating fumes escaped. There is every likelihood that the priestess was high.

mored to have—please lower your voice and whisper this one—a golden thigh. Born probably at Samos early in the sixth century, he immigrated to Croton in Sicily, where, attracting a multitude of followers, he formed a community of men and women who lived apart from other human beings according to his rule. He taught, among many other things, a doctrine of *metempsychōsis* (transmigration of souls, or reincarnation). He claimed to remember his own previous incarnations: as a son of the god Mercury, then as a Trojan hero, then as a prophet, and, more recently, as a fisherman. Another doctrine was the immortality of the human soul, which Pythagoras imagined to be an immortal and unchanging divinity fallen from heaven and imprisoned in the corruption of the fleshly body as in a tomb. ("*Sōma sēma*" [Body-tomb] was an aphorism of the Pythagoreans, who detected profound significance in similarities of sounds.) The choices for good or ill that a soul makes in one life determine what kind of body it will find itself inhabiting in its next incarnation. "The most momentous thing in life," taught the sententious guru, "is the art of winning the soul to good or to evil"—just what Pythagoras was confident he could do for you.

Creeky old Xenophanes found this business too much altogether and sent around the anecdote—hilarious to Xenophanes—that Pythagoras had recognized the voice of a dead friend in the howling of a whipped puppy. Fiery Heraclitus, who had no patience for airy mystification, curtly dismissed Pythagoras as a fraud. Parmenides, however, who believed that our senses were deceived by accidental appearances and that deep reality was unchanging, was proud to associate himself with the theories of Pythagoras. And Empedocles, who was much under Pythagorean influence, went so far as to recall that in a former life he had been a bush.

The Pythagoreans ate no flesh, fish, or fowl and only certain kinds of vegetables (apparently the ones that didn't contain imprisoned souls). They utterly eschewed beans—whether out of respect for souls or for the quality of their communal air we don't know—and must have been subject to all the wasting afflictions of a protein-poor diet. They scorned public sacrifices and other rituals of Greek religion and, burning only incense, spent their days in silence, examining their consciences and disciplining themselves in self-control. "Troubles are good," went a Pythagorean saying, "but pleasures are always evil; for whoever has merited punishment must be punished." "*Pathei mathos*" (Through suffering, understanding), went another of their sayings, entranced as they were by similarities of sounds. Sex was permitted but only to married couples under specially designated circumstances. Each initiate renounced all private possessions; and in the event that he or she returned to the extra-Pythagorean world, the departure was considered death and a gravestone was erected in commemoration of the apostasy.

None of these things—neither the core doctrines nor the extreme discipline—had any precedents in Greek society. Though we no longer have the evidence to trace the route of transmission, we must assume that Pythagoras had come in contact with ideas and practices from the East, absorbing elements of Babylonian numerology, Persian dualism, and especially classical Indian culture with its central tenet of metempsychosis and its monastic practices. Out of this culture, after all, rose the reforms of Siddhartha Gautama, better known to history as the Buddha; and Pythagoras and the Buddha were almost exact contemporaries. Even the mysterious Pythagorean saying carved at Delphi—"*E*" ("Thou art")—probably owes its origin to the key mantra of the Upanishads, "*Tat tvam asi*" ("Thou art the One"). The sense of both sayings lies in the affirmation of the eternal union of the soul with That-Which-Truly-IS, with divinity, with the eternal substance from which all mutable things spring—oneness with Oneness.

Pythagoras found deep meaning in numbers. He is credited with discovering that the chief musical intervals produced on the vibrating strings of a lyre can be expressed as ratios: an octave as 2:1, a fifth as 3:2, a fourth as 4:3. Though these relationships still form the basis of Western musicology, Pythagoras went further. Everything, he thought, could be explained by numbers and their relationships to one another. Since the ratios between the basic musical intervals employ only the first four whole numbers, these numbers must be expressive of the deep harmony of the universe, in which the "spheres" or heavenly bodies sing while whirling through space and their music combines in harmonic chords to create the Music of the Spheres, which we are unable to hear only because the sounds are with us from birth and, there being no contrasting silence, we do not hear the harmonies. Pythagoras could hear them.

Pythagoras played with these numbers till he hit on a particularly seductive arrangement:

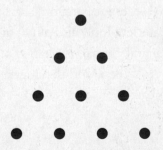

This pattern, an equilateral triangle using only the first four whole numbers (one dot at the head, followed by lines of two, three, and four dots) and composed nonetheless of a decade, took on mystical significance, somehow enunciating not only the nature of number but the nature of the universe itself. Nevertheless, Pythagoras's playing with numbers and triangles also bequeathed us an exceedingly useful discovery, the Pythagorean theorem, which assures us that, no matter whose body we may be inhabiting for the moment, the square of the hypotenuse of a right triangle is always equal to the sum of the squares of the other two sides.

The superior air that emanated from the Pythagoreans earned them enemies. In the mid-fifth century, their main foundations in southern Italy were set afire and many of their number were massacred. "Civil war was no rarity in Greek cities; yet here for the first time," concludes the renowned German classicist Walter Burkert, "it seems to have led to a kind of pogrom, the persecution of those who were different from others in their way of life and disposition." We know nothing more about the oppressors of the Pythagoreans, but we do know that southern Italy was also a stronghold of the most fanatical devotees of pleasure-inducing Dionysus—of whom, except for his philosophy, the beautiful, long-haired Pythagoras might have seemed the incarnation. But Dionysus was no friend to moderation, let alone discipline; and his disciples, the torchbearing *bacchai* and *bacchoi*, were not averse to a little dismemberment now and then, and their secret rites were always conducted in darkness.

IT IS A REMARKABLE IRONY in the history of philosophy that, though Pythagoras was the least mainstream of the Presocratic philosophers—the least Greek, really—he exerted the greatest influence of all on Plato, who would in the fourth century B.C. become the philosopher of philosophers not only for the Greeks but for the entire Western tradition. As the philosopher-mathematician Alfred North Whitehead would say definitively in the twentieth century, "The safest general characterization of the European philosophical tradition is that it consists of a series of footnotes to Plato." Another safe generalization may be stated thus: Though all great figures rise from their culture, they must, in some radical way, contradict that culture—and this Plato certainly set out to do.

One of the first Greeks to write extensively in prose, Plato hit upon a lively format that puts him at a far remove from the vast majority of his sleep-inducing philosophical successors. Rather than lecturing at us about his ideas, he offers what he calls "dialogues," theater-pieces that can be read aloud at a gathering of friends, with actors taking different parts. (That Plato could write so extensively in prose rather than in poetry is evidence that books were now circulating widely in the Greek world. An extended work of prose, unlike sung poetry, is necessarily based on a reading rather than a listening public.) Though each dialogue is intended to explore a particular philosophical theme, Plato's interlocutors behave as human beings do: one character may be too dim to follow the argument, a second may become incensed over the intellectual position of a third or over what he takes to be the disparagement of his own ideas, a latecomer may arrive argumentative and inebriated. As the dialogue approaches its crux—the resolution of the theme, the main point of the whole discussion—one must pay close attention, but along the way to that moment Plato inserts many of the inconsequential (and entertaining) digressions that constitute normal human conversation. This witty format Plato modeled on short theater-pieces of his day called "mimes," which were not silent, Chaplinesque affairs but noisy vaudeville sketches based on the comedy of daily life ("The Quack Doctor," "The Unreliable Servant"). That he was quick to imagine such an unlikely use for this vulgar genre while single-handedly launching the lofty tradition of Greek prose is suggestive of his keen originality.

It is somewhat difficult to separate Plato from his teacher Socrates, since Socrates never wrote anything down but appears as the central character in almost all of Plato's voluminous writings. While it is clear that Plato, especially in the later dialogues, has advanced into philosophical territory far beyond what the oral teachings of his revered Socrates could have contained, he continues to employ the character "Socrates" as his mouthpiece. Luckily, we have fairly extensive news of Socrates from other sources—especially from another student of his, Xenophon—and so may venture a portrait that does not rely exclusively on Plato's highly literary (and therefore somewhat suspect) presentations.

In Greek eyes, Socrates was a squat, ugly, barefoot man who did not bathe too often and was easy to spot shuffling through the *agora* or passing the time in his favorite hangout, the shop of Simon the Cobbler. Looking nothing like a god or hero, he had bulging eyes, a flat, pug nose, prominent lips, and a pot belly. Though a stonemason and the son of a stonemason—and therefore an artisan from the lower reaches of the middle class—he wasn't big on exercise and, when he could, declined involvement even in civic and political affairs. He wasn't big on much of anything except his favorite pursuit: asking questions. While doing this, he maintained his famously unattractive posture, keeping his head down and squinting at people sideways or from under his brow. His series of questions, ever after known as "the Socratic method," irked a great many citizens, since the abysmal ignorance of the person being questioned would be gradually, painfully, inexorably exposed to public view.

Socrates seemed to take special delight in puncturing the pomposity of Athens's leading citizens—which made him popular with young people, who enjoyed the spectacle of their elders' discomfort. So Socrates became recognizable not only by his ugliness but by the crowd of admiring youths who clustered about him hoping to hear a zinger. Like an aging rock star whose unsavory lifestyle and consummate cool make him a favorite target of parents, Socrates was in danger of becoming the victim of his own success as "the Socratic method" turned into a byword for smart-assed, if inscrutable, backtalk. The loathing of the older generation only increased the chorus of adolescent admirers who flocked to his side; and there were times when he could barely open his mouth without hearing rowdy cheers of confirmation.

All the same, except when he was dealing with the most insufferable blowhards, Socrates was respectful of those he questioned. But the questioning was relentless. Socrates thought of himself as serving his fellow Athenians in the role of "a gadfly," impatient with imprecision, goading them to adequate formulations, stinging them out of their complacency. Even to friends, however, a gadfly can be intolerably irritating; to passing acquaintances, Socrates could be, as one of his young admirers put it, more like "a stingray," reducing his interlocutors to a state of numb helplessness.

In Book I of Plato's masterwork, the *Republic*—which probably dates to an earlier phase than the subsequent dialogues that make up the bulk of the work—Socrates finds himself in conversation with his friend Polemarchus at the latter's house in seaside Piraeus, while others listen in. Polemarchus, citing a line from the lyric poet Simonides, has opined that "morality lies in helping one's friends and harming one's enemies." "When you say 'friends,'" queries Socrates meekly,

"do you mean those who appear to a person to be good, or those who genuinely are good (even if they don't appear to be)? And likewise for enemies."

"It seems plausible to suggest," [Polemarchus] said, "that one treats as friends those one regards as good, and as enemies those one regards as bad."

"Isn't it common to make mistakes about this, and think that people are good when they aren't, and vice versa?"

"Yes."

"When this happens, then, doesn't one regard good people as enemies and bad people as friends?"

"Yes."

"But all the same, in these circumstances it's right for one to help bad people and harm good people, is it?"

"Apparently."

"But good people are moral and not the kind to do wrong."

"True."

"On your line of reasoning, then, it's right to harm people who do no wrong."

"Not at all, Socrates," he said. "My reasoning must be flawed, I suppose."

"It's right to harm wrongdoers, then," I [that is, Socrates, who is giving the account of what transpired] said, "and to help those who do right?"

"That sounds better."

"But since there are lots of people who are completely mistaken, Polemarchus, then it will commonly turn out to be right for people to harm friends (whom they regard as bad) and to help enemies (whom they regard as good). And in affirming this, we'll be contradicting what we said Simonides meant."

"Yes," he said, "that is a consequence of what we're saying. Let's change tack, however: we're probably making a wrong assumption about friends and enemies."

"What assumption, Polemarchus?"

"That someone who appears good is a friend."

"What shall we change that to instead?" I asked.

"That someone who doesn't just appear good, but actually is good, is a friend; and that someone who seems good, but actually isn't, is an apparent friend, not a genuine one. And the same goes for enemies."

"So on this line of reasoning, it's a good man who is a friend, and a bad man who is an enemy."

"Yes."

"You're telling us, then, that our original description of morality, when we said that it was right to do good to a friend and harm to an enemy, was incomplete. Now you want us to add that it is right to do good to a friend, provided he is good, and to harm an enemy, provided he is bad. Is that right?"

"Yes," he said, "I think that's a good way to put it."

"Can a moral person harm *anyone*?" I asked.

"Yes, he can," he replied. "He has to harm bad men, people who are his enemies."

"When horses are harmed, do they improve or deteriorate?"

"Deteriorate."

"In respect of a state of goodness for dogs or of a state of goodness for horses?"

"In respect of a state of goodness for horses."

"So the same goes for dogs too: when they are harmed, they deteriorate in respect of what it is to be a good dog, not in respect of what it is to be a good horse. Is that right?"

"No doubt about it."

"And where people are concerned, my friend, shouldn't we say that when they're harmed they deteriorate in respect of what it is to be a good human?"

"Yes."

"And isn't a moral person a good human?"

"There's no doubt about that either."

"It necessarily follows, Polemarchus, that people who are harmed become less moral."

"So it seems."

"Now, can musicians use music to make people unmusical?"

"Impossible."

"Can skilled horsemen use their skill to make people bad horsemen?"

"No."

"So can moral people use morality to make people immoral? Or in general can good people use their goodness to make people bad?"

"No, that's impossible."

"I imagine this is because cooling things down, for instance, is not the function of warmth but of its opposite."

"Yes."

"And moistening things is not the function of dryness but of its opposite."

"Yes."

"So harming people is not the function of a good person, but of his opposite."

"I suppose so."

"And a moral person is a good person?"

"Of course."

"It is not the job of a moral person, then, Polemarchus, to harm a friend or anyone else; it is the job of his opposite, an immoral person."

"I think you're absolutely correct, Socrates," he said.

"So the claim that it's right and moral to give back to people what they are owed—if this is taken to mean that a moral person owes harm to his enemies and help to his friends—turns out to be a claim no clever person would make. I mean, it's false: we've found that it is never right to harm anyone."

"I agree," he said.

The reader may find the Socratic method—the small-step-by-small-step analysis that is Socrates's stock-in-trade—alluring or annoying, depending on temperament. Logical, philosophical types are fascinated, whereas the artistic and intuitive may find the process excruciating, especially when extended to book length—in the case of the *Republic*, nearly 150 times the length of the preceding excerpt—even though the discussions are punctuated by comical interludes. Immediately after the exchange between Socrates and Polemarchus, for instance, Thrasymachus comes on "like a wild animal," "hurl[ing] himself at us," relates Socrates, "as if to tear us apart." "What a lot of drivel, Socrates!" bellows Thrasymachus, who belittles Socrates for "feigning ignorance" and goes on to enunciate what was probably a common, if cynical, view—"that morality is nothing other than the advantage of the stronger party." Socrates, who claims to have been "terrified and panic-stricken" by Thrasymachus's aggression, goes on—ever so meekly, ever so reasonably—to make mincemeat of his antagonist, much to the satisfaction of his audience (whether ancient or modern). Though the operation takes up the balance of

Book I (and runs about ten times as long as the excerpt), by the time Socrates has defanged Thrasymachus he also has the man eating out of his hand.

Besides taking account of the general Socratic procedure of question and response, the reader cannot fail to notice the characteristically Greek turn of mind evident in Socrates's approach: the essence of wetness is to moisten things, the essence of the musician is to make people more musical, the essence of the moral man is to make others more moral. The predilection for articulating the essence—and, therefore, the function or purpose—of something or someone, for defining its necessary qualities, builds on the original search of the Presocratics for the ultimate substance that lies beyond accidental appearances. We, suspicious of detached philosophical pronouncements on essences and far more comfortable with wisdom wrested from lived experience, must bear in mind how novel and fascinating this pursuit of essences—this insistence on precision rather than impressions—was in its time and how truly . . . essential it has proved to Western traditions of science and thought.

Besides the Socratic method and the Greek attraction to essences, another striking feature of Socrates's discourses—especially evident in the preceding excerpt—is what the translator Robin Waterfield[β] calls Socrates's "startling an-

β Most translations of Plato make him sound like your old philosophy prof, the one whose sere notes flaked like the last leaves of autumn as he drew them delicately from his battered portfolio. But in Greek, Plato still sounds fresh, piquant, and provocative. He is even a sly mimic, able to reproduce the characteristic speech of each of his players—the earnest hesitations of Polymarchus, for instance, the bull-in-a-china-shop huffings of Thrasymachus, the foxy subtleties of Socrates. Robin Waterfield is, so far as I know, the first English-language translator to give each of Plato's players a characteristic voice with a contemporary ring, while at the same time capturing many of the ambiguities and allusions of Plato's argument (if, necessarily, abandoning an attempt to reproduce the knotted eloquence of Plato's Greek). I use his translations throughout this section.

ticipation of Christian ethics." In the New Testament, Jesus makes use not of Greek logic but of scriptural citation, rabbinical precedent, and a Hebrew mode of argument that proceeds by assertion and contrast rather than step-by-step reasoning, but he certainly comes out the same door as Socrates:

> You have heard that it was said: "Love your neighbor" and hate your enemy. But I say to you: Love your enemies and pray for those who persecute you, so that you may be children of your Father in Heaven—for "he makes his sun to rise on the evil and the good, and sends his rain to fall on the just and the unjust." For if you love those who love you, what reward can you expect? Don't even the tax collectors do as much? And if you save your greeting for your brother, what are you doing that's so wonderful? Don't even the gentiles do as much? You must, therefore, include everyone, just as your heavenly Father includes everyone.

There are, most surely, significant differences between the Socratic and the Christian presentations. But the fathers of the early church were blown away by the similarities, especially given what they knew (all too well) of the fucker-fuckee aspect of Greek life. How unlikely it was that the competitive Athenians, striving for excellence and always pushing one another out of the way, should have—on their own and without the assistance of revelation—adduced such a "doctrine." The fathers, therefore, came up with an odd formulation to explain how this could have happened: *homo naturaliter Christianus*, the naturally Christian man, who in his attraction to goodness is given sufficient grace to lead a moral life without the support of biblical revelation. Not only did this explanation make Socrates the first Greco-Roman secular saint of the Judeo-Christian tradition; it opened up even to simple believers of the early Christian centuries the possibility that there was goodness and morality to be found among those who had never come in contact with the authority of sacred scripture or the divine grace that flooded from the sacraments. Even though Socrates was an unusual specimen, the undeniable existence of someone who had thought such thoughts showed that grace and wisdom could sometimes be found even in pagan literature. This line of reasoning enabled Christians, who later came to monopolize power in Europe, to cherish pagan texts, some more than others and none more than Plato—which is why we still possess his entire *oeuvre*.γ

If there was one text of Plato's that the church fathers, meaning to remain faithful to the Judaic repugnance toward homosexuality, might have been tempted to toss to the Mediterranean winds, it was the *Symposium*, Plato's account of an unusually sober drinking party at which the main subject was homosexual love. The guests gather in the *andron* of Agathon's house, where they arrange themselves comfortably on his banqueting couches and prepare to tackle their dinner, which they finish off in grumpy semi-silence, Socrates, who cares little for food, arriving late. After they have performed the necessary libations and hymns, they are supposedly ready for the serious drinking to commence, but it soon turns out that, except for Socrates, they are all terribly hung over from last night's festivities—in celebration of Agathon, who has just taken

γ Plato published about twenty-five dialogues of widely differing lengths over a period of fifty years, as well as the *Apology*, the speech given by Socrates in his own defense. Though the authenticity of a few of these dialogues is disputed, there is no reason to doubt that we have them all. There are also extant thirteen letters, though whether these should be attributed to Plato or to his circle is still hotly debated. The vagaries of history by which we came to possess some but not all the books of the Greco-Roman library is the subject of *How the Irish Saved Civilization*, the introductory volume in this series. Despite the depredations of time and barbarians, however, all (or nearly all) the works of certain authors—especially first prize at the Lenaia for his very first tragic trilogy. "In no state to carry on," they agree to a proposal that no president be elected and that each one be allowed to drink as little as he pleases. Normally, the president would determine the exact mixture of wine and water and how often the guests' goblets would be refilled. In such a regimen, each drinker was expected to hold up his end and keep pace—an impossible goal for this group.

Next, they decide to dismiss the naked flute girl, who was enlisted as Act I in the evening's entertainment and who would usually end up sharing a couch or two before the night was through. So they are too wasted even for sex—though Agathon's provision of only one flute girl suggests either that he is a cheap so-and-so (unlikely, given his theatrical triumph) or that he assumes that heterosexual coupling is not what most of his guests would be in the mood for, anyway. The physician Eryximachus then proposes that for their evening's entertainment each imbiber "make the best speech in praise of Love he can, moving around the couches from left to right and starting with Phaedrus." So, no riddles or games, no dancing or flutes, no songs or sex, just speeches—ooee, an *intellectuals'* drinking party (which will need just one more step, the total elimination of booze, in order to achieve its final form, the academic "symposium" of our age). The proposal is "carried unanimously," and Phaedrus begins.

Plato, Virgil, and Cicero—were saved because their texts came to be thought of as quasi-sacred scriptures, penned by specimen *homines naturaliter Christiani.* The complete works of Homer, who certainly didn't fit this category, were saved because he was the inventor of literary Greek (and innumerable passages in subsequent Greek texts would be almost impenetrable without reference to the *Iliad* and the *Odyssey*). The saving or loss of works by most other authors, however, must be chalked up to such circumstances as which collections of books were torched by barbarians. Surely no copyist in any age would have chosen to save, say, the mounds of Pindar's athletic odes that we still possess in preference to the few sad scraps of Sappho that are her only legacy.

Phaedrus's account of Love owes its origin to the military usefulness of banding men together inseparably, which engenders "shame at disgraceful behavior and pride at good behavior." "My claim," intones Phaedrus, "is that being found out by his boyfriend would cause [a man] more distress than being found out by his father, his friends, or anyone else. And the same evidently goes for the boyfriend: he feels particularly ashamed at being caught behaving badly by his lovers. The best conceivable organization (supposing it were somehow possible) for a community or a battalion would be for it to consist of lovers and their boyfriends, since they'd compete with one another in avoiding any kind of shameful act. It's hardly an exaggeration to say that a handful of such men, fighting side by side, could conquer the whole world."

Phaedrus's world—a femaleless world of military conquest based on male-male loyalty—is very unlike ours. We'd have to go to a contemporary prison to find anything comparable. But it is just this aggressive male bonding that will bring Greece its most spectacular international success when in the following century the armies of Alexander the Great will conquer nearly the whole of the known world in the name of Greek culture. Plato, however, places Phaedrus first not because he agrees with him but because he represents the most obvious and least interesting point of view.

The next reported speech is by Agathon's lover, Pausanias, who praises the lifelong fidelity of homosexual couples who "are motivated by a pure form of Celestial Love" and disparages those who specialize in one-night stands or "have affairs with boys who are younger than the age at which intelligence begins to form"—that is, the prepubescent. "There even ought to be a law against having affairs with young boys, to prevent all that time and effort [that goes into wooing] being spent" on boys who may turn out callous and common in the end. Well, Pausanias, nowadays there is such a law—and not just to prevent your wasting your time. Pausanias and the much younger Agathon were revered in Athens as a model homosexual couple, but Pausanias's world, though closer to ours than Phaedrus's, remains alien in important respects, especially in his grudging tolerance for sex with children (as well as for forced sex with women who are not "freeborn"). He comes a bit closer to our attitudes, however, in casting aspersions on those who use sex as an excuse for every kind of bad behavior: "Society sanctions approval of the most extraordinary actions on a lover's part—actions which . . . well, if anyone else were to dare to behave in these ways in pursuit of any other object, with any other goal in mind, he would earn unmitigated disapproval." A little prissy, our Pausanias, but more interesting than his predecessor, especially for the light he throws on the deep need for society's good opinion as the driving mechanism of Greek behavior.

Before we get to Socrates's speech—for whom, in Plato's construction, all the other speeches are but foils—we must hear three more. Eryximachus tells us that as a doctor he knows that "the body of every creature on earth is pervaded by Love, as every plant is too"; then with medical sagacity he urges moderation. His is the voice of the Presocratics. Aristophanes, the great comic playwright, then offers the idea that human beings were once rounded wholes containing "two faces (which were on opposite sides), four ears, two sets of genitals, and every other part of their bodies was how you'd imagine it on the basis of what I've said . . . and when it came to running, they supported themselves on all eight of their limbs and moved rapidly round and round." However we might imagine it, Aristophanes is not trying for comedy; his is a serious metaphor. Because these proto-humans were too powerful, Zeus cut them in half and, with a little remodeling by Apollo, created the human race as we have it today. "It was their very essence that had been split in two," Aristophanes goes on, "so each half missed the other half and tried to be with it." To this day, those who had once been hermaphrodite wholes—that is, half male and half female—are heterosexuals; those who had been male-male wholes are homosexual males; those who had been female-female wholes are lesbians. And all of us are desperate to reunite with our lost halves: "We human beings will never attain happiness unless we find perfect love, unless we each come across the love of our lives and thereby recover our original nature."

This, it seems to me, is an imaginative contribution—symbolic, poetic, but real and consonant with the historical Aristophanes's quirky genius. The last speech before Socrates gets under way, however, is the silliest of all, Agathon's. Though Agathon gained his reputation as a tragic dramatist, it is hard to imagine what kind of tragedies he might have written. All of them have been lost, and only a few scattered lines remain. On the evidence of Plato's parody of his speechifying, however, I'm willing to wager that if a drama of Agathon's ever surfaces it will read something like *The Sound of Music*. When in his peroration he tells the company, "I am moved to express myself in verse," he seems about to break into "Climb Ev'ry Mountain":

"O Love without equal in good looks and grace,
You love to unite us all over the place.
Gracious and gentle, adored by the wise,
Beloved of the gods, only you do we prize.
With you we will feel ev'ry zap of delight;
You guide all our moves, tuck us in for the night.

Follow him, people, sing him your hymn,
His song will bewitch us, both gods and men!"^δ

This one has mistaken tickles for thoughts. The Greeks didn't *always* have a word for it; they could sometimes be as soppy as a Liza Minnelli concert, though "Agathon's speech was greeted with cries of admiration from everyone in the room." We love ya, Liza. Socrates remarks drily, "I was so naive that I thought the point of any eulogy was to tell the truth about the subject! . . . But it now looks as though this isn't the way to deliver a proper eulogy after all. . . . Nevertheless," insists Socrates, "I am prepared to tell the truth."

Socrates goes on in his customary question-and-answer mode to elicit agreements from the drinkers that, all balderdash aside, "first, love is *of* something; second, that something is something a person currently lacks." But readers familiar with earlier dialogues must wonder how Socrates, who claims ignorance of all things but his own ignorance, can ever bring himself to articulate a positive theory of Love, which the rule for participation in this symposium requires of him. Socrates's—or, more likely, Plato's—solution is to introduce a mysterious figure, Diotima, priestess of Mantinea in Arcadia, whom Socrates calls "an expert in love" and his teacher on the subject. Priestess she may be, even an "itinerant charismatic who provides for various needs," the category no less a scholar than Burkert places her in. To me, she seems very like a high-class courtesan—a figure well known in ancient Greece (as in Renaissance Italy), the sort of woman who was allowed more freedom and power than her enslaved or properly married sisters, the only type of female allowed

δ These verses are my condensed version of Agathon's peroration. The actual text in Plato goes on and on. Agathon's cheap use of rhyme is intended by Plato as evidence of airheadedness.

to move more or less as she pleased through society and to say whatever she liked. After all, she enters (at least in imagination) even this exclusively male precinct and becomes the center of its attention, the priestess of Love, revealing her solution to the riddle of Love.

Love, explains Diotima (in Plato's recounting of Socrates's recounting), is not beautiful in himself, since Love, at its most basic level, is an attraction to what is beautiful. We are not attracted to what we already possess, only to what we lack— and, therefore, Love is not a god (as all the other speakers have assumed), by definition deathless and beautiful, but a spirit existing somewhere "between mortality and immortality." "Divinity and humanity," Diotima patiently instructs Socrates, "cannot meet directly; the gods only ever communicate and converse with men (in their sleep or when conscious) by means of spirits. Skill in this area makes a person spiritual, whereas skill in any other art or craft ties a person to the material world. There are many different kinds of spirits, then, and one of them is Love."

Socrates asks the naive question "Who are his parents?," to which Diotima, like Aristophanes, offers a mythological explanation, a common Greek device for illuminating difficult matters:

"Because his parents are [his father] Plenty and [his mother] Poverty, Love's situation is as follows. In the first place, he never has any money, and the usual notion that he's sensitive and attractive is quite wrong: he's a vagrant, with tough, dry skin and no shoes on his feet. He never has a bed to sleep on, but stretches out on the ground and sleeps in the open in doorways and by the roadside. He takes after his mother in having need as a constant companion. From his father, however, he gets his ingenuity in going after things of beauty and value, his courage, impetuosity, and energy, his skill at hunting (he's constantly thinking up captivating stratagems), his desire for knowledge, his resourcefulness, his life-long pursuit of education, and his skills with magic, herbs, and words.

"He isn't essentially either immortal or mortal. Sometimes within a single day he starts by being full of life in abundance, when things are going his way, but then he dies away . . . only to take after his father and come back to life again. He has an income, but it is constantly trickling away, and consequently Love isn't ever destitute, but isn't ever well off either. He also falls between knowledge and ignorance, and the reason for this is as follows. No god loves knowledge or desires wisdom, because gods are already wise; by the same token, no one else who is wise loves knowledge. On the other hand, ignorant people don't love knowledge or de-sire wisdom either, because the trouble with ignorance is precisely that if a person lacks virtue and knowledge, he is perfectly satis-fied with the way he is. If a person isn't aware of a lack, he can't desire the thing which he isn't aware of lacking."

"But Diotima," I [Socrates] said, "if it isn't either wise people or ignorant people who love wisdom, then who is it?"

"Even a child would have realized by now that it is those who fall between wisdom and ignorance," Diotima said, "a category which includes Love, because knowledge is one of the most at-tractive things there is, and attractive things are Love's province. Love is bound, therefore, to love knowledge, and anyone who loves knowledge is bound to fall between knowledge and igno-rance."

In unveiling this compelling myth, even more graceful than Aristophanes's contribution, Diotima handily surpasses all the other speakers and gives us confidence that she can lead us to arcane truths. Diotima's Magical Mystery Tour is accomplished with much recircling over the same territory, as Socrates asks his seemingly simple-minded questions and Diotima leads him gradually upward into new realms of insight, as if she were leading a child by the hand. It is self-evident that all human beings seek *eudaimonia* (good fortune, happiness); and it is the possession of good things that makes for *eudaimonia*. Love—the word that has been used all along is *Eros* (Sexual Desire, viewed as a god or spirit)ᵉ—is, therefore, larger than any "particular kind of love." Once it is conceded that we must make allowance for all sorts of loves ("business, sport, or philosophy" are the examples Diotima gives), it can be seen that "the sole object of people's love is goodness"—"the permanent possession of goodness for oneself."

Diotima then goes off on a kind of detour in which she equates male sexual tumescence with pregnancy. "Love's purpose," announces Diotima, "is physical and mental procreation in an attractive medium." Her model here is seed (procreation) into vagina (an attractive medium), but because this won't serve literally for every "particular kind of love," she takes refuge in analogy. "The point is, Socrates, that every human being is both physically and mentally pregnant," and "the reason why, when pregnant and swollen, ready to burst, we get so excited in the presence of beauty is that the bearer of beauty releases us

ᵉ In the common Greek view, the passions that move us are instances of divine possession, even if, like anger or *eros*, they can lead to destruction. Other Greek words are also translated into English as "love": *philia*, which implies filial respect (as in *philosophia*), and *agapē*, which indicates an affectionate kindness (as between siblings) but lacks erotic coloring. *Agapē* was the word Jews chose to translate the Hebrew *ahava* (in earliest times, pronounced "ahaba") into Greek (as in the commandment "Thou shalt *love* thy neighbor as thyself"); and Christians would employ it with similar force. When God is called "love" in the New Testament, the word used is not *eros* but *agapē*. *Ahava* and *agapē* are so close phonetically as to lead one to suspect that the Greeks may have borrowed the word from the Jews and then altered it slightly to suit their sense of sound.

from our agony." This forced linking of a man about to spurt semen with a woman about to give birth to a child is probably our best evidence that Diotima, unlike the symposiasts, is merely a creature of Plato's imagination. While it is possible to claim that a man—especially Plato the celibate bachelor, who lived his spare life in the monastic mode of Pythagoras—might judge this an apt linkage, it is impossible to think that a woman (and certainly not one who had ever given birth) would invent such a spurious analogy.

The aim of procreation, whether actual or analogous, is immortality. "Everything"—humans, as well as all "mortal nature"—"instinctively values its own offspring: it is immortality which makes this devotion, which is love, a universal feature." Diotima points out that "undying virtue and fame . . . motivates people to do anything, and . . . the better they are, the more this is their motivation. The point is, they're in love with immortality." Furthermore,

there are people whose minds are far more pregnant than their bodies; they're filled with the offspring you might expect a mind to bear and produce. What offspring? Virtue, and especially wisdom. For instance, there are the creations brought into the world by the poets and any craftsmen who count as having done original work, and then there's the most important and attractive kind of wisdom by far, the kind which enables people to manage political and domestic affairs—in other words, self-discipline and justice. And here's another case: when someone's mind has been pregnant with virtue from an early age and he's never had a partner, then once he reaches adulthood, he longs to procreate and give birth, and so he's another one, in my opinion, who goes around searching for beauty, so that he can give birth there, since he'll never do it in an unattractive medium. Since he's pregnant, he prefers physical beauty to ugliness, and he's particularly pleased if he comes across a mind which is attractive, upright, and gifted at the same time. This is a person he immediately finds he can talk fluently to about virtue and about what qualities and practices it takes for a man to be good. In short, he takes on this person's education.

Diotima explains that such a "relationship involves a far stronger bond and far more constant affection than is experienced by people who are united by ordinary children, because the offspring of this relationship are particularly attractive and are closer to immortality than ordinary children [who provide only quasi-immortality by surviving their parents]. We'd all prefer to have children of this sort rather than the human kind, and we cast envious glances at good poets like Homer and Hesiod because the kind of children they leave behind are those that earn their parents renown and 'fame immortal,' since the children themselves are immortal."

Once you've got all this straight, you're ready for the last rungs of the ascent. By all means, counsels Diotima, a young man should start out by "focusing on physical beauty and initially . . . love just one person's body." Then, he must come "to regard the beauty of all bodies as absolutely identical. Once he's realized this and so become capable of loving every single beautiful body in the world, his obsession with just one body grows less intense and strikes him as ridiculous and petty." Next, he must come "to value mental beauty so much more than physical beauty" that he can love "an attractive mind," even if it resides in an aging or unattractive body. Then, "he must press on toward the things people know, until he can see the beauty there too." Soon, "the slavish love of isolated cases of youthful beauty or human beauty of any kind is a thing of the past," as our seeker embarks on "the vast sea of beauty," enabled to do so by "his boundless love of knowledge," which "becomes the medium in which he gives birth to plenty of beautiful, expansive reasoning and thinking," until he catches sight of Beauty "in itself and by itself, constant and eternal" and comes to "see that every other beautiful object somehow partakes of it, but in such a way that their coming to be and ceasing to be don't increase or diminish it at all, and it remains entirely unaffected." At last, the seeker has reached the unchanging One of Parmenides, for this Beauty is also Truth and Goodness, the eternal ultimate.

In her summation, Diotima recommends that "the right kind of love for a boy can help you ascend from the things of this world until you begin to catch sight of *that* Beauty." But one must ever bear in mind that "the things of this world" are to be used only "as rungs in a ladder," assisting your ascent "to that final intellectual endeavor . . . the sight of Beauty itself, in its perfect, immaculate purity—not beauty tainted by human flesh and coloring and all that mortal rubbish, but absolute Beauty, divine and constant." One who reaches the absolute can then "give birth to true goodness instead of phantom goodness, because it is truth rather than illusion whose company he is in. And don't you realize that the gods smile on a person who bears and nurtures true goodness and that, to the extent that any human being does, it is he who has the potential for immortality?" But because each of us must begin on the lowest rung in the ladder of ascent, "in the business of acquiring immortality, it would be hard for human nature to find a better partner than Love."

Plato's innate sense of drama reminds him that his audience can take only so much of this stuff, so he brings us down to earth with the introduction of the *Symposium*'s final character, the dashing and very drunk Alcibiades, who now clamors in, garlanded in a chaplet of ivy and violets, and interrupts the proceedings. Perhaps even the most sober banqueter has had his fill of seriousness, for they all welcome Alcibiades—the tall, muscular, aristocratic darling of Athens, universally acknowledged as its most beautiful young man—with much cheer. Finding himself seated next to Socrates, Alcibiades professes fear, hinting teasingly that he and Socrates have a kinky relationship. "If he starts to get violent, please protect me," Alcibiades begs the slight Agathon, probably the symposiast least able to protect anyone. "He gets insanely attached to his lovers and it terrifies me."

With very little coaxing, Alcibiades launches into a long tale of his relationship with Socrates, whom he finds irresistibly attractive. Plato is using Alcibiades as an example of one stuck at a middle rung in the ladder of ascent, one who has come "to value mental beauty" but has yet to progress further. Vain, fun-loving Alcibiades keeps falling backward, however, to lower rungs: "[Socrates is] the only person in the world in whose company I've felt something which people wouldn't think I was capable of feeling—shame: I feel shame before him and him alone. What happens is that although I'm perfectly well aware of the inescapable force of his recommendations as to what I should do, yet as soon as I'm away from him, I get seduced by the adulation of the masses!"

Alcibiades relates that he has become the suitor of Socrates, wooing him, attempting to charm him into a sexual encounter, to no avail. That the toast of Athens, who can always expect to find himself in the position of *erēmenos* (boy-beloved), should feel compelled to assume the role of *erastēs* (elder lover, pursuer) is intolerably shameful. Alcibiades, therefore, convinces himself that Socrates is in love with him ("the only lover I've got who's good enough for me") and is just "too shy to bring it up." At last, as Alcibiades tells it, he tricks Socrates into staying the night at his house and slips naked into bed with him: "I put my arms around this remarkable, wonderful man—he is, you know—and lay there all night long." But Socrates does nothing. "I call on all the gods and goddesses in heaven to witness the truth of this—that I got up the next morning, after having spent the night with Socrates, and for all the naughtiness we'd got up to, I might as well have been sleeping with my father!"

We are not to take from this story that Socrates does not find Alcibiades just as beautiful as does every other Athenian. True, Socrates has a wife—the shrewish Xanthippe, whom he married late in life—and three small sons, but no Greek constructed a wall of separation between heterosexual and homosexual activity. We are to understand that Socrates has already climbed to the top of Diotima's ladder and glimpsed the One— the Beautiful, the Good, the True—and is no longer obsessed by this earth's limited instances of beauty, whether Alcibiades or any of the other handsome students who constantly cluster about him. He is the exemplar of "Platonic love," as it will be called down the ages.

Alcibiades is given the final speech because he brings us down to earth, the realm that we, the audience, inhabit. The symposiasts found the candor of Alcibiades amusing "because he was evidently still in love with Socrates," just as you, dear Reader, are still in love with————. At the *Symposium*'s end, Plato reminds each of us of where we stand now, as well as what heights the ladder beckons us to.

After that, Plato informs us, "everything went utterly out of control; all there was left to do was to drink a great deal, and even that was completely unsystematic"—that is, without the direction of the customary president. Morning broke to find some sleeping, others gone home, Socrates still asking questions of the two who stayed awake. After those two fell asleep, Socrates, still sober, "got up and left."

T HOUGH SOCRATES remains ever the questing philosopher, knowledgeable only about his own ignorance, it would be hard to miss Plato's seething contempt for ordinary human beings and their pedestrian lives. What would Sappho have said to Plato's (supposedly Diotima's) teaching that, as one climbs the ladder of wisdom, "obsession with just one body grows less intense and strikes [one] as ridiculous and petty"? Love of a single human being—"black earth's most beautiful thing"—ridiculous and petty? How would Andromache have responded to Plato's high-handed dismissal of childrearing as inferior to writing poetry? Would Plato have even been willing to entertain objections by women—real women, whose real female bodies have known real pleasure and real pain, unlike the purring phantasm Diotima? It would be hard to imagine Plato finding any area of agreement with his younger contemporary the Chinese philosopher Mencius, who proclaimed that "all the babies who are smiled at and hugged will know how to love. Spread these virtues through the world; nothing else need be done." *Nothing* else? Plato would have deemed such elementary twaddle unworthy of the noble name "philosophy."

The silent sense of superiority that Plato's mentor, Socrates, exuded in his relentless questioning got him finally into very hot water. He was brought before an Athenian popular court to answer charges of impiety and corrupting the youth of the city. The charge of impiety—really of atheism—Socrates vigorously denied, claiming (probably truthfully) that he was devoted to the gods; nor had he corrupted anyone, only asked them questions. But his radical challenges to the unexamined assumptions of his fellow citizens had led many young people, listening in, to question everything their elders had taught them to revere, causing upsets of all kinds in family life throughout the city. "Corrupting the young" was a charge that must have had for many of his opponents the ring of truth. Furthermore, Socrates confided to the court that he had been entrusted with a *daimonion* (a godlike something), a divine sign, an inner voice that prompted him since childhood to turn away from the civic obligations expected of every Athenian citizen and toward the exclusive pursuit of truth. A what? A *daimonion*? This befuddling claim must have struck many jurors—who were probably no more qualified to sit in judgment than were the jurors who sat on the popular courts that followed the French Revolution—as evidence of the impiety of the accused. Socrates was convicted and the death penalty proposed.

At this point, the convict was allowed by custom to propose a lesser sentence, such as temporary exile—which, in the case of Socrates, would almost certainly have been allowed. Socrates, however, chose a more high-minded route. He proposed that, as the city's benefactor, he should not be punished in any way but rewarded by his fellow citizens and at the least dined at state expense for life. Exile, imprisonment, a fine—these would all be unjust punishments, whereas death . . . well, is death a punishment? Who can say? One can almost see the dull, contorted faces of the jurors trying to take this in. Dimly, the suspicion rises in their minds that they are being toyed with, that the convict may not even grant the legitimacy of their august proceedings. Of course, they sentence him to death.

In the famous last scene of Plato's *Phaedo*, before he drinks the hemlock Socrates comforts his friends, assuring them that death—which is either a dreamless sleep or a passage to the place of true Justice—is nothing to fear. He hopes to meet at last Homer and Hesiod and the heroes of the *Iliad*. No evil can befall a man who is good. As his last act, he forgives his accusers and the jurors who convicted and sentenced him. In peace and calm, Socrates takes the poison and dies. This exemplary "martyrdom" on behalf of the Truth will be seen by the intellectuals of the early Christian centuries as further proof of the saintliness of Socrates, whose life and death contain so many surprising parallels to the life and death of Christ as related in the four gospels of the New Testament.

The death of Socrates was certainly a watershed in Plato's life, turning him into a vocal opponent of democracy, convinced forever after that this celebrated Athenian political invention was a dangerous sham, which could only be destructive of goodness and wisdom. The relationship between a man's life and his thought is always a conundrum. Nietzsche's idea, quoted at the beginning of this chapter, that every philosophy can be read as a disguised personal confession, an involuntary memoir, has much validity, but it can't settle the question of whether Socrates's execution was solely responsible for turning Plato against democracy or whether this event was simply confirmation of the trajectory Plato was already on. Did this death provide Plato with a road-to-Damascus revelation, turning his whole life upside down, or did it merely strengthen long-established prejudices? The latter is more likely. Years before Socrates was put on trial, he was seen to be intimate with a group of young aristocrats, Alcibiades among them, who were openly contemptuous of democracy (as well as of Athenian religious beliefs) and who may have come by their contempt as a result of listening to Socrates's relentless questioning.

In Plato's middle and later writings, especially in the *Republic* and the *Laws*, he paints a detailed picture of the ideal Greek *polis*, a state without a whiff of democracy, solidly built on enlightened Socratic-Platonic principles. Most people are like the inhabitants of the Cave, the Platonic "myth" excerpted at the head of this chapter, able to see only flickering shadows, many levels removed from anything real. They need to be governed by guardians, philosopher-kings who have been strictly educated to know always what is right and just for themselves and for others. Knowing what is right, they will always choose what is right, provided all the usual temptations—such as the foolishness of the poets and the wildness of the musicians—have been strictly eliminated from their education. Because of their purified education, the philosopher-kings will be able to rise to the World of the Forms, to commune with absolute Truth, Goodness, Justice, though the great mass of humanity will remain ever trapped in the obscurities of the Cave, hopeless "lovers of sights and sounds," mistaking the paltry pleasures of evanescent physical phenomena for truth. Because of such inherent human weakness, Plato reluctantly banished all poetry, art, and music from his ideal state; these things only lead people into trouble. (What would the real-life Socrates, the carver of stone whose fondest hope was to meet Homer and Hesiod the other side of the grave, have thought of these exclusions?)

Besides the guardians, the keepers of wisdom, Plato's society has two lesser classes: the soldiers, whose virtue is courage, and the producers, of whom little is expected except that they do their jobs and satisfy their low appetites with as much restraint as possible. Though such an "ideal" has little appeal to those who lived through the bleak twentieth-century utopias of fascism and communism, there seems always to be someone somewhere who dreams of implementing a new version of Plato's *polis*, a world of puritanical perfection, controlled by a narrow elite, who know what is best for everyone. Plato made the fatal error of equating knowledge with virtue and assuming that if one knows what is right he will do what is right. After so much additional history, after so many failed utopias, we should know better, we who should try to envision only pretty good societies—relatively balanced, more or less functioning societies in which happiness is made as general as possible without anyone (or any class) ever getting everything he wants. Moderate Solon was far more down-to-earth than the haunted author of the *Republic*.

Am I being unfair to Plato? Maybe. If, as Nietzsche claimed, one can read a person's life in his philosophy, one can also read almost any book that way, including this one. And I confess that certain formative experiences have left me with little patience for those who "know what is best" for everyone else. Others are more receptive to Plato—not a few of them as different from one another as the novelists Carson McCullers and Iris Murdoch and the philosopher Luce Irigaray. These contemporary and near-contemporary Platonists have been receptive not so much to Plato's dictatorship by the enlightened as to his eloquent descriptions of the *psyche* (soul), the immortal principle within each of us, that openness to immortality that yearns for absolute Goodness, the Goodness that is our ultimate goal but that we find finally wanting in every earthly being we turn to. "Too late have I loved thee, O Beauty ever ancient and ever new!" was the famous prayer of the great Christian Platonist Augustine of Hippo in the fourth century A.D. "Too late have

I loved thee! And, behold, thou wast within me, and I out of myself, and there I searched for thee." There are resonances in Plato so profound and humane that even the most convinced anti-Platonist cannot ignore him entirely.

P LATO SPENT HIS LIFE educating his followers—pro-creating, as Diotima would put it, in the "attractive medium" of their minds. He taught in a shrine of olive groves, sacred to the Greek hero Academos and called, therefore, *Academia* (whence our words *academy* and *academic*), and shared the grounds with a public *gymnasium* (place of nude exercise), a physical training facility where Athenian citizens, especially adolescents, kept themselves in shape for the rigors of hoplite service. The naked gymnasts were stalked by older men, hoping to attract the boy of their dreams to "procreative" activities in a less cerebral medium. But this was also an excellent site for luring young men to Plato's educational activities. He opened his Academy in the 380s; and it would continue to thrive for nine centuries—into the early sixth century A.D., when it would be shut down for good by the Byzantine emperor Justinian, who thought that stamping out the last vestiges of paganism was the best way to curry the Christian god's favor and so win back the lost Western provinces of the Roman empire. In the twentieth century, archaeologists have found, buried on the Academy grounds, the slates of ancient schoolboys, some with lessons scratched on them.

One of these schoolboys was Aristotle, Plato's greatest student, who, like all great students, took exception to his master's teachings. He taught first at the Academy, later in direct competition to the Platonists at his own Athenian establishment, a *gymnasium* built in a grove sacred to Apollo Lykeios and called the Lyceum. In the Stanza della Segnatura in the Vatican, Raphael painted his famous Renaissance fresco *The School of Athens*. At its center stand two men, the broad-browed Plato, hoary with age, pointing upward, the young, dark-haired Aristotle pointing down—a brilliant iconic summation of the radical difference between the two philosophers.

For Plato, ultimate reality is the World of the Forms, the dwelling place of the One—the Good, the True, the Beautiful, the Just. Plato never makes quite clear whether these essences are simply qualities of the One or separate entities (or, most likely, occupy some middle ground). Rather, he reasons, if there are examples of good men in the world (and there are), this can only be because they have a share in Goodness itself, which must therefore exist somewhere beyond all mortal instances of goodness. So it goes with all the other abstractions—as we saw, for instance, in Diotima's explanation of how beautiful boys participate in some aspect of Beauty itself, as well as in Socrates's hope of encountering after his death the Justice that exists beyond all our faulty attempts to establish just procedures in this world. For that matter, all the things we know in this world are but feeble examples of their ultimate Forms, which exist beyond all physical instances. Thus, in the World of the Forms, there must be the Form of Tableness and Chairness, the exemplars for all the tables and chairs we find in our world. It is to this World of the Forms, the ultimate reality beyond the top of Diotima's ladder, that Plato points in Raphael's circular fresco.

Pointing downward, Aristotle says that no such world exists and that even broad-browed Plato has never glimpsed such a "reality," except in fantasy. The World of the Forms is the result of a mistake in logic. Forms do not exist apart from the beings they *in*form. Every table does indeed have a form, that is, a principle of organization by which the carpenter constructs a wooden platform supported by four legs or by three legs or by whatever he has in mind. This form, which exists in the carpenter's mind, is the formal cause of the table—but it can have no existence except in the carpenter's mind and at length in his work. To speak otherwise—to say that there is an absolute Tableness floating somewhere that gives form to all particular tables—is "to speak abstractly and idly," said Aristotle. Plato was an idealist, that is, someone who believes that ideas constitute a higher reality, separate from material things. Aristotle was a materialist—a qualified materialist, however, since he believed with Plato that the rational part of a human being, the *psyche*, is immortal.

But more than being a philosopher—it must be confessed, of lesser creativity and inherent interest than his master—Aristotle was a categorizer, in fact the greatest categorizer who ever lived. It was he who divided different forms of knowledge from one another—especially, philosophy from the physical sciences—and gave us the academic categories we still use today. He is responsible for the filing cabinet of the Western world—all those *-ologies*, *-ses*, and *-ics*—every term from *analysis* to *biology* (which science he invented outright), from *metaphysics* (the term is his alone) to *meteorology*, from *politics* (that is, the theory and practice of the *polis*) to *zoology*.

He was especially drawn to the study of logic—he was, indeed, its formal inventor—and he laid out all the basic rules for rational thinking and enumerated all the fallacies by which we may fall into logical error. He divided causes into four kinds: the efficient cause (which produces the effect; say, the carpenter), the material cause (the "matter" to be worked; say, the wood), the formal cause (the essence or "form" introduced by the efficient cause; say, the idea in the carpenter's mind), and the final cause (the purpose for which the thing exists; say, to serve food). God, thought Aristotle, was the ultimate final cause, though his god, the Unmoved Mover, was quite unlike ours, a being with no interest in the universe that depended on him. Aristotle invented the syllogism and pointed out the difference between *a priori* and *a posteriori* reasoning.ζ

In the words of the great British classicist Paul Harvey, "Aristotelian logic more than any other single influence formed the European mind." Many of Aristotle's observations—especially the scientific ones about, for instance, the movements of celestial bodies and about procreation as the sole purpose of human sexuality—have not weathered the test of time. (Galileo's trouble with the Catholic hierarchy was caused by his unraveling the Aristotelian cosmology to which the hierarchs had wedded themselves. Everyone's trouble with the Catholic hierarchy in our day is caused by its continued adherence to Aristotelian observations on human sexuality that everyone else knows are inadequate.) But the principal problem in reading Aristotle today is that, unlike the far more eloquent Plato, he is so very dull.

One could make a good case that Aristotle's real intellectual father—not of his tiresome prose but of the universality of his interests—was not so much Plato as Herodotus of Halicarnassus. Born early in the fifth century B.C. in an Ionian-influenced city on the southwest coast of Asia, Herodotus, in common with the Presocratics, was a figure of insatiable curiosity. He wrote a nine-book account of the Persian Wars—the Greek term for the long struggle between the feisty little Greek city-states and the endlessly powerful empire that lay to their east, the sup-

ζ In *a priori* ("from what went before") reasoning, we deduce an effect from a cause or a result from a principle—as we always do, for instance, in mathematical proofs. In *a posteriori* ("from what came after") reasoning, we argue from the effect to the cause—which is how court cases are argued, inferring, for instance, the interior disposition of malice from the act of murder.

posedly unbeatable Persians, who occupied most of the known world. This epic struggle, which began on the plain of Marathon and encompassed the tragic defeat of the Spartan Legion at Thermopylae,[η] ended eleven years later in 479 B.C. with decisive victory for the Greek forces and solidified their consciousness of themselves as a nation, a nation superior even to the most powerful empire of all time. Herodotus called his accounts *historiai* (investigations), a word that soon took on the connotation it retains to this day. Herodotus indeed was called by subsequent generations "the father of history." But his nine books range far and wide, Book 2, for instance, being devoted almost solely to a description of exotic Egypt, which the Persians had invaded. Within his historical narrative Herodotus pursued matters scientific, archaeological, anthropological, ethnographic; and in this way—in his astonishing diversity of interests—he was the predecessor of Aristotle.

Thucydides, the masterful Athenian historian of the generation after Herodotus, took Herodotus's techniques—his

[η] Many of Greece's historical events have entered our language as symbolic milestones. Before the battle of Marathon in 490 B.C., the Athenian runner Phidippides was sent to ask Sparta's help. He ran the first "marathon" by covering the distance between Athens and Sparta, about 125 miles, in one day and then by running back to Athens. According to legend, he then ran on (26 miles farther) to join the battle at Marathon, then ran back to Athens to announce the Greek victory and then dropped dead. The valor of the Greek soldiers who fought at Marathon—the *Marathonomachoi*, as they were called—so inspired Greece that Aeschylus, for one, asked that his epitaph not speak of his plays but state that his only glory was that he fought at Marathon.

A decade later, a small force of Spartans perished at Thermopylae, a supposedly indefensible pass between steep cliffs and sea, but their deaths proved the decisive turning point of the war, preventing the Persian army from descending on Greece—which would have spelled the end of everything that came later. It would, in a real sense, have spelled the end of Western history. The touching epitaph for the Spartans, who called themselves Lacedaemonians, was written by the lyric poet Simonides and carved in stone on the walls of the pass:

Tell them in Lacedaemon, passer-by,
That here obedient to their words we lie.

John Ruskin thought these the noblest words ever uttered by man.

endless strings of gossipy inquiries—and raised them to a new level of seriousness. His subject was the Peloponnesian War, the war between Athens and Sparta. Seafaring Athens, perfectly positioned to maintain ties throughout the Aegean and into the Black Sea, over to the Mediterranean, into the Adriatic, and as far as the Tyrrhenian Sea, had turned out to be the principal beneficiary of the Persian defeat, coming to control the alliance of diverse city-states that had coalesced to save Greece. But as Athens gained more and more power, the sheer threat of its seemingly global influence made war with threatened, land-locked Sparta inevitable; after many skirmishes and attempts at peace, war was joined decisively in 431 and lasted nearly thirty years. Thucydides in his high seriousness wished his work to become a "possession for all time," not a clever bauble "written for display, to make an immediate impression." In his tightly compressed prose, he eschewed altogether the impressionistic effects of the storyteller; he saw himself, rather, as a scientist or physician who searches below surface phenomena to determine exact underlying causes. He distinguished sharply between the immediate pretexts for the war—quarrels about Athens's alliances with lesser cities—and the principal cause, which Thucydides saw clearly as Sparta's fear of Athens's never-ending expansion. Men go to war, he concluded, out of "honor, fear, and interest"—a conclusion that has never been improved on. Unlike Herodotus, Thucydides had no truck with oracles and omens; gods are entirely absent from his narrative.

His determination to look reality in the face was unswerving, even to the point of showing how war—this war and all wars—causes the degeneration of society:

Practically the whole of the Hellenic world was convulsed, with rival parties in every state—democratic leaders trying to bring in the Athenians, and oligarchs trying to bring in the Spartans. . . . To fit in with the change of events, words, too, had to change their usual meanings. What used to be described as a thoughtless act of aggression was now regarded as the courage one would ex- pect to find in a party member; to think of the future and wait was merely another way of saying one was a coward; any idea of moderation was just an attempt to disguise one's unmanly charac- ter; ability to understand a question from all sides meant that one was totally unfitted for action. Fanatical enthusiasm was the mark of a real man, and to plot against an enemy behind his back was perfectly legitimate self-defense. Anyone who held violent opin- ions could always be trusted, and anyone who objected to them became a suspect. . . . As a result . . . there was a general deterio- ration of character throughout the Greek world. The plain way of looking at things, which is so much the mark of a noble nature, was regarded as a ridiculous quality and soon ceased to exist. Society became divided into camps in which no man trusted his fellow.

Thucydides, always looking for the skull beneath the skin, em- ploys abstractions—aggression, courage, moderation, fanatical enthusiasm—as if they were actors in his drama. Though he at- tempts complete impartiality (and largely succeeds), his admira- tion for Pericles, Athens's embattled, larger-than-life leader, shines through, as does his love for his ancestral city.

In 404 B.C., Athens lost the war, from which it would never entirely recover. For a short time, it even lost its democracy and had to bow to Spartan tyranny. But its brilliant son Thucydides, following the path blazed by Herodotus, had succeeded in cre- ating an entirely new mode of knowledge, independent of philosophical inquiry. No longer would knowledge be the sole province of scientists, mathematicians, and philosophers, those who observed natural phemomena or tried to discover the essences of things or contemplated a world beyond the world. Close attention to human action—society and politics, war and peace—could yield another kind of knowledge. And this knowledge, the result of meditation on the past and close consideration of human affairs, could yield new principles, quite unlike anything established by philosophy or the sciences, to guide humanity in the future.

VI
THE
ARTIST

HOW TO SEE

Daedalus was Greece's fabled artist, an Athenian architect and sculptor who may have lived in the late Bronze Age. He was hired by King Minos of Crete to design a tortuous maze, called the Labyrinth, in which to imprison the Minotaur, a powerful monster with the head of a bull and the body of a man. The Minotaur, insatiable for human blood, had to be regularly fed boys and girls, who were left in the Labyrinth, from whose confounding complex of corridors there could be no escape. In what seems the essential childhood nightmare, each child was hunted down and eaten by the Minotaur. At last, one boy, Theseus, was able to slay the monster and escape the Labyrinth, retracing his steps by means of a thread given him by Minos's daughter, the princess Ariadne.

Theseus went on to serve as king of Athens, where his graciousness and courage became the stuff of legend. He gave asylum to the blind outcast Oedipus; and even after Theseus's death, his spirit was thought to animate the Athenians in their wars. As late as the fifth century B.C. he was believed to be the ghostly giant seen fighting with the Athenians at the battle of Marathon. The Cretan Labyrinth appears repeatedly in Western art and literature—in expressions as diverse as the labyrinth laid out on the medieval floor of Chartres cathedral and Stephen King's The Shining, in which a boy outwits a mad bull of a father by escaping from a modern labyrinth. Those who have seen the film version will have no trouble imagining Jack Nicholson as the Minotaur.

Daedalus in his old age was forced by Minos to remain on Crete, but he devised a novel means of escape: a pair of wings with which to fly away.

He lays out feathers—all in order, first
the shorter, then the longer (you'd have said

they'd grown along a slope); just like the kind
of pipes that country people used to fashion,
where from unequal reed to reed the rise
is gradual. And these he held together
with twine around the center; at the base
he fastened them with wax; and thus arranged—
he'd bent them slightly—they could imitate
the wings of true birds.

This is from Ovid's retelling of the story of Daedalus, whose name means "cunning fabricator," a man able "to work on unknown arts, to alter nature"—that is, to be an artist of unfathomable power. Daedalus made a smaller pair of wings for his beloved son Icarus and warned him to "fly a middle course," avoiding both the sea's spray and the sun's scorching heat.

The old man worked and warned; his cheeks grew damp
with tears; and with a father's fears, his hands
began to tremble.

They take off, Daedalus leading the way, up over the Cyclades.

A fisherman, who with his pliant rod
was angling there below, caught sight of them;
and then a shepherd leaning on his staff
and, too, a peasant leaning on his plow
saw them and were dismayed: they thought that these
must surely be some gods, sky-voyaging.

Artists may be truly godlike in their effects, but Daedalus's fears were well founded. Icarus, taking "delight / in his audacity" and "fascinated by the open sky, / flew higher." The sun melted the wax and

Icarus plunged into the Aegean. His horrified father—"though that word is hollow now"—buried "his dear son's body" on the island now known as Icaria.

The reverberations down the millennia from this mythological cycle of Cretan stories are multiform, taking us from Le Morte d'Arthur *of Thomas Malory (whose young King Arthur is partly modeled on Theseus) to the* Ariadne auf Naxos *of Richard Strauss, from Jean Racine to Eugene O'Neill (both dramatists wrote plays—*Phèdre *and* Desire under the Elms—*based on the complications of Theseus's adulthood and the sexual tragedy of his second wife, Phaedra). In what is surely one of the most memorable reverberations, Daedalus, the archetypal artist who takes his chances even in the face of great risk, was used by James Joyce to create the figure of Stephen Dedalus, artist-hero of* A Portrait of the Artist as a Young Man, *who then goes on to serve as the more ambiguous figure of a yet-to-bloom Telemachus in* Ulysses.

RHYMES, like those Agathon delivered at his symposium, were looked down on by entitled and educated Greeks of the classical period, not only because they gave off the odor of a monger in the market but because they suggested a lack of attention to one's language. If you were serious about your Greek, you would eliminate the occurrence of such childish, jingly elements—which, because they can occur by accident, should not occur in the controlled speech of a serious person. Because, however, there are accidents of language—some words rhyme, while others are extremely similar in sound, and there's nothing to be done about it—these linguistic phenomena beyond our control must Mean Something; they must be there as *daimonia*, signposts of divine intention, which the more profound of our fellows may be able to discern. This line of reasoning was what convinced the Pythagoreans that they had hit upon hidden depths of meaning by coming across certain rhymes that struck them as full of portent and by noting other close similarities of sounds between words. It may also be that the extraordinary richness of Greek made such verbal oddities seem more singular than they would have appeared in other ancient tongues.

Each human language has its strengths and weaknesses and, like a musical instrument, is better designed to express certain information, thoughts, and feelings than others. A violin and a trombone have little in common; and though each can be drafted to sound the same melody, the melody will have a different texture and make a quite different impression on the hearer, depending on the instrument employed. Ancient Hebrew is tense and terse, a desert language of spare muscularity, as tightly economical in its movements and effects as a desert nomad, who, because of the constant threat of dehydration, must always think before he moves and think before he speaks, who never uses two words when one will do, who never uses one word when silence can express his meaning. (Not a little of the meaning of the Hebrew Bible is contained in its silences.) Ancient Latin is a language ideal for recordkeeping, simple maxims, and obvious subordinations, the perfect language for a tribe of parsimonious farmers who transformed themselves into land-grabbing real estate developers, then into colonial masters, and finally into imperialists who believed the whole world belonged to them by right. Only with immense exertions—by poets like Virgil, studiously imitating Homer—was Latin forged into an instrument fit for the emotional modulations of poetry and the subtleties of thought. With all that, no Latin dramatist ever came close to the Greek achievement; and the unoriginal Latin philosophers were all weak imitators of their Greek forebears.

Though ancient languages are notable for their modest vocabularies (the world still being young and the phenomena to be named far fewer than what we face today), Greek is an exception: the abundance of words in a dictionary of ancient Greek is staggering not only to the student but to the expert. The Spartans, the Achaeans, the Athenians, the Boeotians, the Aetolians, the Euboeans, the Thessalonians, the Macedonians, the Lydians, the Ionians, the speakers who hailed from the various Adriatic and Aegean islands, the colonists of Sicily, southern Italy, and the Black Sea—these and many more contributed their finely shaded regional vocabularies (not unlike their characteristic musical modes) to the whole language, which became like a vast orchestra of diverse instruments, able to produce modulations of extraordinary refinement. Unlike the Jews, the Greeks could never stop talking, and as is always the case with such people, their favorite subject was themselves.

The entire library of ancient Hebrew runs to a compact cabinet of twenty-four scrolls; the books of the Greek library are close to countless. Not only this, but Greek proceeds in a naturally discursive style, constantly turning this way and that in elegant riffs and delicate variations, like a spring river running to tributaries, curling into rivulets, bubbling into pools. Even when you are thinking or speaking another language altogether, Greek can scratch away impishly at the back of your brain. Neither as compressed as Hebrew, coiled and ready to spring, nor as mellifluous and tidy as Latin, it is, by contrast, a spiky language as full of sharp ups and downs as an economist's graph. No wonder that when Virginia Woolf went mad, she heard the birds singing in ancient Greek, the language her father had taught her; and when she heard them, many years later, singing again in that same tongue, she knew it was time to depart and, filling her pockets with stones, walked into the Ouse.

WORSHIPING AT THE ALTAR of their own superiority, the Greeks refused to learn anyone else's language, convinced as they were that all other languages were so deficient as to be a kind of baby talk. The barbarians prattled nonsense: "bar, bar bar," equivalent to our "blah, blah, blah." Had they bothered to learn other languages, the Pythagoreans might also have learned some lessons in cultural relativity and not been so convinced that accidental similarities of sounds between certain Greek words were celestial signposts. But abiding contempt for whatever was not Greek—the flip side of

Greek superiority—limited Hellenic sensibility, confining *to hellenikon* to its own backyard, blocking the likelihood of cultural cross-pollination and stunting the ability of Greece to absorb outside influences.

One needn't sail the wine-dark sea for long before realizing that the classical Greeks were classically classist, sexist, and racist. Nor does it take all that much perspicacity to understand that hidden behind the show of contempt lay irrational fears. (Does not our studied eloquence dispel all taint of barbarian prattle? Is not our lively democracy like a well-aired *andron*, revealing all other political systems to be stale contrivances? Surely, freemen are the only worthy associates of freemen—and why are slaves always such blundering dunderheads? Am I not, glossy from my workout, a paragon of hardened strength?—and how awful to be a woman, a weak, confined receptacle, as deficient in body and mind as is a barbarian tongue in sound and sense!) How often, I wonder, did these paragons of excellence hear a softly whispered question: But are not barbarians somewhat like you? Do you not share with slaves a common humanity? Are men and women so different that there is nothing feminine within you, nothing masculine within her? The fear of Otherness ran so deep that even Dionysus, almost certainly a homegrown Greek god going back to earliest times—but also the epitome of Otherness—was always spoken of as a foreigner, an intromission from the effete East. But in nothing did ambivalence toward the Other appear so starkly as in the twists and turns of Greek art.

Like Thales's invention of geometry, Greek art and architecture had its origin in Egyptian measurement. There were of course other strands of influence on the arts of the Greeks; and many of the archaic statuettes and examples of pottery that have come down to us from the time of Homer and earlier could almost belong to the Phoenicians, the Mesopotamians, and even the sub-Saharan Africans, so closely imitative are they of artistic conventions far afield [see figure 10]. But in the seventh and sixth centuries—that is, in the time of the lyric poets and the Presocratic philosophers—Egypt provided Greece with fresh inspiration. Before that time, monumental building, whether of temples or of statuary, was unknown to the Greeks. Greek temples were small, almost temporary enclosures of mud brick, reinforced by timber. Apart from martial metalwork, the plastic arts were limited to geometric pottery and votive offerings in wood and clay, primitive representations no more than a few inches high of a god or human, designed to be left at the god's little temple in thanksgiving or in hope of divine favor.

Increasing affluence, however, allowed some Greeks to travel, and northeast Africa proved more alluring—and provided a warmer welcome—than did the vast lands of the Persian enemy to the East. In the static, unchanging home of the pharaohs, these travelers admired the awesome architecture and imposing depictions in statuary of the pharaohs and their gods. To build such immensities, architect and artist would require precise plans based on exacting measurements, and these the Egyptians supplied to their Greek guests, as well as their methods of quarrying stone and dressing it. The result was a new building program in the principal Greek cities, which gave us in short order all the essential elements that would over time come to make up the visual ambience of the Western world.

Though the Greeks borrowed the idea of monumentality from the Egyptians, their actual work quickly took on characteristically Greek expressiveness. The new temples (and, soon thereafter, other public buildings) were now large and lasting, built of stone and set on hillsides, culminations of the human settlements from which they sprang. Unlike the looming

Egyptian buildings—which, with their massive walls, their forbidding portals, and the granite pharaohs and impassive animal gods that served as great stone guardians, seemed to be imposed from above—the Greek temples did not bellow "Bow down and keep out!" Rather, like their humble predecessors of mud and wood, these new Greek buildings maintained a harmony with their surroundings, as if they had somehow grown from the landscape itself. Their walls could hardly be seen: what presented itself to the viewer was a gracefully stepped porch that rose in massive but slender columns to a mildly pitched roof. The colonnades that surrounded the temple served, in their airy openness, as invitations to mount the steps and enter the precinct. As one approached the building, one could see high up between the columns and the roof a decorative frieze running horizontally.

The startlingly various Greek landscape cooperated in this new architectural venture by providing some of the most dramatic backdrops the world has to offer. Stark and dizzying heights fall off in sudden and graceful valleys and, beyond the land, haloed swaths of sea, intersected by rugged peninsulas and shrouded islands, provide visual dramas all their own. For light, water, and vegetation combine to produce bays, vivid in pools of aquamarine near their shorelines, but, farther out, raddled in purple, as if Phoenician cloths lay trembling on the sea floor far below the shimmering surface of the wine-dark sea. Today, one may still climb the magnificent Acropolis at Athens, visit the sun-blinding Temple of Poseidon that towers above the blue Gulf of Sounion, ascend to the profoundly mysterious ruins of Delphi on the wild, exhilarating slopes of Mount Parnassus, and feel in one's depths how much the ancient Greeks loved the look of their land—more than two-and-a-half millennia before humanity's appreciation of landscape is thought to have developed.

Not all the architectural elements fell into place at once. It took some experimenting to render everything in optimal proportions; and the earliest attempts at monumental temple building look squat and earthbound [see figure 2] when compared with the soaring weightlessness of the later examples. But by trial and error the architects reached a feeling for the ideal relationships of mass and line—what the Latin poet Horace would term *aurea mediocritas* (the golden mean)—so that their later work, even when seen today in a ruinous state, has the power to lift the spirit [3,4]. Much of this effect depends on the way in which they dealt with the proportions of the columns, solid at the base but seeming to taper toward the roof. In actuality, the columns incline ever so slightly inward and their seemingly straight lines are subtly curved to correct what would otherwise be the optical illusion that they fan outward. In time, the Greek architects learned many such refinements to enhance proportions and make their work more and more satisfying to the eye.

Within the cella, the walled chamber at the heart of the structure, one came into the presence of the god or goddess to whom the temple was dedicated—this in the form of a monumental statue, many meters high, of his or her presumed likeness, illuminated by lamps and often fronted by a shallow reflecting pool that cast additional light upon the image. This central statue was housed in a very un-Egyptian "inner sanctum," no more off-limits than is the cella of the Lincoln Memorial. In addition to the statue of the god, the architects came to provide sculptors with additional occasions to display their art, especially in the frieze of the facade—the long horizontal band running between the cornice that supported the roof and the architrave that rested atop the columns and that gave sculptors the opportunity to tell a whole story in successive panels. The facade's tympanum, the elongated triangular panel formed by the pitched roof and the cornice, offered a spectacular site for a tableau of figures [5].

But the sixth century also saw an explosion in monumental sculpture that went beyond the temple, as statues, life-size and larger, were erected in park and marketplace to commemorate battles, gods, and fallen heroes. In this novel assemblage [6] of temples and, a bit later, theaters [7] (as well as lesser public buildings, such as the *stoa* [8], the covered walkway that was the forerunner of our shopping mall) and open public spaces punctuated by monumental memorials, the look and even the experience of city life as we still know it was coming into being—bustling, diverse, essentially secular though serving many needs, and with pleasant alternative enclosures for retreat and stillness [9].

The monumental statuary of the archaic period (from the late seventh century to about 480 B.C.) betrayed its Egyptian origin in its stiff symmetry, based as it was on the traditional Egyptian grid that accounted for the ins and outs of human anatomy by a rigid apportioning of corporeal shapes into an abstract pattern [11, 12, 13]. The *kouroi* (youths, sons, scions), memorial statues to fallen heroes erected at widely dispersed sites, were the favored depiction of the human form in this period; and though the style of representation will change radically, the *kouros*—the adolescent on the cusp of manhood—will remain the central subject of Greek art. This image of the man-child, examples of which far outnumber all other visual realities, not only is expressive of the Greek ideal but ultimately calls attention to the underlying obsessions of Greek civilization.

In employing the Egyptian pattern, the Greek sculptor at first adhered scrupulously to the overall disposition of corporeal form: the spatial relationships between head and shoulders, between clavicle and chest, between torso and thighs, and so forth, remained exactly as received from Egypt. The arms remained rigidly at the sides, the fists clenched, the left foot striding forward. But there were, from the first, two Greek innovations: the figure was now plainly a youth, rather than the bearded adult of common Egyptian portrayals, and he was naked, his loins no longer skirted as was invariably the case in Egyptian statuary. The Greek propensity for male nudity, both in life and in art, was bothersome to surrounding societies, in which men, though hardly overmodest, thought of complete nudity (at least in public) as a form of humiliation. Slaves and the lower orders of workmen—such as fishermen and quarrymen—might sometimes appear naked in the course of their labors, but dignified social standing, dependent as it was on utter absolution from all forms of manual labor, necessarily implied clothing.

Why did the Greeks see this matter so differently—not only from surrounding societies but from other traditions throughout the history of art in which nudity, if allowed at all, has been occasional? Even the single outstanding exception among foreign traditions of art, Indian temple sculpture of the tenth century A.D., is indebted to Greek models. The Greek choice has become the choice of Western art—from earliest archaic Greece to the fall of Rome and then from the early Renaissance to the present (interrupted by the modest Middle Ages during which only Adam and Eve could provide the artist with an excuse for stripping his subjects to their bare essentials). But the artists of Rome, the Renaissance, and later were consciously imitating Greek models, to which we must turn for an answer to our question.

Scholars are not unanimous as to whether public nudity (in labor, in athletics, and at festive occasions such as symposia) was the precedent for the *kouroi* or whether the *kouroi*, displayed everywhere, precipitated public nudity; but the most sensible guess would seem to be that, in this case, art was imitating life rather than the other way around. At the same time, nudity certainly became more prevalent in art than in life, since all occasions in art became occasions for nudity. But no Greek soldier, almost invariably unclothed in art, would be so mad as to fight naked (all were heavily armed); no athlete left the *gymnasium* for a nude stroll through the *agora*; no inebriated symposiast, however much of a public spectacle he had made of himself the night before, was ever seen exposing himself in the light of day.

Was the society's encouragement of nudity, especially among young males—whether in statuary or at the *gymnasium*—just a manifestation of another of its peculiar institutions, socially sanctioned pederasty? If this were so, we should expect to find more sexual content in the statues than we do. The *kouroi* are never sculpted in arousal. In fact, after the archaic period—as the artists achieve greater flexibility and control over their medium—the genitals of the *kouroi*, as well as the genitals of virtually all males depicted in Greek art, shrink to a size most modern males would find embarrassing. There are exceptions to this: slaves and foreigners, who are usually shown as ugly, are sometimes depicted with enormous schlongs, as are the Dionysiac satyrs, normally deformed and demented as well; and artists who portray sympotic orgies and bedroom encounters are not shy about showing us exactly what is going on. But all this sort of thing is found on pottery (slaves, foreigners, satyrs, and orgies) and the backs of mirrors (sequestered lovemaking), intended for private titillation, not for public display.

Sexual passion, as we have seen, is a god named Eros. To suffer sexual passion is, therefore, to be bested by a god. One must of course give in—there is no sense in trying to overcome a god—but the very idea of being bested by anyone was to a Greek sufficient humiliation as not to be a fit subject of high art. There is a difference between being realistic about sexual passion—admitting its existence, naming it openly, enjoying it blatantly—and giving it pride of place in the *agora*. An orgy could therefore be the very thing for a drinking goblet [34, 35, 36, 37, 38, 39] or lovemaking be prized as an apt subject for a boudoir mirror [40, 41], but neither belonged in a public space, where only ideal dignity should reign. Better to draw and sculpt male genitals with a certain reticence—retracted against the groin as they might appear in combat or during a hard workout or emerging from what Joyce, parodying Homeric epithet, called the "scrotum-tightening sea." Athletes were even known to tie up the foreskin as if it were sausage casing, so as to prevent the comedy of an involuntary erection in the course of exercise.

Because, however, theatrical comedy was the realm in which no portrayal could be considered too provocative, comic actors were the only class of Greeks to draw public attention to their sexual equipment. They wore enormous penises and testicles, flopping down almost to their knees—an effect hardly more erotic than a clown's red mouth [42]. For productions of *Lysistrata*, however, in which the sex-starved male choristers appear with enormous erections, the genitalia were no doubt well stuffed, as was the case for actors playing satyrs, who always appeared with erect *phalloi* attached to loin harnesses. Hopeless sexual passion (of a mature woman—Phaedra, wife of Theseus—for her handsome stepson) is the subject of Euripides's *Hippolytus*, which of course ends tragically. But this is an exception in the *oeuvre* of an exceptional playwright. Almost all direct references to sex in Greek art are brutish, comic, or intended for private use—which only serve to underscore the public chastity of the *kouroi*, whose bold existence still presents us with a conundrum.

Nakedness has signaled humiliation, not only to the neighbors of the Greeks, but throughout human history. We have only to think of the emaciated and naked victims being fed by the Nazis into the gas chambers of central Europe and thence into mass graves or the dead American soldier being dragged through the streets of Mogadishu to remind ourselves of the universal meaning of public nakedness. The Romans understood well that the shame of crucifixion lay not just in its hideous pain but in the fact that the victim died publicly naked, every corporeal quiver of his final agony a show for all to see.$^{\alpha}$ Nudity bespeaks defenselessness—and can, therefore, evoke pity and a sense of solidarity, not just with the naked victim but with all of defenseless humanity, as when Shakespeare's Henry V, in the night before the battle of Agincourt, asks his troops to remember that "in his nakedness [the King] appears but a man."

How, then, did this universal sign of shame—and, perhaps at a deeper level, of piteous solidarity—come to serve the Greeks (and the subsequent Western tradition) as symbolic of heroism? The *kouros* is the Greek in his idealized state, eternally young, eternally about to bud, eternally strong, but fixed for all time—not in process, not on his way from boyhood to manhood, but eternally achieved, eternally One. As the ultimate ideal, he must be naked, for no costume but his own skin could serve his eternity. But he is eternally absolved from all becoming, whether further growth, further sexual blossoming, or further decay. Forever beyond all development (which would necessarily imply disintegration

α Retributive punishment of individuals by a political power is not the only course in which nudity can appear shameful. As the director Stanley Donen, no show business virgin himself, exclaimed recently of Kathleen Turner's nude turn in the Broadway production of *The Graduate*: "I never even went to see Kathleen Turner naked, because I knew what my reaction would be: 'That's how Kathleen Turner looks naked!' I'd be embarrassed for her, and for all of us staring at her nakedness, and I'd be out the door."

in a later stage), he belongs to the World of the Forms. He is the Form of Man, the perfection, of which all beautiful and heroic men partake as partial examples, the man that all men would wish to be. And it is this wish, this impossible wish, that lends the *kouros* the pathos we attribute to it.

The *kouros*, then, is not merely the expression of a Greek idea but of a profoundly human longing that the Greeks were the first to uncover and that reverberates through art and literature ever after. It is the longing that breaks forth from John Keats, dying in his twenties, on beholding in the British Museum a "Grecian urn"[β] on which a sylvan scene was shown:

> Fair youth, beneath the trees, thou canst not leave
>   Thy song, nor ever can those trees be bare;
>   Bold lover, never, never canst thou kiss,
>   Though winning near the goal—yet, do not grieve;
> She cannot fade, though thou hast not thy bliss,
>   Forever wilt thou love, and she be fair!
>
>
> Ah, happy, happy boughs! that cannot shed
>   Your leaves, nor ever bid the spring adieu;
> And, happy melodist, unwearièd,
>   Forever piping songs forever new;
> More happy love! more happy, happy love!
>   Forever warm and still to be enjoyed,
>   Forever panting and forever young;
>   All breathing human passion far
>   above,
> That leaves a heart high-sorrowful and
>   cloyed,
>   A burning forehead, and a
>   parching tongue.

β Since no one has ever discovered the urn Keats describes, the suspicion has arisen that what he actually viewed were the so-called Elgin Marbles, plundered by Lord Elgin from the Athenian Parthenon and still harbored by the British Museum.

It is the sentiment expressed with shuddering resignation by
W. B. Yeats, grown old, in "Sailing to Byzantium":

O sages standing in God's holy fire
As in the gold mosaic of a wall,
Come from the holy fire, perne in a gyre,
And be the singing-masters of my soul.
Consume my heart away; sick with desire
And fastened to a dying animal
It knows not what it is; and gather me
Into the artifice of eternity.

Once out of nature I shall never take
My bodily form from any natural thing,
But such a form as Grecian goldsmiths make
Of hammered gold and gold enamelling
To keep a drowsy Emperor awake;
Or set upon a golden bough to sing
To lords and ladies of Byzantium
Of what is past, or passing, or to come.

The poet, now a golden bird, will sing from his golden
bough—for, as in Keats's poem, nature itself has been absolved
from all becoming—and though the poet will take becoming as
his theme ("what is past, or passing, or to come"), he himself
will soar above all mortal change—far above, as Keats puts it,
"all breathing human passion."

Though both these examples (not surprisingly) make reference to Greece, the feeling, the wish to be absolved from becoming—from the "change and decay in all around I see"—is
deeply human. And its expression in notes high and low, in
measures quick and slow—whether in Homer's lost utopias of

Troy and Ithaca or in Sappho's plangently expressed desire for youth and regret over age, whether in Socrates's earnest aspiration to "shuffle off this mortal coil" and ascend to the World of the Forms or in the molded pathos of the *kouroi*—is Greece's most complex and valuable gift to the Western tradition.

Not that this is all there is to say about nudity. The shards of obscene pottery remain, visual equivalents of Archilochus's dirty jokes. And the figures of the herms remain, plinths without bodies except for head and phallus, not retracted but exceedingly erect [33]. But the pottery was as private as is most pornography, created for momentary enjoyment far beyond the bustling *agora*. The herms had an opposite function: set at boundary lines and, therefore, markedly public, they were apotropaic guardians of the *polis* itself, meant (not unlike the monumental pharaohs and animal gods of Egypt) to ward off evil and keep all enemies at bay by their primitive display of masculine power. The *kouros*, neither joke nor charm, gathers up all the divergent, nonstop Greek talk and speaks with one authoritative voice: "Here is our ideal, the best we have to offer."

This is not unlike the message that NASA delivered to the *kosmos* when in 1972 it sent a probe into deep space in the hopes of greeting intelligent life elsewhere in the universe. The spacecraft, now billions of miles into its journey, carries examples of Earth's nature and culture (images, sounds, music, greetings in fifty-five languages) on a gold-plated copper disk. Bolted to the craft's main frame is an anodized plaque carrying graphic messages: a star map, locating Earth, and alongside it the figures of a human male and a human female, both nude [69]. (After all, we wouldn't want those extraterrestrials to think that our bodies grew clothing the way a turtle grows its shell.) Neither the man nor the woman, however, could serve as a median representative of humanity, since both are members of a minority race—that is, white—nor do they resemble average Americans, being a good deal leaner than Pickup Pete and Supermarket Sally. The oddest detail is that, though both are clearly meant to be adults, they have no hint of hair except on their heads. What NASA chose to project into the universe by way of greeting is a couple of well-muscled humans who, despite their twenty-year-old faces, are prepubescent. So the ideal of the Greek *kouroi*, somewhat modified by American tastes (no skanky pubic hair, please), is perhaps at this moment being examined by faraway aliens who are trying to figure out how human reproduction takes place on that inhabited planet in the third concentric circle from a certain Milky Way star. Scratching their little green heads, they can't quite make it out.

If this American idealization is a somewhat debased version of its Greek predecessor and lacks the sheer dignity of the original, it nonetheless owes to the *kouroi* of the sixth century B.C. the idea of a transcendent visual ideal, absolved from time—surely a strange notion to send out, voyaging forever, through our space-time continuum. But then, we are what we have been, and the images we concoct do not float free like balloons but own deep historical roots—and, apparently, there's nothing even NASA can do about the way human history has shaped human imagination.

THE STIFF SYMMETRY of the *kouroi* of the seventh and sixth centuries began, in the fifth, to give way to a revolutionary relaxation of Athenian models that rapidly brought all of Greek sculpture to its acme. The "Kritian boy" [14] from the Acropolis is patently a *kouros* with the usual placid facial expression, his arms at his side, his left foot forward. But the sculptor's eye and hand are no longer in thrall to tradition, and he—probably Kritios, because the work is so like others known to be his—is no longer merely making what has been made before. Instead of standing alert with weight equally distributed, as are all earlier *kouroi*, this boy stands as would any boy at leisure, his weight on his left leg, his looser right leg bent at the knee, which sends his whole body into a gentle curve, his hips and shoulders no longer placed in stark parallels but occupying subtly slanted rather than rigidly horizontal planes, the head no longer squarely set atop its neck but slightly, so very slightly, inclined forward and to his right. The tactile appreciation of human anatomy and the grace of the whole conception leave one amazed. Though the subject may remain as virginally chaste as its muscle-bound predecessors, there can be no doubt that the beholder is meant to respond erotically. Viewed against its predecessors, the "Kritian boy" is an astonishing work of genius, a genius of head and heart, for never before in the already long history of human artifacts had a human being so lovingly shaped a human body—the balance between straight and bent limbs, the tension between taut and slack muscles—that he seems to have penetrated to its soul. Here is an artisan who understands the body of a boy as if he were the creator not merely of a marble statue but of the boy himself. Henceforth, a Greek statue will be unified by the underlying structure of the human body, not by surface patterning [15].

This innovative softening of the body of the *kouros* precipitates further diversity. The "Kritian boy" is so obviously a boy—much more so than his superbodied archaic predecessors—that he clearly embodies boyishness rather than a more generalized maleness; and this suggested additional variations to the sculptors. Other depictions of idealized maleness—rougher, more mature, in different poses—are now possible; and soon enough one encounters sculpted ideal males of different kinds: archers in battle, horsemen on campaign, athletes submitting their bodies to various physical disciplines, revolutionary heroes, gods of fearful beauty [16, 17, 18, 19, 20, 21, 22]. But the new variety hides an underlying sameness, for all these portrayals, however different each may be from the other, are of male perfection. Greek art of the high classical period serves as a mirror in which the Greek male admires himself—his perfectly proportioned, remarkably adept self.

Of course, women are depicted too, though rarely, and always clothed [23, 24, 25]. The ideal woman, therefore, is the secluded virgin or the secluded matron. Unlike men, "Greek women have no prime," writes the Canadian poet and classicist Anne Carson, "only a season of unripe virginity followed by a season of overripe maturity, with the moment of defloration as the dividing line." This describes only girls of good families, who begin as presexual beings, are tamed by conjugal penetration, and forthwith settle down to the work that is properly theirs—keeping the man's house and raising his children. There is no true ideal for the Greek woman, no naked eternality, only the tasks of becoming: preparation, marriage, childbirth, childrearing, suffering society's toleration if she survives past menopause, death. As the Berkeley art historian Andrew Stewart puts it, "whether *parthenos* [virgin], wife, or widow, since she is and always will be a creature of both excess and lack [that is, emotion rather than mind, receptacle rather than tool], her *aretē* is to recognize male supremacy and to do what her male guardian (father, brother, husband) thinks is right." Stewart adds wryly, "Needless to say, this directive was no doubt often honored as much in the breach as in the observance."

We know almost by instinct that Stewart must be right even

though our evidence of female resistance lies in fragments. We can point to Sappho's magisterial confidence, to the women revolutionaries of Aristophanes, to the unyielding Medea of Euripides and be certain that far more heat bubbled beneath the cool surface of Greek ideality than can be read in its public message. The Irish-English critic Terry Eagleton is particularly illuminating:

For a male-dominated society, man is the founding principle and woman the excluded opposite of this; and as long as such a distinction is held in place the system can function effectively. . . . Woman is the opposite, the "other" of man: She is non-man, defective man, assigned a chiefly negative role in relation to the male first principle. But equally man is what he is only by virtue of ceaselessly shutting out this other or opposite, defining himself in antithesis to it, and his whole identity is therefore caught up and put at risk in the very gesture by which he seeks to assert his unique, autonomous existence.

Woman is not just an other in the sense of something beyond his ken, but another intimately related to him as the image of what he is not, and therefore an essential reminder of what he is. Man therefore needs this other even as he spurns it, is constrained to give a positive identity to what he regards as no-thing. Not only is his own being parasitically dependent upon the woman, and upon the act of excluding and subordinating her, but one reason why such exclusion is necessary is because she may not be quite so other after all. Perhaps she stands as a sign of something in man that he needs to repress, expel beyond his own being, relegate to a securely alien region beyond his own definitive limits. Perhaps what is outside is also somehow inside, what is alien is also intimate—so that man needs to police the absolute frontier between the two realms as vigilantly as he does just because it may always be transgressed, has always been transgressed already, and is much less absolute than it appears.

But does this female other ever succeed in leaving behind private transgression, domestic tugs of war, and the fictional tropes of poetry and drama [26, 27, 28, 29]? Does she ever break into temple or *agora* as a subversive public statement, even as a sculpted ideal? One way of answering such questions is to ask these further ones: Does the woman ever lose her clothes in Greek art—and, if so, what does she look like?

She does—and she looks marvelous.

In the late fourth century, about 150 years after the carving of the "Kritian boy," the incomparable Praxiteles dared to push into twice forbidden territory. His subject was Aphrodite, goddess of love, whom one might think on the face of it the ideal subject for female nudity. But the myth of Aphrodite showed her to be zealously protective of her *belles choses*. Should any male to whom she had not chosen to proffer her gifts come upon her in her nakedness, the penalty was immediate death. By the late fourth century we must imagine a certain waning of such taboos about the gods, but it remains true that uncovering a female figure was boldness enough. To name her Aphrodite was heartstopping. Praxiteles's Aphrodite [30], fresh from her bath, stands in an elegantly languid *S*-curve, her left hand grasping drapery that conceals nothing (and serves to make her even more naked), her right hand tending—but not quite managing—to shield her private parts. Her sensational, touchable body owes nothing to the ruling Greek convention of depicting women as narrow-hipped boys with breasts—second-class males who lack penises. She is, to employ the inevitable cliché, all woman, an image so unafraid, so devoid of coyness, so shocking as to reduce any Greek male to silence, no small task. Has she just been startled by an intruder? Of course she has, for the intruder is her sculptor, who loved every inch of her with his chisel, as well as every male who down the subsequent centuries has dared to look with longing on the nakedness of the love goddess. Does her haughty face deplore my intrusion or beckon me on? Will she wrap the drapery around herself or let it fall to the ground? Will she kill me or welcome me? Who can say. She is Woman, fickle, unknowable, ineffably mysterious, obsessively desirable.

Here, for the first time in human history, the forbidden power and even the pathos of the female nude is revealed—not tentatively as one might have expected but with the breathtaking confidence of a genius who can picture publicly what before this has been confined to men's dreams. No sculptor will again make such a revolution till Michelangelo brings the Middle Ages to a definitive end by unveiling his *David* to the people of Florence two millennia into the future. What is all the more astounding is that the Greeks, after their initial shock, permitted the public display of this new art and patronized artists who took their inspiration from Praxiteles. After all, artists were not writers like Aristophanes or Euripides. In the Greek class system, they were working-class blokes, people who made their livelihoods by using their hands. No one had to indulge these mere artisans. But they got away with it. Soon the naked goddess was everywhere, sometimes concealing her private parts with one hand; sometimes shielding her breasts with the other; sometimes crouching gracefully at her bath, the folds of her abdomen enveloped by her sculptor in an invisible caress; sometimes reclining and partially draped; sometimes brazenly bare for all to see [31, 32]—and it's hard to imagine now what the history of Western art would have been, had Aphrodite never been undressed.

W HAT ENABLED Praxiteles and his fellow sculptors to get away with it? By the late fourth century, Greece was changing, Athens especially. Not that the Greeks had ever allowed themselves to come to a cultural standstill, but by the time of Praxiteles Greek sensibility was evolving precipitately. For one thing, Hippocrates, born on the island of Cos about 460 B.C. and living to at least 370, had revolutionized medicine, establishing it solidly as a form of experimental science and detaching it forever from mystical folk remedies and general quackery. By Praxiteles's day, Hippocrates's extensive writings were being taken with high seriousness, particularly his studies of human anatomy, a rich resource for sculptors of the human body. Hippocrates's no-nonsense anatomical treatises severed the study of the body from mythological imaginings and bade the student confine himself to careful observation and keep before him always the indissoluble link between cause and effect. In this way, Hippocratic medicine served as an indirect cause of the unveiling of Aphrodite and the freeing of Greek sculpture from its remaining taboos.

Even more important perhaps was the damage Athens had done to its previously impregnable self-confidence. Athens, quintessential city of *aretē*, land of democracy, home of invincibly courageous freemen, had lost the Peloponnesian War—which was a little like the United States losing to North Korea: the paragon of political institutions had been bested by the most bizarre, the most retrograde *polis* in the Greek world. By the time Athens surrendered to Sparta in 404 B.C., the great city had become a dependent basket case, its walls in ruins, its population depleted, all its colonies lost, its famous fleet reduced to a dozen ships [1]. The defeat engendered in Athenians of the fourth century, like Praxiteles, a certain skepticism about the imperviously male ideals of the previous century.

Though Athens recovered some of its wealth and dignity, it had not long to wait before it was assaulted once more, this time by Philip II of Macedon, who ruled over a quasi-Greek kingdom in the Balkans. How Greek the Macedonians were is still a matter of dispute; but the Greeks of the mainland, the islands, and the traditional colonies claimed that the "Greek" spoken by the Macedonians could not be Greek at all, since it was impossible to understand. (I imagine the situation was somewhat parallel to a Scottish movie needing to be distributed with subtitles even in the English-speaking world.) At all events, the Macedonians were surely Greek in their impressive martial abilities, which Philip, an inspired general, knew how to employ to the max. The much-reduced Athenians were no match for him and had finally to reach an unfavorable peace in 346.

Though Athens remained technically a free city, it now fell under the long shadow cast by Philip, who was assassinated ten years later and succeeded by his twenty-year-old son, Alexander, soon to be the Great. Alexander's plans were considerably grander than his father's: he meant to conquer the whole world, and he very nearly succeeded. But before setting out on his first campaign—to capture the Persian empire—he made certain of his hold on Greece by cruelly razing the entire city of Thebes in retribution for its rebelliousness against him. The wholesale massacre of the Thebans kept Greece quiet through the whole of Alexander's short life. His death in 323 brought to a close the classical or Hellenic period, initiating what we call the Hellenistic Age, a falling off (or so it is thought) from the cultural heights of the fifth century and the better part of the fourth. Certainly, Alexander's successors were hardly less adept than he at putting Athens in its place. Alexander's far-flung empire, however, had at length to submit to the growing power of Rome. In 146 all of Greece became a Roman "protectorate"; in 27 the first Roman emperor, Caesar Augustus, made Greece a Roman province. As the Romans themselves would have said, "*Sic transit gloria mundi.*"[γ]

As Athens bowed its neck beneath this long series of catastrophes, serenity and confidence, still evident in the fourth-century works of Praxiteles, waned, and another spirit entirely came to the fore. The shift was already evident in the plays of Euripides, who died while the Peloponnesian War was raging and of whom it was said that he drew men not as the ideals "they ought to be" but "as they were." All the sculpture we have seen so far presents us with idealized figures. Now in the wake of Athenian military losses, the realistic spirit of Euripides invades the minds of the sculptors. It is a general rule of culture that new ideas appear first in literature, only later in the visual arts. This is probably because ideas are so intimately linked to words, which are their primary vehicles, and because the tools of literature are so negligible and transportable, compared with what an artist must use.

The invasion of realism into Athe-

γ "So passes worldly glory." The ultimate source of this most famous of Latin tags has never been identified. It used to be spoken at the ritual of papal coronation but is in all likelihood older than Christianity. For a fuller exposition of the career of Alexander the Great, see Chapter 1 of *Desire of the Everlasting Hills*, Volume III of this series. Alexander—whatever his Greek may have sounded like—had been tutored by Aristotle and loved Greek literature, especially the *Iliad*, a copy of which he always kept under his pillow, along with a very sharp dagger. He is responsible for spreading the Greek language (in a simplified form) and Greek culture as far north as the Danube, as far south as North Africa, and as far east as India. This was the ancient Ecumene, which Rome would inherit and spread farther west—as far as the island of Britain.

nian sculpture that, by degrees, paralleled invasions by Sparta, Macedon, and Rome may have got under way because of an increased desire to memorialize the recently deceased as they actually were in life rather than in idealized images that bore little or no relation to remembered faces and bodies. Such idealization made a certain sense in the case of Greek soldiers cut down in their prime, but what sense does it make to memorialize an old man by such means? The sculptors, having schooled themselves in close observation of human anatomy, were now primed to sculpt from life; and the initial result was bust portraits of men like ugly old Socrates [44] and broad-browed Plato [45], their aspects hardly Apollonian.

Once the divide was crossed we begin to see portraits of all kinds: a defeated Demosthenes [46], the great orator who had tirelessly (and vainly) warned the complacent Athenians of the dangers of Philip of Macedon; an exceedingly preoccupied— and most unheroic—Chrysippus [47], a Stoic philosopher of the third century; a credibly handsome Alexander [48], whose clean-shaven countenance set a new style for the Greeks, who had previously considered the beard to be the sign of manhood, full citizenship, and patriarchal status (as it is still considered by the clergy of the Greek church). The new style lasted well into the Roman imperial period—and to it we still owe the preference of males in the clean-shaven West. (Few, however, could imitate Alexander's head of carelessly thick curls.)

The gods were still being sculpted, of course, but even they seemed to exhibit new individuality. Lysippus's Heracles [49] leans against his club, bulging with inordinate muscles that set him far from the balanced physical ideal of former times—and his labors have plainly exhausted the old bench-presser. Apollo, on the other hand, in the anonymous treatment known as "the Belvedere" [50] is just a bit too slender, a mite too sweet, self-consciously posed, his legs tending toward the feminine, his hairdo straight from the beauty parlor. (What is this, a fashion shoot?) Both figures, however different from one another, have surely been brought to earth.

If the gods are no longer quite so ideal as they had been, the Greek male as the acme of humanity has surely been called into question. The first non-Greeks to be portrayed heroically in Greek art are the Celtic barbarians, whom the Greeks began to encounter in the early third century when Gaulish tribes, bent on conquering Greek cities, crossed into Asia Minor. The Celts looked much more like gods than did the Greeks—they were tall, slender, and white, in contrast to Greeks, who despite their idealization of themselves tended to be short, squat, and swarthy—and in their fathomless courage they elected to enter battle naked, except for the gold torques they wore around their necks. For the chinking, clanking Greeks, armed from head to foot [51], to see men enter battle as if they were ideal-ized statuary was quite a surprise; and though the Celts looked very different from themselves in certain respects (they were clean-shaven except for their bushy mustaches, they wore lime in their hair to make the locks stand out), the Greeks declined to caricature them as they had all other barbarians. In the bat-tle monument at Pergamon, the Celts have been defeated (of course)—but they are truly beautiful, heroic, and godlike in their defeat [52].

Now, suffering—even the suffering of good men—can be depicted with new intensity. The Laocoön group [53], proba-bly sculpted a decade or two after the monument at Pergamon, is an almost excessive tour de force on the suffering of a good man—in this case, Laocoön, priest of Troy during its siege by the Greeks. Two legends circle Laocoön: first, that he was killed by snakes for opposing the entry of the Wooden Horse;

second, that he was a sensualist who had broken his vow of priestly celibacy, his two sons being the proof, and all three had to suffer divine retribution. Take your choice—but the face and torso of Laocoön, attempting with every ounce of his strength to free himself from the twisting, all-enveloping serpents, while knowing full well what the end will be, is a stark nightmare from the depths of the human psyche—a thing impossible to imagine the Greeks creating even a few years earlier.

Scenes of heroic suffering now compete with scenes of daily life and its ordinary brutalities. Marsyas, a satyr who had challenged Apollo to a music contest, is strung up on a tree to be flayed alive [54], the punishment for his *hubris*, while Apollo's Scythian slave [55]—a man of anxious (or cruelly expectant?) visage—crouches beneath the doomed Marsyas, sharpening the knife that will be used in the punishment. Unlike the athletes of old who always stood above us on pedestals, a battered boxer [56] looks up at us, his wounded face a palimpsest of suffering. A bent old woman [57], her body distorted by age and illness, her face disfigured by the effort of walking, hauls herself forward. She is on her way to market, as the dead fowl and basket of live chicks grasped in her left hand attest. But her head is garlanded, her old feet shod in elegant, thin-strapped sandals; and, in her effort, her right breast is about to escape her plunging neckline. Here is an old beauty that Rembrandt might have painted, a country girl come to town for a festival, perhaps her last, and wearing her best for the occasion. In a bronze statue of the second century, a small boy, ordinary and unheroic, sits on an outcrop of stone, carefully removing a thorn from his foot [58].

The new sculptors are as versatile in pleasure as in pain. A sprawling satyr [59] has obviously had a little too much fun and is sleeping off his drunken revel. His body is heroic surely, but the pose, which calls attention to his now-slack genitals, is the polar opposite of the heroic chastity of the *kouroi*. This could have come from any gay magazine. Nor is the satyr, previously a type of ugliness, at all ugly. Here is down-to-earth, in-your-face, erotic realism, enticing, salacious, forbidden, available— and too good to be true, since nothing will wake the satyr. In a separate group that could almost be a reenactment of the sprawling satyr's earlier revel, another fun-loving satyr [60]—a tautly muscled, handsome one, all satyrs now seeming to have shed their previous deformities—beats out time with a foot clapper and strikes his cymbals with gusto. He is the very figure of the young, involved musician, and his earthy smile leaves no doubt as to where his music will lead. The lovely young nymph [61] who responds so delightedly to his lusty invitation is herself far removed from the crazed *bacchae* of old, her open, happy face and firm breasts creating—for the first time in ancient art—an utterly innocent image of freely budding female sexuality. Seated on a rock but already rising toward her musician, she is removing her sandals in preparation for the wild dance to come. Of this extraordinary couple, John Boardman says they represent "the delightful carefree world of the Dionysian outdoors . . . a Hellenistic *fête-champêtre*."

Dionysus himself has been appearing in Greek art with increasing frequency. He seems always on the go. In an early appearance (of the late sixth century), he was already a voyager, shown on the exquisitely detailed interior of an Athenian drinking cup by the potter Exekias, sailing the wine-dark sea in his nicely curved craft [62]. Having turned the pirates who tried to kidnap him into dolphins, garlanded and bearded Dionysus blithely steers his little boat, which has sprouted a vine of large grapes that sway above sail and mast, as the dolphins circle helplessly. This magnificent idea from the tail end of the archaic period parallels Euripides's conception of a Dionysus on pilgrimage, a magical being who arrives from nowhere. Unlike the calmly balanced Apollo, Dionysus precipitates growth and change, rather than ruling over sameness and stasis.

In sculptures of the fourth century, he himself is seen to change and grow. In a work probably by Praxiteles, Dionysus is a baby in the arms of Hermes [63], god of roads and frontiers (in which guise his apotropaic image stood at Greek boundaries), of good luck and interpretation (thus *hermeneutics*). Hermes, when he was the newborn son of Zeus, made a fool of Apollo on the very day he was born, subsequently assuaging Apollo's wrath with the gift of the lyre, which Baby Hermes had just invented. No wonder the adult Hermes should eye Baby Dionysus with amused affection, while Dionysus's little index finger points to Hermes as if to say, "*You*'re my kind of guy." In a contrasting study by Lysippus, Baby Dionysus, already grown much larger, is hugged against the chest of an aging satyr, who needs to lean against a tree trunk to support the infant's weight [64]. The satyr, more rough-hewn and elemental than Hermes, studies the face of cuddly little Dionysus as if to say with admiration, "My day is nearly done—but, god, will you wreak havoc!"

A splendid late-fourth-century floor of pebbled mosaic at Pella, the capital of Macedon, gives us Dionysus once more on the move, this time as a beardless adolescent, muscular but sensual, alert but relaxed, his left hand waving a beribboned *thyrsus*—the customary wand of the god and his devotees, wreathed in ivy and surmounted by a pine cone—his right hand pressing the throat of his leaping steed, a wildly magnificent panther, completely responsive to the god [65]. We can almost hear the *bacchae* send up their thrilling shriek: "*Euoe, euoe!* The god is coming, the god is coming! Dionysus is *here!*"

"What fun we will have!" No doubt this is what is on the mind of the long-legged, elderly satyr who tackles the nubile nymph with such awkward vigor [66]. But the satyr, who has thus far viewed his resisting prey only from behind—and a singularly fetching behind it is—is about to be given a shock, as is the viewer. As one proceeds around the couple, it becomes evident that the soft, round nymph is a hermaphrodite with a prominent penis. Such a *scherzo* becomes more common as the Hellenistic Age runs its course, even as the laughter begins to ring more hollow. Small sculptures (and occasionally monumental studies) of priapic dwarves, hopeless drunks, and other people of the streets serve as measures of the crumbling of the classical ideal and the sudden plummeting of the age's sensibility. A grotesquely deformed figure, seemingly a model for a larger sculpture, dances as he displays his enormous phallus, one hand in his mouth, the other up his ass [67]. A hideously crippled hunchback sits, presumably in public, masturbating his massive erection [68]. The idea behind the French phrase for orgasm, *la petite mort*, here devolves into death-in-life, life-as-death. And there is no pity, just routine comedy—jokes number 67 and 68. Ha, ha, ha.

Apollo, the pristine figure who served as ultimate model for all the heroic statues of gods and men, has been bested, as have the Greeks themselves. He is seldom seen nowadays, and there are rumors of his death. Dionysus has come, Dionysus has come, Dionysus of dark wine and inspiration, Dionysus of growth and change, Dionysus of passion and death. And Dionysus has stayed too long.

VII

THE
WAY THEY
WENT

GRECO-ROMAN MEETS

JUDEO-CHRISTIAN

Psyche *was, to begin with, a Greek word for "life," in the sense of individual human life, and occurs in Homer in such phrases as "to risk one's life" and "to save one's life." Homer also uses it of the ghosts of the underworld—the weak, almost-not-there shades of those who once were men. In the works of the early scientist-philosophers,* psyche *can refer to the ultimate substance, the source of life and consciousness, the spirit of the universe. By the fifth century* B.C., psyche *had come to mean the "conscious self," the "personality," even the "emotional self," and thence it quickly takes on, especially in Plato, the meaning of "immortal self"—the soul, in contrast to the body.* Psyche *was also used by the Greeks as their word for butterfly because of a common belief that butterflies were the souls of the dead. And, finally, Psyche was the name of a girl.*

This girl appears in a story by Apuleius, contained in his picaresque novel The Golden Ass, *the only Latin novel to survive complete, though we are fairly sure Apuleius derived the Psyche story from much older Greek material. Psyche was so beautiful that she incurred the jealousy of Venus, the Roman Aphrodite, who sent her son Cupid to bewitch her. Cupid, whose name refers to cupidity or sexual desire, is the Roman equivalent of Eros and was depicted, as he is to this day, as a childlike god with wings and a quiverful of arrows with which he can make mortals fall in love against their will. His task was to doom Psyche by making her fall in love with the basest of men, but on sight of her the god of Love was himself smitten. To keep his passion on the q.t., he installed Psyche in a magical palace and visited her bed every night, though only in darkness, and warned her that she must never* attempt to see him in the light, for his splendor would be too much for her. Psyche's two older sisters, once they saw Psyche's magical new circumstances, were overcome by jealousy and tried to convince the poor girl that she must be sleeping not with a god but with a monstrous snake that could not bear to be seen. Psyche, deeply in love with her mysterious visitor, was nonetheless confused by her sisters' theory and resolved to learn the truth. The next night she took a lamp and looked on her godly visitor while he slept, falling even more deeply in love with him. But a drop of hot oil fell from her lamp to his shoulder, and the god awoke. Angered by Psyche's disobedience, he towered above her in all his magnificence, spread his shining wings, and disappeared. Needless to say, in Apuleius's conception, Cupid was no fat cherub but a most impressive adolescent.

Psyche, desolate, tried to drown herself in the first river she came to but was saved and upbraided by the shepherd god Pan. After many miseries, she fell into the hands of Venus, who made her a slave, beat her savagely, and sent her to carry out impossible tasks—all of which she was able to accomplish with the help of the beneficent powers of the universe. After the final trial, however, which brought her to Hades itself, Psyche fainted away in a deadly sleep. Cupid, forgiving her at last, came to her aid and petitioned Jupiter to allow their marriage, which Venus was then forced to consent to. Psyche was revived; and Cupid and Psyche, of course, lived happily ever after.

For many in the ancient world, the story of Cupid and Psyche was a Platonic allegory of the journey of the human soul through the trials of life. Having glimpsed the immortal splendor of divinity, she is condemned to banishment and extreme suffering, made all the more acute by her separation from divinity, of which she has had such an unforgettable taste; and she can be reunited with her perfect lover only after the sleep of death. In the later, Christian centuries, the story of Psyche stood as a metaphor of the yearning of the soul for God. Great mys-

tics such as Catherine of Siena, Teresa of Ávila, and John of the Cross, who described in their writings their experience of betrothal and marriage to Christ in highly colored, even carnal terms, were influenced, whether they knew it or not, by a pagan story in a wonderfully trashy Latin novel.

WHAT DID THEY BELIEVE, these Greeks? Were the gods real to them or just metaphors? Certainly, they did not have creeds or dogmas, confessional or doctrinal positions such as we have come to expect from religions. And just as certainly, there was a gradated spectrum of interpretation, as there must always be in things religious, that spanned classes and communities and that shifted in emphasis from one period to another. What is so striking about the Homeric gods—as opposed to the One that most of us are familiar with (though *familiar* is surely the wrong word)—is their lack of godliness. Oh sure, they have power beyond the dreams of the world's most powerful king, but they exercise this power just the way he would—heavy-handedly, often mercilessly, even spitefully. And they are taken up with their own predictable domestic crises—who's sleeping with whom, who's getting back at whom, who's belittling whom. Could anyone actually *believe* in such gods?

In the absence of something better, yes. It is hard for us—after so many centuries of monotheism (and more recent centuries of agnosticism and atheism)—to retroject ourselves into the Greek religious consciousness. The stories of the gods, which were multiform and seemingly limitless, came down to the Greeks from many streams of oral tradition, which they had no way of critiquing. They could not say, for instance, as we can, that the story with which this book began, of Demeter and her daughter, Persephone, was just a clever metaphor that gave a preliterate society an "explanation" for the changing seasons—in a class with such things as "Why the Snake Has No Legs" or "How the Giraffe Got Its Neck," which we have long since banished to the nursery. But if we look seriously at the Demeter story, we may find ourselves even in the twenty-first century captivated by its poetry and depth of emotion—which may lead us to exclaim something like "Well, this doesn't explain anything scientifically, but there is something very satisfying about it. It has the truth of a dream."

Dreams, we all know, can be very truthful, even if at the level of conscious critique they are full of mad illogic. Some such thoughts surely occurred to men like Socrates and Plato, who advised their followers to reconceive the myths as metaphors—not metaphors as naive explanations of natural phenomena but as attempts by society's dreamers to find a language that can penetrate to the heart of reality. These philosophers understood that though the myths were naive in the sense that they were anthropomorphic, presenting the gods as if they were men, the myths were also attempting—at a deeper level— to feel the intangible and say the unsayable.

The Greek gods changed as the Greeks themselves were changed by the events of their history. The rigid figures of the archaic *kouroi* have much in common with the gods of Homer, Hesiod, Solon, and even Aeschylus: these gods are human beings made gigantic, as full of needs as of power and requiring the stateliness of ritual—soothing actions performed in the same way over and over again—in order to be assuaged. Such actions always require loss for men and gain for the gods—libation, animal sacrifice, in great crises even human sacrifice—but there is also an exchange, an economy of the divine. For by our ritual, carried out with punctilious sincerity, we may avoid divine displeasure and find ourselves the recipients of heavenly grace.

When the house of Oedipus is plunged into confusion over what seem to be conflicting oracles, Jocasta emerges from the palace, carrying her suppliant's branch, wound in wool, determined to perform the ritual of supplication that can avert the wrath of the god. She addresses the chorus, as she makes her way to Apollo's shrine:

> Lords of the realm, it occurred to me,
> just now, to visit the temples of the gods,
> so I have my branch in hand and incense too.
>
> Oedipus is beside himself. Racked with anguish,
> no longer a man of sense, he won't admit
> the latest prophecies are hollow as the old—
> he's at the mercy of every passing voice
> if the voice tells of terror.
> I urge him gently, nothing seems to help,
> so I turn to you, Apollo, you are nearest.

She places her branch on the altar of Apollo and continues her prayer:

> I come with prayers and offerings . . . I beg you,
> cleanse us, set us free from defilement!
> Look at us, passengers in the grip of fear,
> watching the pilot of the vessel go to pieces.

Though Jocasta performs the prescribed rites, we know that these cannot avail because the defilement within the palace is too grave to be washed away by a few prayers and a well-placed olive branch. Lord Apollo, principle of justice and the terrifyingly unseen presence throughout the play—"nearest" in a way

Jocasta has failed to reckon with—will not, in the end, be mocked. He will bring his justice to perfection, and this will entail the suicide of Jocasta, the blinding of Oedipus, and the permanent humiliation of the entire family. Jocasta cannot know all this at this point and therefore cannot be aware how insufficient are her paltry rites. At the center of Greek religion is the belief that, though we can at times successfully invoke the mercy of the gods on us and our causes, we must pay for our sins, whether these are conscious or not—and if the sins are big, we must pay big time. How different is this from common belief and practice even in our day, whatever the particular doctrines of a given religion may be? We can understand Greek religion because, at its heart, it operates on the same internal dynamic that fuels all (or certainly almost all) religion. The aboriginal Christian prayer *Kyrie eleison* (Lord, have mercy) is a Greek prayer far more ancient than Christianity.

But there is also an undercurrent in Jocasta's speech that suggests a shift in religious perspective—not so much in the time of the tyrants as in the time of Sophocles, the play's author. For there is something a tad slapdash about Jocasta's approach to the gods. She doesn't believe in oracles, which she finds "hollow." It has "just now" "occurred" to her "to visit the temples of the gods," and she chooses the temple of Apollo because it's "nearest" to her palace. Does she believe or doesn't she? She seems a skeptic in trouble beyond her usual coping mechanisms, the sort of person who in our day might slip into a church when her world is falling apart but would otherwise give scant thought to divinity.

In the period when Sophocles was writing *Oedipus*, Athens was reaching the acme of its *aretē*, its moment of supreme artistic and political confidence. Its empire was booming: the Athenian colonies and sister cities from mainland Greece to

Italy, from the Aegean coast of Asia to the coast of the Black Sea, were creating greater general wealth through the growing exchanges of staples and exotica, and Athenian democracy and military power—which went hand in hand—were the envy of the world. Athenians held themselves, not the gods, responsible for this turn of events; and though they certainly continued to fulfill the rites and rituals of Greek religion, as does Jocasta, they relied on their own native strengths and smarts to keep their enterprise going. They had become an essentially secular people.

There is a speech, probably the most famous speech in all of Western history, that sheds much light on the Athenian *esprit* of the fifth century, Pericles's Funeral Oration over the Athenian dead in the first year of the Peloponnesian War. Though it is a speech of some length (if brief by Greek standards), I quote it in full, because there is no other single cultural expression that so enables us to penetrate the Athenian frame of mind. Thucydides, in whose exacting *History of the Peloponnesian War* the speech occurs, explains "the ancient custom" of the Athenians, carried out annually over the bones of those who had died for Athens in the previous year: "When the bones have been laid in the earth, a man chosen by the city for his intellectual gifts and for his general reputation makes an appropriate speech in praise of the dead, and after the speech all depart." Pericles, coming "forward from the tomb and, standing on a high platform, so that he might be heard by as many people as possible in the crowd," began:

Most of those who have stood in this place before me have praised the tradition of this speech that closes our ceremony. It is good, they have felt, that solemn words should be spoken over our fallen soldiers. I do not share this sentiment. Acts deserve acts, not words, in their honor; and to me a state funeral, such as you have witnessed, would have been honor enough. Our trust in the great bravery of this great number of the fallen should not depend on one man's eloquence. Moreover, it is very hard to speak appropriately when many of a speaker's hearers will scarce believe that he is truthful. For those who have known and loved the dead may think his words scant justice to the memories they would hear honored, while those who did not know them may occasionally, from jealousy, suspect me of overstatement when they hear of feats beyond their own powers. For it is only human for men not to bear praise of others beyond the point at which they still feel they can rival their exploits. Transgress that boundary and they are jealous and incredulous. But since the wisdom of our ancestors enacted this law I too must submit and try to suit as best I can the wishes and feelings of every member of this gathering.

My first words shall be for our ancestors; for it is both just to them and fitting that on an occasion such as this our tribute of memory should be paid to them. For, dwelling always in this country, generation after generation in unchanging and unbroken succession, they have, by their hard work and courage, handed down to us a free country. So they are worthy of our praise; and still more so are our fathers. For they added to our ancestral patrimony the empire that we hold today and they delivered it, not without blood and toil, into the hands of our own generation; while it is we ourselves, those of us now in midlife, who consolidated our power throughout the greater part of the empire and secured our City's complete independence both in war and peace.

Of the battles that we and our fathers fought, whether we were winning power abroad or gallantly withstanding nearby enemies, whether Greek or foreign, I will say no more: these are too familiar to you all. I'd rather set forth the spirit in which we faced them, and the Athenian constitution and Athenian way of life that brought us to greatness, and to pass from these things to the dead themselves. For I think it not unfitting for these things to be recalled in today's solemnity; and it is appropriate that this whole assembly of both citizens and strangers should hear these things.

For our system of government does not copy the systems of our neighbors: we are a model to them, not they to us. Our constitution is called a democracy, because power rests in the hands not of the few but of the many. Our laws guarantee equal justice for all in their private disputes; and as for the election of public officials, we welcome talent to every arena of achievement, nor do we make our choices on the grounds of class but on the grounds of excellence alone. And as we give free play to all in our public life, so we carry the same spirit into our daily relations with one another. We have no black looks or angry words for our neighbor if he enjoys himself in his own way, and we even abstain from little acts of churlishness that, though they do no mortal damage, leave hurt feelings in their wake. Open and tolerant in our private lives, in our public affairs we keep within the law. We acknowledge the restraint of reverence; we are obedient to those in authority and to the laws, especially to those that give protection to the oppressed and those unwritten laws of the heart whose transgression brings admitted shame.

Yet ours is no workaday city only. No other city provides so many recreations for the spirit—contests and sacrifices all the year round, and beauty in our public buildings to cheer the spirit and delight the eye day by day. Moreover, the City is so large and powerful that all the wealth of all the world flows in to her, so that our own Attic products seem no more familiar to us than the fruits of the labors of other nations.

And how different from our enemies is our attitude toward military security! The gates of our City are flung open to the world. We practice no periodic deportations, nor do we prevent our visitors from observing or discovering whatever "secrets" might prove of military advantage to an enemy. For we do not place our trust in secret weapons but in our own faithful courage.

So too with education. The Spartans toil from early childhood in the laborious pursuit of courage, while we, free to live and wander as we please, march out nonetheless to face the selfsame dangers. Here is the proof of my words: when the Spartans advance into our country, they do not come alone but with all their allies; but when we invade our neighbors we have little difficulty as a rule, even on foreign soil, in defeating men who are fighting for their own homes. Moreover, no enemy has ever met us in our full strength, for we have our navy to look after at the same time that our soldiers are sent on service to many scattered possessions; but if our enemies chance to encounter some portion of our forces and defeat a few of us, they boast that they have driven back our whole army, or, if they are defeated, that the victors were in full strength. Indeed, if we choose to face danger with an easy mind rather than after rigorous training and to trust rather in our native manliness than in state-sponsored courage, the advantage lies with us; for we are spared all the tedium of practicing for future hardships, and when we find ourselves among them we are as brave as our plodding rivals. Here as elsewhere, then, the City sets an example that deserves admiration.

We are lovers of beauty without extravagance, and lovers of wisdom without effeminacy. Wealth to us is not mere material for vainglory but an opportunity for achievement; and we think poverty nothing to be ashamed of unless one makes no effort to overcome it. Our citizens attend both to public and private duties and do not allow absorption in their own affairs to diminish their knowledge of the City's business. We differ from other states in regarding the man who keeps aloof from public life not as "private" but as useless; we decide or debate, carefully and in person, all matters of policy, and we hold, not that words and deeds go ill together, but that acts are foredoomed to failure when undertaken undiscussed. For we are noted for being at once most adventurous in action and most reflective beforehand. Other men are bold in ignorance, while reflection will stop their going forward. But the bravest are surely those who have the clearest vision of what lies before them, glory and danger alike—and yet go forth to meet it.

In doing good, too, we are the exact opposite of the rest of mankind. We secure our friends not by accepting favors but by granting them. And so this makes friendship with us something that can be counted on: for we are eager, as creditors, to cement by continued kindness our relation to our friends. If they do not respond with the same warmth, it is because they feel that their services will not be given spontaneously but only as repayment of a debt. We are alone among mankind in doing men benefits, not on calculation of self-interest, but in the fearless confidence of freedom.

In a word, I say our City as a whole is an education to Greece, and that our citizens yield to none, man by man, for independence of spirit, many-sidedness of attainment, and complete self-reliance in limbs and brain.

That this is no vainglorious phrase but actual fact is proven by the universal leadership that our way of life has won us. No other city of the present day goes out to her ordeal greater than ever man dreamed; no other is so powerful that the invader feels no bitterness when he suffers at her hands, and her subjects no shame at the indignity of their dependence. Great indeed are the signs and symbols of our power. Men of the future will wonder at us, as all men do today. We need no Homer or other man of words to praise us; for such give pleasure for a moment, but the truth will put to shame their imaginings of our deeds. For our pioneers have forced a way into every sea and every land, establishing among all mankind, in punishment or beneficence, eternal memorials of their settlement.

Such then is the City for whom, lest they should lose her, the men whom we celebrate died a soldier's death; and it is but natural that each of us, who survive them, should wish to spend ourselves in her service. That, indeed, is why I have spent many words on the City. I wished to show that we have more at stake than men who have no such inheritance, and to support my praise of the dead by making clear to you what they have done. For if I have chanted the glories of the City, it was these men, and men like them, who have adorned her with such splendor. With them, as with few among Greeks, words cannot magnify the deeds that they have done.

Such an end as we have here seems indeed to show us what a good life is, from its first signs of power to its final consummation. For even where life's previous record showed faults and failures, it is just to weigh the last full measure of devotion against them all. There they wiped out evil with good and did the City more service as soldiers than they did her harm in private life. There no hearts grew faint because they loved their riches more than honor; no poor man shirked his duty in the hope of future wealth. All these they put aside to strike a blow for the City. Counting the quest to avenge her honor as the most glorious of all ventures, and leaving Hope, the uncertain goddess, to send them what she would, they faced the foe as they drew near him in the strength of their own manhood; and when the shock of battle came, they chose rather to suffer the utmost than to win life by weakness. So their memory has escaped the reproaches of men's lips, but they bore instead on their bodies the marks of men's hands, and in a moment of time, at the climax of their lives, were rapt away from a world filled, for their dying eyes, not with terror but with glory.

Such were the men who lie here and such the City that inspired them. We survivors may pray to be spared their bitter hour but must disdain to meet the foe with a spirit less daring. Fix your eyes on the greatness of Athens as you have it before you day by day, fall in love with her, and when you feel her great, remember that this greatness was won by men with courage, with knowledge of their duty, and with a sense of honor in action, who, if they failed in private life, disdained to deprive the City of their services but sacrificed their lives as their best offerings on her behalf. So they gave their bodies to the commonwealth and received, each for his own memory, praise that will never die, and with it the grandest of all sepulchres, not that in which their mortal bones are laid, but a home in the minds of men, where their glory remains fresh to stir to speech or action as the occasion may require.

For the whole earth is the sepulchre of famous men; and their story is not graven only on stone over their native earth but lives on far away, without visible symbol, woven into the stuff of other men's lives. For you now, it remains to rival what they have done and, knowing that the secret of happiness is freedom and the secret of freedom a brave heart, not idly to stand aside from the enemy's onslaught. For it is not the poor and luckless, the ones who have no hope of prosperity, who have most cause to reckon death as little loss, but those for whom fortune may yet keep reversal in store and who would feel the change most if trouble befell them. Moreover, weakly to decline the trial is more painful to a man of spirit than death coming sudden and unperceived in the hour of strength and confidence.

Therefore I do not mourn with the parents of the dead who are here with us. Rather, I will comfort them. For they know that they have been born into a world of manifold chances and that he is to be accounted happy to whom the best lot falls—the best sorrow, such as is yours today, or the best death, such as fell to these, for whom life and happiness were bound together. I know it is not easy to give you comfort. I know how often in the joy of others you will have reminders of what was once your own, and how men feel sorrow, not for the loss of what they have never tasted, but when something that has grown dear to them has been snatched away. But you must keep a brave heart in the hope of other children, those of you who are still of an age to bear them. For the newcomers will help you forget the gap in your own circle, and will help the City to fill up the ranks of its workers and its soldiers. For no man is fitted to give fair and honest advice in council if he has not, like his fellows, a family at stake in the hour of the City's danger. To you who are past the age of vigor I would say: count the long years of happiness so much gain to set off against the brief space that yet remains, and let your burden be lightened by the glory of the dead. For the love of honor alone is not staled by age, and it is by honor, not, as some say, by gold, that the helpless end of life is cheered.

I turn to those among you who are children or brothers of the fallen, for whom I foresee a mighty contest with the memory of the dead. Their praise is in all men's mouths; and even if you should rise to heroic heights, you will be judged harshly for achieving less than they. For the living have the jealousy of rivals to contend with, but the dead are honored with unchallenged admiration.

If I must speak a word to those who are now in widowhood on the powers and duties of women, I will cast all my advice into one brief sentence. Great will be your glory if you do not lower the nature that is within you—hers greatest of all whose praise or blame is least bruited on the lips of men.

I have said what I had to say, according to the law, and the graveside offerings to the dead have been duly made. Henceforward the City will support their children till they come of age:

such is the crown and benefit she holds out to the dead and to their kin for the trials they have undergone for her. For where the prize is highest, there, too, will you find the best and the bravest.

And now, when you have finished your lamentation, let each of you depart.

Pericles's words are echoed in other critical speeches of later Western history. His modest beginning cannot but remind us of Lincoln at Gettysburg—"The world will little note nor long remember what we say here"—even to the point of Lincoln's exact phrase "the last full measure of devotion." Pericles's resolve—"the secret of happiness is freedom and the secret of freedom a brave heart"—and his rhetorical emphases on blood and toil are so very reminiscent of Churchill's in his repeated promise to the British people during the Second World War of "blood, toil, tears, and sweat." And no wonder, for both orators knew their Thucydides and knew this speech.

For me at least, the most obvious later parallel is the 1961 presidential inauguration address of John F. Kennedy. America was then at the height of its power and prestige, the unembarrassed leader of the free world, whose classless way of life, civil tolerance, and freedom of speech were the envy of humanity. We were, or so we thought, without peer or precedent, an open society dedicated to "the pursuit of happiness," the opposite of the secretive Soviet Union and its dreary militarism, generous in victory, openhanded to those who sought our help. Kennedy's cadences were as measured—and as tough—as those of Pericles: "Let every nation know, whether it wishes us well or ill, that we shall pay any price, bear any burden, meet any hardship, support any friend, oppose any foe to assure the survival and the success of liberty." When Kennedy admitted that his was "a call to bear the burden of a long twilight struggle,

year in and year out," he exhibited Periclean modesty and balance, and there was none of the exaggeration and bombast that
clangs through current political discourse. When he told of sacrifices yet to come, like Pericles he pulled no punches. It is hard
today to imagine an American president reminding individuals
of their obligations to the nation as a whole—or even daring to
suggest that we must give up something as trivial as our SUVs
for the sake of the common good. What an incredible moment
it would be if we were once more to hear a president say with
a straight face, "Ask not what your country can do for you; ask
what you can do for your country."

Kennedy may remind us, if distantly, of Pericles in other
ways as well. Known as the First Citizen of Athens and fifteen
times elected *stratēgos*, Pericles [43] dominated not only
Athenian politics but Athenian imagination. For he was not
merely a political animal but a man of genuine intellectual and
artistic interests, and he counted among his close friends the
sculptor Phidias (who created the great statue of *Athēnē
Promachos* at his request), the dramatist Sophocles (who gave
us the skeptical Jocasta), Herodotus (the father of history), and
the debunking philosopher Anaxagoras, who had called into
question the existence of the gods. Though his first marriage
ended in divorce, Pericles formed a lasting union with the cultivated Aspasia, an Athenian celebrity who had once been a
courtesan (and therefore a woman of far more freedom and
worldly experience than most of her sisters). The call to share
the company of this romantic couple and the conversation of
their table was the invitation most prized by fifth-century
Athenians. Pericles's death—by plague in the second year of the
war—was a blow from which Athens never completely recovered, as it drifted politically and militarily from one disaster to

another till the unthinkable happened and the empire itself was irrecoverably lost and with it most of the city's power and prestige.

Of course, all ages and all leaders have their blind spots. The City of Freedom that Pericles lauded was full of slaves—and of freeborn women whose lives were lived in an obscurity that Pericles's closing reference makes all too clear. But the Athenian empire was for Pericles an unquestioned good. The Land of the Free and the Home of the Brave that Kennedy presided over was a land where dark-skinned people were relegated to a fearful obscurity that was not so far from slavery—and women, if known at all, were normally known as their husband's wives. But American power was in Kennedy's presentation always on the side of right.

One cannot fail to note how secular are the language and the overall approach of Pericles. The gods are hardly mentioned; Athenians must rely on themselves. No more does Kennedy take refuge in invocations of divinity; and only at the very end of his speech does he mention God: "Here on earth God's work must truly be our own." In other words, let's stick to the world as we know it and leave God out of it. This is not a theology (or an anti-theology) but a strategy. In neither case is there a confession of atheism, just an implied acknowledgment that a politician is no oracle and has no business speaking on behalf of heaven. It was this lack of knee-jerk religiosity that prompted Harvey Cox, then a young, little-known Baptist minister, to write admiringly of Kennedy in *The Secular City* as the ideal secular politician, who refused, in a religiously diverse society, to tart up his speeches with pious cant: "Though there can be little doubt that [Kennedy's] Christian conscience informed many of his decisions, especially in the area of racial justice, he stalwartly declined to accept the semireligious halo that Americans, deprived of a monarch who reigns *gratia dei*, have often tried to attach to their chief executive."

After the Age of Pericles, as Athenian confidence dimmed, that famous confidence was all too often replaced by cynicism, modesty by cockiness, sincerity by manipulation, strength by bluster. Though the gods were more and more loudly invoked, the prayers rang hollow, the appeal to conscience turned mute, and any reference to social justice tended to be met with a knowing smirk. And though the parallels to our present day are only partial, they are vivid enough to give us pause, as God, now strangely shorn of his justice, appears to direct our every national move.α

α The Second Gulf War has sent classicists scurrying back to their Thucydides, where they have found frightening parallels between the *hubris* of seemingly unbeatable Athens—in its fearless resolve to dominate the world even without allies—and the dismissive attitude of the Bush administration toward America's traditional friends, toward the UN and its member nations, and toward world opinion. See, for instance, "The Melian Dialogue," Book V, *History of the Peloponnesian War,* in which the Athenian delegates, brushing aside all appeals to fairness, threaten the existence of the small state of Melos, if the Melians do not do exactly what the Athenians demand and join their exceedingly underpopulated alliance: "We recommend that you should try to get what it is

THE FINAL CRUMBLING of Athenian confidence left a large social vacuum. In the arts, as we have seen, idealism was succeeded by realism, realism by a jaded desire for momentary stimulation (as in the surprise hermaphrodites— of which there were many), flagging desire by crabbed pessimism. In philosophy, the loss of Athenian independence precipitated a narrowing of subject matter. No longer did philosophers aspire to the deep spiritual insights and broad moral vision of Socrates, Plato, and Aristotle. They divided into conflicting schools and wandered through the Greco-Roman world as permanent immigrants, picking up tutoring jobs as they could. The names of their schools are still with us, not so much as descriptions of current schools of philosophy as of human temperaments and mind-sets. There were the Sophists, who taught their charges how to win an argument without regard to the truth; the Skeptics, who believed that no certain knowledge was possible; the Cynics, who taught self-sufficiency; the Stoics, who taught virtuous detachment from material things; the Epicureans, who taught that "pleasure is the beginning and end of living happily." All these schools (and many more) were in competition with one another—for the minds of men as well as for tutoring jobs—and within each school were serious thinkers whose philosophies were far more modulated and subtle than my broadside characterizations of their teachings would suggest. But the upshot was a debased intellectual climate, fragmented and agnostic. Well, the Stoics may be right, so I think I'll spend the rest of the day practicing self-denial. On the other hand, the Epicureans may be right, so I think I'll tuck into another plate of that scrumptious wild boar.

Religion also fragmented. The Greeks and the Romans tended to interact with one another in prickly, high-handed ways. The conquered Greeks, knowing they were the cultural and intellectual superiors of their conquerors, could be touchy, resentful, and unbending. The Romans, having the inferiority complex of all *arrivistes*, took refuge too easily in shouting, bullying, and otherwise throwing their weight around. Greek artists and philosophers, dependent as they now

possible for you to get, taking into consideration what both of us really do think; since you know as well as we do that, when these matters are discussed by practical people, the standard of justice depends on the equality of power to compel and that in fact the strong do what they have the power to do and the weak accept what they have to accept." When Donald Rumsfeld, a practical imperialist if ever there was one, took over the Pentagon, he commissioned a study of how ancient empires maintained their hegemony. Might he more profitably study how they lost all they had gained?

were on Roman wealth and patronage, were not unlike contemporary Frenchmen who cannot bear to acknowledge that
France is no longer the cultural and economic navel of the world.
Often enough, in the eyes of the Romans, there seemed no way
to placate Greek outrage. But the Romans did try. They sat at the
feet of Greek tutors to improve their minds, they read and imitated Greek literature, and they commissioned myriad copies of
Greek buildings and sculptures to enhance their simple towns.
And they copied, insofar as they could, the external manifestations of Greek religion.

Of the many peoples of Earth, the Romans may have had
the most boring religion of all. They had a pantheon of gods,
patron-protectors of various families and tribes, but most of
these gods were little more than names. Contact with the impressive stories of Greek mythology and the thrilling art that
accompanied them—a contact that began as a result of the
Greek colonization of southern Italy—encouraged the Romans
to dress up their own religion in Greek fashions. Their high
God, Jupiter, they reinterpreted as a variant of Greek Zeus. (In
this, they were certainly right. The prehistoric people who
lived in an area of southern Russia and spoke the original Indo-
European language worshiped the Sky-Father and called him
"Diespiter"—the word that became "Zeu Pater," or "Father
Zeus," to their primeval Greek-speaking descendants and "Jup-
piter" to their primeval Latin-speaking descendants.) Roman
Venus was assigned the Greek stories about Aphrodite, Juno
took on the stories of Hera, Minerva those of Athena, Mars
those of Ares, Vulcan those of Hephaestus, and so forth. This
instant mythmaking gave the Roman gods faces as well as stories and considerably enlivened Roman imagination.

Roman religion was basically a businessman's religion of
contractual obligations. Though scrupulous attention was paid

to the details of the public rituals, which had been handed down from time immemorial, it was all pretty much in the spirit of "You scratch my back, I'll scratch yours"—rituals for favors. Not only were there few Roman myths, there was virtually no theology or interest in the theoretical aspects of religion, the very enigmas that had sparked the speculations of the earliest Greek philosophers. Sometimes, even the name of a god was forgotten. In the *Aeneid* Virgil presents the Trojan prince Aeneas, the supposed ancestor of the Romans, being led by Evander, a local Latin king, to the Capitoline Hill, where the king informs the Trojan: "This grove, this hill, tree-topped, are some god's home . . . although we do not know which god."

The Romans, being practical, can-do folk, did at length take some interest in the ethical end of philosophy—the question of how best to live—which encouraged them to sit still long enough to gain some tips from the later Greek philosophers, especially the self-denying Stoics and the pleasure-loving Epicureans—the two philosophical vogues that most caught Roman fancy (such as it was). Love of Order, the very quality that made the Romans such skilled administrators of their vast empire, limited their aptitude for things intellectual and artistic. The creative curiosity that made the Greeks such cultural giants limited and, finally, undid their earlier imperial successes. Their vibrant energy was far more stirred by art, ideas, and political innovation than it ever was by the day-to-day business of empire.

But the diminution of Greek religion preceded Roman influence. Religion for the Greeks, though certainly more exciting than the Roman variety, was a public exercise, a demonstration that at some level all Greeks were united in their reverence for the same gods—and it tended toward the bland predictability of a stadium of Americans reciting the Pledge of

Allegiance. There were, however, many alternatives, not a few of them shadowy and fugitive. These were called "the Mysteries" (from the Greek *mystēs*, an initiate, and *mysteria*, the rites of initiation). The Mysteries were secret cults into which one had to be initiated—and they have kept their secrets. To this day, we have little more than informed speculation as to what the majority of them entailed.

The most populous of the Mysteries was held at Eleusis, about twelve miles from Athens, in honor of Demeter, goddess of the harvest, and her daughter Persephone, goddess of spring-time. The rites began in Athens in late September at the time of sowing. The devotees of Demeter purified themselves by bathing in the sea. After a tremendous sacrifice of piglets, the initiates set off on their procession to Eleusis along the Sacred Way, reenacting scenes from the myth of Demeter and Persephone, as Christians reenact the Way of the Cross on Good Friday. We know that the initiates fasted, then broke their fast with mint tea; we know that obscene jokes were told along the procession—of an old crone who had got the sor-rowing harvest goddess to laugh by twisting her ancient labia into a smile—and that there was some connection between Demeter of the grain and Dionysus of the grape. We know that when the great procession reached Eleusis, the initiates poured into the Telesterion, a hall that held several thousand, and that the culmination of the festival was the exhibition of "sacred things" by the initiating priest. But what the initiates were shown we do not know. Their secret was kept through the thousand years the rites took place—till their suppression by a Christian emperor in A.D. 393, after which the sanctuary itself was leveled by Alaric and his Visigoths. And the Eleusinian se-cret is now safe with the dead.

The Eleusinian Mysteries were the most public and popular

of the Mysteries. Most Athenians were initiates, and women and even *metics* were welcome. Only murderers and dyed-in-the-wool barbarians ("those who speak an incomprehensible tongue") were kept out. Many other Mysteries owned no designated sanctuary and were far more secretive. What went on in them is more obscure to us than the rites of Demeter. By the time Rome conquered Greece, even more exotic religious rites were being imported from Egypt and Asia. Not a few of these shadowy religions made the men who ran the Roman imperial machinery nervous, for they gave off a smell of political dissent and sometimes even the noxious threat of insurrection. They provided intellectual and cultural harbors for the powerless and dispossessed. Women and slaves, mercenaries and foreigners flocked to their underground rituals and listened attentively to god-knows-what rubbish that might undermine the security of the state. One particularly obscure and troublesome sect was gaining a foothold in important cities throughout the Greco-Roman world. It was led by Jews from the Roman province of Syria-Palestine. In time, it would come to be called Christianity.

W E HAVE REACHED the Meeting of the Waters, the point at which the two great rivers of our cultural patrimony—the Greco-Roman and the Judeo-Christian—flow into each other to become the mighty torrent of Western civilization. It is an irony of our cultural history that the plodding Romans became the channel through which all the delicacies and distinctions of Greek culture flowed into the West. It is no less ironic that, given its subsequent history of Jew-hatred, Christianity should become the vehicle by which Jewish values entered the mainstream. But such and so are the case.

Many aspects of this immense confluence are dealt with in earlier books in this series. The seminal Jewish contribution to our common Western history—without which nothing else could have happened—is the subject of Volume II, *The Gifts of the Jews*. The contribution of early Christianity and its dependence on ancient Judaism are the subjects of Volume III, *Desire of the Everlasting Hills*. Nor have the Romans been neglected. Even if they don't have a volume of their own, they are the subject of the first two chapters of the introductory Volume I, *How the Irish Saved Civilization,* and they form an important strand throughout *Desire of the Everlasting Hills.* (Nor are we quite done with them: they are scheduled to make another appearance—early in Volume V, when we investigate the question of how the Romans became the Italians.) It remains for me here and now to tie up only a few loose ends.

The obscure "mystery" religion of Christianity went from being a threat to the Roman establishment—scapegoated by the emperor Nero in A.D. 64—to becoming part of the establishment 249 years later when it was adopted by its most illustrious convert, the emperor Constantine. Despite its exceedingly Jewish roots, Christianity became a player in the Greco-Roman world, a world shaped by Greek culture and Roman power. Greek, not ancient Hebrew (nor even the Aramaic of the first Christians), became the language of Christianity. Its sacred writings, which came to be known as the New Testament, were written in Greek, and the gospel—the "good news" of Jesus Christ—was preached throughout the ancient world in the Greek tongue. The terms of this new religion, though based on Hebrew models, were Greek terms. Christ, *Ekklēsia* (Church), Baptism, Eucharist, *Agapē* (Lovingkindness)—all of Christianity's central words were Greek words. Christian patterns of thought, like strips of precious inlaid wood, could indeed be traced to their Jewish origins in the coastal Levant, but they often shone with a Greek patina. Paul and Luke, who together account for about fifty percent of the writings of the New Testament, display a familiarity with Greek philosophy and even an attachment to Stoicism. This philosophy of self-denial also taught the brotherhood of man, based on the Stoical belief that every human being without distinction possesses a spark of divinity that is in communion with God, who in the Stoical system is called *Logos* (Word, Reason, Meaning)—the word John's Gospel uses to describe Jesus.

In the first five centuries of Christianity, whenever theological controversy erupted, it almost always erupted in Greek. The Christians of what would become "the Latin West" were not terribly interested in fine intellectual distinctions; it was "the Greek East" that was the sizzling hotbed of theological strife. Was Jesus God or man or both? If both, how so? The terms that flew back and forth were Greek terms—*person, substance, nature.* The man Jesus, it was finally decided, was *homoousios patri* (of the same substance as the Father God). *Ousia* (substance), a term forged by the Presocratic philosophers of the sixth century B.C. to designate immutable reality, was drafted to settle a Christian theological argument more than a thousand years later, as it is still drafted each Sunday in Christian churches throughout the world when the Creed is recited.

The Christian world became a world of Greek vocabulary, Greek distinctions, Greek categories. Nor was it only a question of language. Languages carry values with them; and the Greek divisions between matter and spirit, body and soul, lived in Christian consciousness and shaped Christian sensibility, breaking out repeatedly like an inescapable virus—which owed its origins not to Jesus the Jew but to a Greek language of discourse, shaped by Plato, by his philosophical predecessors, and before them by the large cultural context of Greek perceptions and prejudices. Indeed, the categories of "matter" and "spirit" were so expertly woven into the Greek language by the time Christianity came along that they were unquestioned and unseen.

It is no coincidence that Christian monasticism began in the Greek East in imitation of the Pythagoreans and their spiritual sons the Platonists, who sometimes lived in communities under vow, renounced a normal life in the world, and waited in some lonely place for a final revelation. Even the special appurtenances of Christian monasticism—silence, meditation, chanting, distinctive costumes, beads, incense, kneeling, hands raised in prayer—all too likely go back to the Pythagoreans and beyond them to *their* influences, the Indian Buddhists and their predecessors. (To find the *ultimate* source of Christian monasticism, we might better look to the Dalai Lama than to anything we know of Jesus.) The liturgies elaborated in these monasteries certainly built on pagan Greek models of public prayer and ritual in their litanies, hymns, pageants, and processions.

But these developments were exceptional. For the most part, in the union of Greco-Roman with Judeo-Christian, the Greco-Roman turn of mind combined with Judeo-Christian values. While the outward form of the Western world remained Greco-Roman, its content became gradually Judeo-Christian. The worldview that underlay the New Testament was so different from that of the Greeks and the Romans as to be almost its opposite. It was a worldview that stressed not excellence of public achievement but the adventure of a personal journey with God, a lifetime journey in which a human being was invited to unite himself to God by imitating God's justice and mercy. It was far more individualized than anything the

Greeks had ever come up with and stressed the experience of a call, a personal vocation, a unique destiny for each human being. The one God of the Jews had created the world and everyone in it, and God would bring the world to its end. There was no eternal cosmos, circling round and round. Time is real, not cyclical; it does not repeat itself but proceeds forward inexorably, which makes each moment—and the decisions I make each moment—precious. I am not merely an instance of Man, I am this particular, unrepeatable man, who never existed before and will never exist again. I create a real future in the present by what I do *now*. Whereas fate was central to Greeks and Romans, hope is central to Jews and Christians. Anyone who doubts the great gulf between these two worldviews has only to reread the speeches Hector makes to Andromache (in Chapter I) and to realize the impossibility of putting such speeches on the lips of any believing Jew or Christian:

> "And fate? No one alive has ever escaped it,
> neither brave man nor coward, I tell you—
> it's born with us the day that we are born."

Everything about the core values of the Jews and Christians was foreign to the Greeks and Romans, who in their philosophy had decided that whatever is unique is monstrous and unintelligible. Only that which *is* forever is truly intelligible and worthy of contemplation. The ideal is what is interesting; the individual is beside the point. But as Greek confidence ebbed and Greek philosophy split into scores of yip-yapping schools, the Greeks became more and more puzzled. They had lost their way, philosophically—and the Romans, who were just aping them, had nothing original to propose by way of saving them all from their dilemmas.

Christianity, at first, seemed just another woo-woo wave to cultivated Greeks. Some Greeks had begun to hope faintly for the happiness of their souls in a spiritual afterlife—and this was just what Mysteries like Demeter's promised. But the idea of *physical* resurrection struck them as ghoulish. Who wants his body back, anyway, once he's got rid of it? Matter is the very principle of unintelligibility. Best to be done with it. For the Jews, who had little or no belief in the immortality of the soul, only salvation *in one's body* could have any meaning. For a long time, the Greeks and the Jews talked at cross-purposes.

Gradually, however, as men educated in Greek learning began to explain Judeo-Christian beliefs, the beliefs came to hold out more meaning to the Greeks and Romans in a time when their own traditional religions were being drained of vigor. The philosophers knitted their brows and moaned about the impossibility of reaching truth; Christianity seemed to offer answers. The result of all this was that, just as the Judeo-Christian world had learned the Greek language and internalized Greek categories, the Greco-Roman world gradually abandoned its dying gods and became monotheist. At times, this union of two such disparate cultures went smoothly enough; at other times the union was (and still can be) bizarre and even internally contradictory.

In A.D. 330, Constantine, the first Christian emperor, transferred his capital from Rome to Byzantium and renamed the city Constantinople. In 395, the empire was permanently divided between the sons of Theodosius the Great, the emperor Arcadius ruling the Greek East from Constantinople, the Emperor Honorius ruling the Latin West from Rome. From then on, there was a complete separation of administration and even succession between the two realms. Less than a century later, in 476, the Western empire fell permanently to the northern barbarians, the pillaging Germanic tribes. But life in the Byzantine empire continued more or less unchanged till the mid-fifteenth century, when it fell at last to the Ottoman Turks. This was an ornate, refined, stratified, and largely static society that had less and less to do with Western Europe. Sadly, its form of Christianity, which came to be called Orthodoxy and is full of rarefied spiritual insight, has never been well known in the West.

In the West, Christianity found itself confronting the barbarian hordes, who in their crazy way redirected the Judeo-Christian stream at least as much as the Greeks had done. There is an early Irish lyric called "The Hag of Beare," spoken by an old woman who has become a nun and who spends her last days doing penance. She's actually a goddess from Ireland's pagan past, now attempting to adjust to the new Christian order, and her ancient mind keeps mourning, at first ambivalently, over scenes of her lusty youth when she was a beautiful, much beloved princess:

> These arms, now bony, thin
> And useless to younger men,
> Once caressed with skill
> The limbs of princes!

Finally, she gives vent to her real feelings about her pagan past, her joy in what once was—even though it might gain her disapproval in the new order:

> So God be praised
> That I misspent my days!

For whether the plunge be bold
Or timid, the blood runs cold.

Nothing this red-blooded ever issued from Byzantium, where poetry (except for hymnody) was virtually unknown, drama had died, speculation was strictly confined, art had turned into imitation of past models, and the draperies that had once revealed goddesses in all their splendor were used to cloak every figure in layers of virtuous solemnity. Even the one relatively undraped figure, the dour John the Baptist, speaks of the transformation that a Plato-influenced Christianity wrought on Greek art. In *Dinner with Persephone*, Patricia Storace's delicious repast, a contemporary Greek woman comments: "Think how our ideal of the body changed with Christianity from the beautiful athlete's body to the ruined emaciated saint's body you see in icons. John the Baptist is always shown nearly naked, like the old gods and the boy athletes, but his arms and legs are stick-like, tortured-looking, as if he is diseased. And yet this body is a kind of ideal, the ideal Christian body, with its hollow throat, the sacralized misery of its limbs and the sacred torment on its face, with which it bargains for the eternal life that beauty couldn't win." The Greeks no longer strove to emulate Apollo and Aphrodite; they came to resemble more and more the frowning, storm-browed Christs and sad, resigned Madonnas of their own icons. They even stopped calling themselves Greeks (or Hellenes); they were Christians, nothing else.

In this last stage, there was some continuity with the Greece that had been, if only in a pushing of the body-soul duality to logical, if absurd, conclusions, but there was also dreadful calcification in the building of this Byzantine "artifice of eternity." In another of history's terrible ironies, the barbarian influence on Western Christianity enlivened it beyond anything the diluted Greeks of Byzantium were now capable of. The mad bar-barians pushed Western Christianity into retaining some of the pluralistic abundance, the inventive plasticity, the fathomless versatility that had once been incomparably characteristic of the Greeks. If these currents were not always ascendant in the new Christian order, they were never entirely lost; and by such in-direct means was the lambent flame of the Greek legacy kept alight in the West.

But to find something Greek that is as emotional and singu-lar as "The Hag," we must go back to the lyric poets. Here, then, one last time, is Sappho—in an apostrophe to Hesperus, the god who lights the evening sky, her poem as bold and, es-pecially in the way it builds to its resonant last line, as tender as anything from the barbarians:

> Star of Evening, herd them home
> whom Dawn dispersed, now Day is over:
> kid to its, lamb to its, child to its
> mother.

Human connectedness to all of nature has an immediacy here that we seldom experience today—even if this ritual is still re-peated every evening as shepherd children and their flocks de-scend the forested slopes of Lesbos.

Of course, it is the Greeks who came after Sappho who were largely responsible for the levels of cerebral mediation that now intervene between us and nature. To understand why the Greeks matter to us today, we must appreciate their careering variety of human responses—the lightning-quick transmuta-tions, the Odyssean resourcefulness, the inexhaustible creativ-ity—that came to its final end only in the contractions of the Byzantine state after so many centuries of constant change and renewal. There was nothing the ancient Greeks did not poke their noses into, no experience they shunned, no problem they did not attempt to solve. When the world was still young, they set off at the first light and returned early from the *agora*, their arms full and their carts loaded down with every purchase, domestic and foreign, natural and artificial, they could lay their hands on. Whatever we experience in our day, whatever we hope to learn, whatever we most desire, whatever we set out to find, we see that the Greeks have been there before us, and we meet them on their way back.

THE GREEK ALPHABET ✍

GREEK LETTER		GREEK NAME	TRANSLITERATION
A	α	alpha	a
B	β	beta	b
Γ	γ	gamma	g
Δ	δ	delta	d
E	ε	epsilon	e
Z	ζ	zeta	z
H	η	eta	ē (sometimes a)
Θ	θ	theta	th
I	ι	iota	i
K	κ	kappa	c, k
Λ	λ	lambda	l
M	μ	mu	m
N	ν	nu	n
Ξ	ξ	xi	x

GREEK LETTER		GREEK NAME	TRANSLITERATION
O	o	omicron	o
Π	π	pi	p
P	ρ	rho	r
Σ	σ, ς	sigma	s
T	τ	tau	t
Υ	υ	upsilon	y
Φ	φ	phi	ph
X	χ	chi	ch
Ψ	ψ	psi	ps
Ω	ω	omega	ō

PRONOUNCING GLOSSARY ✍

Achaeans (a-*kee*-unz): One of Homer's terms for the Greeks who attacked Troy. Also called Argives and Danaans.

Achilles (a-*kil*-eez): Son of Peleus and Thetis, a sea nymph; greatest of the Greek warriors at Troy.

Aegisthus (ee-*jis*-thus): Son of Thyestes, lover of Clytemnestra, murderer of Agamemnon.

Aeneas (e-*nee*-as): Son of Aphrodite and Anchises; sails from Troy to Italy to found a dynasty that will produce Romulus and Remus, the founders of Rome.

Aeschylus (*ee*-skull-us): Athenian writer of tragedies (525/24–456 B.C.).

Agamemnon (a-ga-*mem*-non): Son of Atreus, brother of Menelaus, commander in chief of the Greek forces at Troy, murdered by his wife, Clytemnestra.

Agathon (*a*-ga-thon): Fifth-century B.C. Athenian writer of tragedies, character in Plato's *Symposium*.

Agave (a-*ga*-vee): Mother of Pentheus, king of Thebes.

Alcibiades (al-suh-*bye*-a-deez): Athenian general and statesman (c. 450–404 B.C.), pupil of Socrates.

Alcman (*alk*-mun): Seventh-century B.C. lyric poet of Sparta.

Alexander the Great (al-ek-*sand*-er): Macedonian conqueror of the Greek city-states (356–323 B.C.), son of Philip II, pupil of Aristotle.

Anacreon (a-*nak*-ree-on): Lyric poet born c. 550 B.C.

Anaxagoras (a-nak-*sag*-ah-rus): Philosopher born c. 500 B.C.

Andromache (an-*drom*-ah-kee): Wife of Hector, mother of Astyanax.

Aphrodite (a-fro-*dye*-tee): Goddess of love and beauty.

Apollo (a-*pol*-oh): God of light, music, and prophecy, son of Zeus and Leto, brother of Artemis.

Apuleius (a-pyoo-*lay*-us): Roman writer born in Numidia c. A.D. 130.

Arcadius (ar-*kay*-dee-us): Roman emperor, A.D. 395–408.

Archilochus (ar-*kill*-oh-kus): Seventh-century B.C. lyric poet, writer of lampoons.

Ariadne (a-ri-*ad*-nee): Daughter of Minos, king of Crete; helps Theseus.

Aristophanes (*ar*-i-*stof*-a-neez): Athenian writer of comedy (444–388 B.C.).

Aristotle (*ar*-i-*staht*-ul): Philosopher (384–322 B.C.), pupil of Plato and teacher of Alexander the Great.

Artemis (*ar*-te-mis): Virgin goddess of the hunt, daughter of Zeus and Leto, sister of Apollo.

Astyanax (a-*stye*-a-naks): Son of Hector and Andromache.

Atreus (*ay*-tryoos): Father of Agamemnon and Menelaus.

Bacchae (*bak*-ay): Tragedy written by Euripides.

Boeotia (bee-o-sha): District in ancient Greece northwest of Athens.

Calchas (*kal*-kas): Prophet who accompanied the Achaeans to Troy.

Cassandra (ka-*san*-dra): Trojan prophetess of Apollo, daughter of Priam and Hecuba.

Chryses (*krye*-seez): Trojan priest whose daughter is carried off by Agamemnon as a war prize.

Chrysippus (krye-*sip*-us): Stoic philosopher (c. 280–207 B.C.).

Circe (*sir*-see): Enchantress who turns Odysseus's men into swine.

Clytemnestra (klye-tem-*nes*-tra): Wife of Agamemnon; murders her husband.

Cnossos (*knos*-os): City on the northern coast of Crete.

Cronus (*kro*-nos): Titan, father of Zeus and son of Uranus and Gaea.

Cupid (*kyoo*-pid): Roman god of love, equivalent of Eros.

Daedalus (*dee*-da-lus): Athenian architect who designs the labyrinth in Crete, father of Icarus.

Demeter (de-*mee*-tur): Goddess of agriculture, mother of Persephone, sister of Zeus.

Democritus (dem-*ok*-ri-tus): Fifth-century B.C. philosopher.

Demodocus (dem-*od*-ik-us): Phaeacian bard in the *Odyssey*.

Demosthenes (de-*mos*-the-neez): Athenian orator (384–322 B.C.).

Dionysus (dye-o-*nye*-sus): God of fertility, wine, and drama, son of Zeus and Semele.

Diotima (dye-*ot*-i-ma): Legendary priestess of Mantinea and teacher of Socrates.

Electra (e-*lek*-tra): Daughter of Agamemnon and Clytemnestra, sister of Orestes and Iphigenia.

Empedocles (em-*ped*-o-kleez): Fifth-century B.C. philosopher and statesman.

Eris (*er* -is): Goddess of discord.

Eryximachus (er-ik-*sim*-a-kus): Fifth-century B.C. medical doctor, character in Plato's *Symposium*.

Euboea (you-*bee*-a): Island off the coast of eastern Greece.

Euripides (you-*rip*-i-deez): Athenian writer of tragedies (485–406 B.C.).

Evander (e-*van*-der): Arcadian king whose son Pallas fights beside Aeneas.

Exekias (eks-*ee*-kee-us): Sixth-century B.C. Athenian potter and vase painter.

Hades (*hay*-deez) God of the underworld, brother of Zeus, husband of Persephone; also, by attribution, the name given to the underworld.

Hector (*hek*-tor): Greatest of the Trojan warriors, son of Priam and Hecuba, husband of Andromache, brother of Paris.

Hecuba (*hek*-you-ba): Wife of Priam, mother of Hector, Paris, and Cassandra, queen of Troy.

Hegelochus (hay-*gel*-o-kus): Athenian tragic actor.

Helen (*he*-len): Wife of Menelaus, daughter of Zeus; her affair with Paris ignites the Trojan War.

Hephaestus (he-*fees*-tus): God of fire, metallurgy, and the forge, husband of Aphrodite.

Heraclitus (her-a-*klye*-tus): Philosopher of Ephesus, lived c. 535–475 B.C.

Herodotus (her-*a*-doh-tus): Fifth-century B.C. historian, author of *The Persian Wars.*

Hesiod (*hee*-see-od): Eighth- to seventh-century B.C. author of the *Theogony* and *Works and Days.*

Hippocrates (hi-*pok*-rah-teez): Fifth-century B.C. physician, "the father of medicine."

Hippolytus (hi-*pol*-i-tus): Son of Theseus, accused of rape by his stepmother, Phaedra.

Icarus (*ik*-a-rus): Son of Daedalus, ignores his father's warning not to fly too close to the sun.

Jocasta (joh-*kas*-ta): Mother and wife of Oedipus, widow of Laius.

Kritios (*krit*-ee-us): Fifth-century B.C. sculptor.

Laertes (lay-*ur*-teez): Father of Odysseus.

Laius (*lay*-us): First husband of Jocasta, father of Oedipus.

Laocoon (lay-*ok*-oh-on): Trojan priest who warns the Trojans not to take the Wooden Horse into the city.

Leucippus (loo-*sip*-us): Fifth-century B.C. philosopher, joint author with Democritus of the Atomic theory.

Lysippus (lye-*sip*-us): Fourth-century B.C. sculptor.

Lysistrata (lis-*is*-tra-ta): Comedy written by Aristophanes (411 B.C.).

Marsyas (*mar*-see-us): Satyr who engages in musical contest with Apollo.

Medea (me-*dee*-a): Colchian witch, wife of Jason.

Menelaus (me-ne-*lay*-us): Brother of Agamemnon, husband of Helen.

Mycenae (mye-*see*-nee): City in ancient Greece, home of Agamemnon.

Nausicaa (naw-*si*-kay-a): Phaeacian princess, daughter of Alcinous and Arete; befriends Odysseus.

Niobe (*nye*-o-bee): Mother whose children were all slain by the arrows of Apollo and Artemis, because she had boasted that her many children made her more important than *their* mother, the goddess Leto, who had only two children.

Odysseus (o-*dis*-yoos): King of Ithaca, husband of Penelope, father of Telemachus.

Oedipus (*ee*-di-pus, *e*-di-pus): Son of Laius and Jocasta, king of Thebes.

Orestes (o-*res*-teez): Son of Agamemnon and Clytemnestra, brother of Electra and Iphigenia.

Ovid (*ov*-id): Roman author (43 B.C.–17 A.D.) of the *Metamorphoses* and *Ars Amatoria*.

Paris (*pa*-ris): Trojan prince, son of Priam and Hecuba, brother of Hector; abducts Helen from Menelaus.

Parmenides (par-*men*-i-deez): Fifth-century B.C. philosopher and poet.

Patroclus (pa-*tro*-klus): Companion of Achilles, killed by Hector.

Pausanias (po-*say*-nee-us): Lover of Agathon, character in Plato's *Symposium*.

Peleus (*peel*-yoos): Father of Achilles, husband of the sea nymph Thetis.

Penelope (pe-*ne*-lo-pee): Faithful wife of Odysseus.

Pentheus (*penth*-yoos): Young king of Thebes, ripped to shreds by his mother, Agave.

Pericles (*per*-ik-leez): Greatest of Athenian statesmen; ruled Athens from 460 to 429 B.C.

Persephone (pur-*se*-fo-nee): Queen of the underworld, wife of Hades, daughter of Zeus and Demeter.

Phaeacians (fee-*ay*-shuns): Inhabitants of the island Scheria who offer hospitality to the shipwrecked Odysseus.

Phaedra (*feed*-ra): Wife of Theseus, stepmother of Hippolytus.

Phaedrus (*feed*-rus): Pupil of Socrates, character in Plato's *Symposium*.

Phidippides (fye-*dip*-a-deez): Runner sent by the Athenians to Sparta in 490 B.C. to secure aid against the Persians.

Philostratus (fil-*os*-tra-tus): Sophistic writer of the second century A.D.

Phoebus (*fee*-bus): Epithet of Apollo, "the shining one."

Pisistratus (pye-*sis*-tra-tus): Tyrant of Athens from 560 B.C. to 527 B.C.

Plato (*play*-toh): Philosopher (428–347 B.C.), pupil of Socrates, teacher of Aristotle.

Pnyx (*pniks*): Open-air setting in Athens where assemblies of the people were held.

Polemarchus (po-le-*mar*-kus): Pupil of Socrates, character in Plato's *Republic*.

Poseidon (po-*sye*-don): God of the sea and earthquakes, brother of Zeus and Hades, son of Cronus.

Praxiteles (prak-*si*-te-leez): Fourth-century B.C. Athenian sculptor.

Priam (*prye*-am): King of Troy, husband of Hecuba, father of Hector, Paris, and Cassandra.

Psyche (*sye*-kee): Wife of Cupid; her name means "soul."

Pythagoras (pi-*thag*-o-ras): Sixth-century B.C. mathematician, philosopher, and religious leader.

Sappho (*saf*-oh): Lyric poet born on the island of Lesbos c. 612 B.C.

Scaean (*see*-an) **Gates**: Main gates of Troy.

Socrates (*sok*-ra-teez): Athenian philosopher (469–399 B.C.), teacher of Plato, Xenophon, and Alcibiades.

Solon (*so*-lon): Athenian statesman and legislator (c. 640–560 B.C.).

Sophocles (*sof*-oh-kleez): Athenian writer of tragedies (496–406 B.C.).

Thales (*thay*-leez): Ionian philosopher (c. 635–546 B.C.).

Theodosius the Great (*thee*-o-*doh*-shus): Emperor, A.D. 378–395.

Theognis (thee-*og*-nis): Sixth-century B.C. elegiac poet.

Theseus (*thees*-yoos): King of Athens, husband of Phaedra, father of Hippolytus.

Thespis (*thes*-pis): Father of Greek tragedy, contemporary of Pisistratus.

Thessalonians (thes-a-*lon*-i-anz): Inhabitants of Thessalonica (also called Salonika), a seaport in northwestern Greece.

Thetis (*thee*-tis): Sea nymph married to Peleus, mother of Achilles.

Thrasymachus (thra-*sim*-a-kus): Fifth-century B.C. Sophist, character in Plato's *Republic*.

Thucydides (thoo-*sid*-a-deez): Fifth-century B.C. historian, author of *The Peloponnesian War*.

Thyestes (thye-*es*-teez): Brother of Atreus, father of Aegisthus.

Xanthippe (zan-*thip*-pee): Wife of Socrates.

Xenophanes (zen-*o*-fa-neez): Philosopher and poet; founded the Eleatic school (c. 560–480 B.C.).

Xenophon (*zen*-o-fon): Historian (c. 430–c. 354 B.C.), disciple of Socrates.

Zeus (*zyoos*): King of the Olympian gods, son of Cronus, husband of Hera.

NOTES AND SOURCES ✍

What follows is not an exhaustive bibliography of all the books I consulted (which would perilously weigh down this modest book), merely what I found most valuable and wish to point out to readers interested in the further pursuit of particular themes. In approaching my overall subject, I found especially helpful a book by a gifted amateur, Charles Freeman, *The Greek Achievement* (London and New York, 1999), and another by a collection of distinguished scholars at the top of their game, *Literature in the Greek World*, edited by Oliver Taplin (Oxford and New York, 2000). Both books review in different ways principal theories of current scholarship, the latter focused on the "receivers" of the literature, whether readers, spectators, or audiences. *The Oxford Companion to Classical Civilization*, edited by Simon Hornblower and Antony Spawforth (1993), and *The Oxford Companion to Classical Literature*, edited by M. C. Howatson (1990), provided indispensable checklists. Because the various parts of our ancient world were hardly sealed off from one another, I found that my old friend the six-volume *Anchor Bible Dictionary* (New York, 1992) also came in handy, as well as, from time to time, *The Oxford Companion to the Bible* (1993). Everyone's old friend Edith Hamilton's *Mythology* (New York, 1942) was useful in choosing the myths that introduce each chapter, as were innumerable other sources. For original Greek texts, my usual source was the Loeb series (see the notes for Chapter I).

INTRODUCTION
Besides the books listed above, the following were useful in preparing the Introduction and throughout my study: *The Oxford Illustrated*

History of Greece and the Hellenistic World, edited by John Boardman et al. (1988); Oswyn Murray, *Early Greece* (Cambridge, MA, 1993); Thomas R. Martin, *Ancient Greece* (New Haven and London, 1996). An exciting example of insightful scholarship from the middle of the last century is Stringfellow Barr, *The Will of Zeus: A History of Greece from the Origins of Hellenic Culture to the Death of Alexander* (Philadelphia and New York, 1961).

There is at present a raging controversy over the origins of the Greeks. The high likelihood of their racial origin in the Caucasus, as well as the certainty of their linguistic origin as a branch of the Indo-European tree, was perverted by the Nazis to confirm their racial theories—somehow, the Greeks turned out to be Germans. This perversion has impelled some contemporary scholars, especially among the French, to search far and wide for other (if not racial or linguistic, at least cultural) antecedents. There can be little doubt that both Africa and Asia exerted pervasive, if somewhat distant, influence on the formation of Greek culture, Africa through Egyptian-Nubian-Ethiopian connections, Asia through Sumerian-Akkadian connections. But, despite scholarly special pleading (by, for example, Martin Bernal in his fashionably notorious *Black Athena*), these connections—save for similarities between certain Sumerian-Akkadian myths and corresponding Greek myths and between narrative elements of the *Epic of Gilgamesh* and that of the *Odyssey*—are difficult to demonstrate.

One can easily exhaust the reader by alluding to one too many scholarly controversies. I cannot refrain, however, from at least mentioning that many reputable scholars—Peter Ucko, Ruth Tringham, Mary Lefkowitz, and Colin Renfrew, to name a few—doubt (or even vigorously dispute) the importance of earth goddess worship in prehistoric Greece.

I: THE WARRIOR

I was lucky to be able to quote from Robert Fagles's fresh translations of the *Iliad* (New York and London, 1990) and the *Odyssey* (New York and London, 1996), which can hardly be praised too highly. The introduction and notes to each volume, by Bernard Knox, are also uncommonly valuable. As to the Greek originals, I consulted the texts as published in four volumes of the splendidly never-ending Loeb Classical Library, published by Harvard. (The series of "Loebs" was my usual source for the Greek texts referred to throughout this book.)

The subjects of the Greeks at war and their influence on the military traditions of the Western world are ably covered, I found, in several books by Victor Davis Hanson, the most useful being *The Wars of the Ancient Greeks* (New York, 1999, and London, 2000) and *Carnage and Culture: Landmark Battles in the Rise of Western Power* (New York, 2001). Dick Cheney's keen interest in Hanson's histories has been reported by several journalists, among them Michiko Kakutani, "How Books Have Shaped U.S. Policy" (*New York Times*, April 5, 2003).

Another book on the subject of the wars of the West, Philip Bobbit's *The Shield of Achilles: War, Peace, and the Course of History* (New York, 2002), though not as directly related to my subject as its title might suggest, has proved a powerful catalyst to my own thinking. The closing quotation is from my favorite Dr. Seuss book, *The 500 Hats of Bartholomew Cubbins*.

II: THE WANDERER

As to orality, literacy, and the alphabet, I have been considering these phenomena for so long (see especially the first two volumes in this series, *How the Irish Saved Civilization* and *The Gifts of the Jews*) that it is difficult now to name all the books that have influenced me. For those wishing additional, easily digestible information about Mesopotamian cuneiform, Samuel Noah Kramer's books, especially *The Sumerians* (Chicago, 1963), still provide the best starting point. For an introduction to the enigmas of deciphering the oldest writing systems, Andrew Robinson offers in *Lost Languages* (New York, 2002) an immensely entertaining romp, as well as a splendid bibliography. Recently, I have found the essays of Clarisse Herrenschmidt in *L'Orient ancien et nous: L'Écriture, la raison, les dieux* (Paris, 1996) to be truly provocative. Her collaborators in that collection, whose essays are also of considerable value, are Jean Bottéro and Jean-Pierre Vernant; and the collection has now been translated into English under the title *Ancestor of the West: Writing, Reasoning, and Religion in Mesopotamia, Elam, and Greece* (Chicago, 2000). Another study of consequence, excellent at providing social contexts, is Rosalind Thomas, *Literacy and Orality in Ancient Greece* (Cambridge, 1992). The translations of the inscriptions on two seventh-century cups are mine.

In the controversy over orality versus literacy in Homer, the benchmark study is Milman Parry's *L'Épithète traditionnelle dans Homère* (Paris, 1928), translated into English as *The Making of Homeric Verse* (Oxford, 1971). Parry's groundbreaking work was continued after his untimely death by Albert B. Lord in *The Singer of Tales* (Cambridge, MA, 1960), by Eric A. Havelock in *Origins of Western Literacy* (Toronto, 1976) and in other works, as well as by Parry's son, Adam. *The Singer of Tales* has recently been reissued in a second edition (Cambridge, MA, 2000) with an accompanying CD that supplements the text with audio and video recordings of Balkan folksingers of the 1930s in whose prodigious memories and battery of techniques Parry found keys for appreciating the performance strategies of Homer and of his predecessors. Thanks to Parry et al., it is no longer in doubt that Homer availed himself of the traditional methods of the performers of oral poetry. None of their findings, however, can settle once and for all the question of whether or not Homer was literate.

Chief among theorists of the cultural consequences of orality versus literacy are Marshall McLuhan (*The Gutenberg Galaxy* and *Understanding Media*), and his disciple Walter J. Ong (*Orality and Literacy: The Technologizing of the Word*). Though I am broadly sympathetic to their approaches, I find them at their best as interpreters of the change from medieval commonalty to the print culture of the Reformation, rather than as assessors of the cultural impact made by divergent writing systems in antiquity.

"Ulysses" by Tennyson is widely available in many collections; the quotation from "Ithaca" by Cavafy is taken from *Before Time Could Change Them: The Complete Poems of Constantine P. Cavafy*, newly translated by Theoharis C. Theoharis (New York, 2001); "The Wanderer" by Auden is from *W. H. Auden: The Complete Poems* (New York, 2003). The quotation from Samuel Johnson first appeared in *The Rambler* for

November 10, 1750. The entire essay is well worth one's attention as it is, in its exaltation of the pleasures of private life over those of public adulation, a milestone in the evolution of Western sensibility.

III: THE POET

The quotation from Hesiod's *Theogony* is from the translation by Richmond Lattimore (Ann Arbor, 1959), though I have taken the liberty of altering Lattimore's spellings of Greek proper names (for example, *Helikon* to *Helicon*) to conform to the style of my text.

I confess to a lifelong love affair with the Greek lyric poets; and finding no one else's translations completely to my taste, I have ventured to make my own. The one exception is the Sapphic fragment that begins "The moon has set. . . ." That translation has been rattling around in my head for so many decades that I can no longer recall where I first saw it. The translations from Eubulus and Aristophanes are also mine.

The mechanisms that drive this poetry—highly specified varieties of set rhythms appropriate to different moods and occasions, tonal values (now lost to us) associated with long and short syllables, musical modes—are so different from most of the mechanisms available in modern English that every translator must despair of re-creating a semblance of the original textures of Greek poetry in English. What is necessary is to live inside the Greek long enough so that one has a chance of making a new English poem that can convey similar sense and feeling by the instruments available to us: the ways in which words may be chosen and combined through stress and rhythm, alliteration and assonance, and rhyme. Though this last is never employed in Greek lyric poetry, it is a useful English tool for binding elements together that in Greek are bound by other means. Readers who wish to push further may find helpful Anne Pippin Burnett, *Three Archaic Poets: Archilochus, Alcaeus, Sappho* (London, 1983).

The connection I make between homosocial societies and homoerotic activity, though perhaps shocking to some simple souls, is well attested in literature, as well as in current news stories. Less known, at least in the West, is the homoerotic thread in upper-class Japanese life, well exposed, for example, in Eiko Ikegami's *The Taming of the Samurai: Honorific Individualism and the Making of Modern Japan* (Cambridge, MA, 1995). Examples of Islamist homosexuality are attested in many recent journalistic reports (see, for instance, Jeffrey Goldberg, "The Education of a Holy Warrior," *New York Times Magazine*, June 25, 2000).

An essential work for understanding Athenian social life is James Davidson's delightful *Courtesans and Fishcakes: The Consuming Passions of Classical Athens* (London, 1997), though I found myself disagreeing with Davidson on certain aspects of his interpretation of the relationship—or nonrelationship, as he sees it—between Greek sexual practices and male political power. The standard work on *that* subject is K. J. Dover, *Greek Homosexuality* (Cambridge, MA, 1978), which I find convincing. Two books by Italian writers also proved helpful: *Secondo natura* (Rome, 1988) by the legal scholar Eva Cantarella, now available in English as *Bisexuality in the Ancient World* (New Haven, 2002), and *Compagni d'amore: Da Ganimede a Batman: Identità e mito nelle omosessualità maschili* (Verona, 1997) by the psychiatrist Vittorio Lingiardi, now available in English as *Men in Love: Male Homosexualities from Ganymede to Batman* (Chicago, 2002).

IV: THE POLITICIAN AND THE PLAYWRIGHT

The translations of Solon's poetic fragments are mine. For Greek democracy, I relied largely on the standard study by J. K. Davies, *Democracy and Classical Greece* (Cambridge, MA, 1973). Though I present Solon as laying the foundations of Athenian democracy, I am of course aware that later figures—Cleisthenes, Ephialtes, Pericles—are responsible for establishing its functioning. But since they belong to the actualizing moments rather than to the drama of origination, I have (largely from space considerations) left them out of this part of my narrative. In addition to Davies, I have been much taken with Volume I, *Freedom in the Making of Western Culture* (New York, 1991), of Orlando Patterson's monumental study *Freedom*. I am finally unpersuaded by his fundamental proposition that the Greek articulation of freedom began in slavery: it seems to me that it began in Greek conversation and general Greek opinionatedness and that the evidence for this is to be found as far back as the *Iliad*, which preceded the burgeoning of Athens's slave population by nearly two centuries. But Patterson's study remains breathtaking in its admirable originality and magisterial sweep.

For drama, *The Cambridge Companion to Greek Tragedy*, edited by P. E. Easterling (Cambridge, 1997), helped bring my own scholarship up to date. The lines from Clytemnestra's speech in *Agamemnon* are taken from the Fagles translation in *Aeschylus: The Oresteia* (London and New York, 1977). The passages from *Oedipus Tyrannos* are taken from the Fagles translation in *Sophocles: Three Theban Plays* (London and New York, 1982), the passage from *Medea* from the spritely vernacular translation by Frederic Raphael and Kenneth McLeish (London, 1994). *The Interpretation of Dreams* (1900), in which Sigmund Freud presents his theory of the Oedipus complex, is available in many editions, as is Friedrich Nietzsche's *The Birth of Tragedy* (1872).

Two excellent books that span much of the material in this chapter and the next are Martha C. Nussbaum, *The Fragility of Goodness: Luck and Ethics in Greek Tragedy and Philosophy* (Cambridge, 1986), and Simon Hornblower, *The Greek World 479–323 B.C.* (London and New York, revised 1991).

V: THE PHILOSOPHER

All of Nietzsche's works are available in a variety of editions. The new theory on why he went mad is to be found in Richard Schain, *The Legend of Nietzsche's Syphilis* (Oxford, 2002). A more rational approach to the irrational may be found in the classic by E. R. Dodds, *The Greeks and the Irrational* (Berkeley, 1951). The translations from Hesiod and Aristophanes are mine. The classic study of Greek religious beliefs is Walter Burkert, *Greek Religion* (Cambridge, MA, 1985).

The passages from Plato's *Republic* were translated by Robin Waterfield (Oxford, 1993), as were the passages from Plato's *Symposium* (Oxford, 1994); nor can I too highly recommend Waterfield's introductions and notes to these volumes. The translation of the passage from the New Testament (Mt 5:43–48) is mine. For readers who wish to delve more deeply into the multifaceted subject of Greek philosophy, there are three books I would especially propose: Anthony

Gottlieb, *The Dream of Reason: A History of Philosophy from the Greeks to the Renaissance* (New York, 2000), for its amazing clarity and wit; Melissa Lane, *Plato's Progeny: How Plato and Socrates Still Captivate the Modern Mind* (London, 2001), an accessible introduction to ancient philosophy's contemporary influence; and Volume I (New York, 1962) of Frederick Copleston's masterful nine-volume *History of Philosophy*, still the standard treatment in English, clear if dense and only for the dedicated student. None of these, however, had as much influence on me as a Plato seminar I was fortunate enough to take forty years ago with the legendary J. Giles Milhaven, who loved Plato much more than I but helped me to see what he was about and even to appreciate somewhat the ins and outs of Platonic prose.

An excellent new translation of Herodotus has been made by the always reliable Robin Waterfield in *Herodotus: The Histories* (Oxford, 1998). The quotation from Thucydides is from his *History of the Peloponnesian War*, translated by Rex Warner (London, 1972). The last two sentences, however, are my translation. For those who would plumb the depths of Athenian history, Mark Munn, *The School of History: Athens in the Age of Socrates* (Berkeley, 2000), makes an articulate guide. A compact and enlightening consideration of the differences between Herodotus and Thucydides may be found in T. J. Luce, *The Greek Historians* (London, 1997).

VI: THE ARTIST

The passages from Ovid are from his *Metamorphoses*, translated by Allen Mandelbaum (New York, 1993).

There are many fine studies of Greek art. Among the best are John Boardman, *The Oxford History of Classical Art* (1993), and Martin Robertson, *A Shorter History of Greek Art* (Cambridge, 1991). But the book that gave me the most to think about was Andrew Stewart, *Art, Desire, and the Body in Ancient Greece* (Cambridge, 1997). I stuck very close to his interpretation of the treatment of women in Greek art. It was in Stewart that I found the quotation from Terry Eagleton, which he took from Eagleton's *Literary Theory* (Minneapolis, 1983).

VII: THE WAY THEY WENT

Robert Graves made a terrific translation of *The Golden Ass* by Apuleius (New York, 1951). For Greek religious beliefs, you may wish to consult—in addition to Burkert, cited in Chapter V—Paul Veyne, *Did the Greeks Believe Their Myths?* (Chicago, 1988). For the passage from Sophocles's *Oedipus Tyrannos*, see the notes to Chapter IV.

For the funeral oration of Pericles, I could find nothing that truly suited my needs, all the available translations being either too inappropriately colloquial or too out-of-date. The speech is beautifully constructed, and I could not bear to have Pericles sound either banal or antiquated. In the end, I used the well-wrought translation contained in the old Oxford edition of Thucydides by Richard Livingstone (1943), a translation that was made long, long ago by Richard Crawley and revised long ago by Richard Feetham—but I, in my turn, have revised it so considerably that I doubt Crawley's shade would recognize it as his own. By starting with a language of dignity (and with an eye on the Greek), I found it fairly easy to recast the whole in a contemporary idiom. The quotation in the note on "The Melian Dialogue," however, is from the Rex Warner translation (see Chapter V). Harvey Cox's immensely influential study *The Secular City* (New York, 1965) was revised in 1966 and republished in an anniversary edition in 1990.

I am aware that in speaking of "being," the Ionian Presocratics used the term *physis* (nature) rather than *ousia* (substance). But *ousia* was also used, and the terms, as used at least by philosophers, were virtually interchangeable. By the time of Plato, *ousia* had become the preferred term; by the time of Aristotle it had become the technical term.

The last part of the last chapter comes from too many sources to name here, though not a few of these are named in these notes and in the endnotes to previous volumes in this series. For the deep cultural divide between Jews and Greeks, the best authors to begin with may be Thorleif Boman, *Hebrew Thought Compared with Greek* (London and New York, 1960), and Martin Hengel, *Judentum und Hellenismus* (Tübingen, 1973), currently available in English translation as *Judaism and Hellenism* from the Eugene, Ore. publisher, Wipf and Stock—though I'd have to say the best beginning is immersion in the Hebrew Bible and the Greek classics. The landmark study of Byzantium is by

John Julius Norwich in three volumes under the series title *Byzantium* (New York, 1988, 1991, 1995), now digested as *A Short History of Byzantium* (New York, 1997). *The Oxford History of Byzantium* (2002), however, a compilation by many hands, is considerably easier to tackle—and full of wonderful pictures. Another excellent study is *Late Antiquity: A Guide to the Postclassical World* (Cambridge, Mass., 1999), edited by G. W. Bowersock, the invaluable Peter Brown, and Oleg Grabar. The classic study of the impact of Greco-Roman attitudes on early Christianity is by Henry Chadwick, *Early Christian Thought and the Classical Tradition* (Oxford, 1966).

The extract from "The Hag of Beare" comes from the translation from the Irish by John Montague in his *Tides* (Dublin and Chicago, 1971). The translation of the Sappho fragment is mine.

CHRONOLOGY ᔑ

3000–1100 B.C.	The Bronze Age in Greece: the Minoans and Mycenaeans.
1600–1400	The Golden Age of the Minoans in Crete.
c. 1400	The destruction of palaces on Crete. The Mycenaeans appear to take over in Crete.
1184	The traditional date for the fall of Troy.
1100	The beginning of the Iron (or Dark) Age in Greece.
800–600	The period of Greek colonization.
750	The founding of Ischia.
750–700	Homer's *Iliad* and *Odyssey*.
621	Draco and the first written laws in Athens. Beginning of the archaic period in architecture.
c. 612	Sappho born on the island of Lesbos.
594	Solon (c. 640–560) given extraordinary powers in Athens. Economic and political reforms.
560–527	The tyranny of Pisistratus in Athens.
499	The revolt of Ionian Greek cities against Persia. The beginning of the Persian War.

490	The Athenians defeat the Persians at Marathon.
480	The Persians win at Thermopylae.
479	The Persians are defeated at Plataea and Mycale. The end of the Persian War. Beginning of the classical period in architecture.
460–430	The Golden Age of Pericles in Athens. Pericles builds up Athens and strengthens democracy. Athens becomes increasingly antagonistic to Sparta. The three tragedians: Aeschylus (525–456), Sophocles (496–406), Euripides (485–406).
431–404	The Peloponnesian War.
431	The first year of the war ends with Pericles's funeral oration.
430	The plague at Athens.
429	The death of Pericles from the plague.
416	The Athenian attack on the island of Melos. The "Melian Dialogue" of Thucydides.
413	The Athenian expedition to Sicily. Athens defeated.
411	The oligarchic revolution at Athens: despotic committee of four hundred.
410	Athens restores democracy.
404	Athens surrenders to Sparta; oligarchy returns to Athens.
404–371	Period of Spartan dominance.
403	Democracy restored to Athens.
399	The death of Socrates at Athens.
359–336	The reign of Philip II of Macedon.

347	The completion of Plato's *Republic*.
336–323	The reign of Alexander the Great.
335	Aristotle (384–322) founds the Lyceum.
323	The death of Alexander the Great.
323–146	The Hellenistic Age.
148	Macedonia becomes a Roman province.
146	Achaea becomes a part of Macedonia.
A.D. 330	Byzantium becomes the capital of the Roman world; named New Rome or Constantinople.

ACKNOWLEDGMENTS ❧

To faithful friends who read the first draft of the manuscript—Susan Cahill, John E. Becker, William J. Cassidy III, Michael D. Coogan, Gary B. Ostrower, Burton Visotzky, Jane G. White, and Robert J. White—I am most grateful, for I owe them much by way of corrections large and small, though what errors remain are mine alone. As the series has progressed, these stalwarts have come to form a kind of familiar repertory theater of critics: there is the one who demands clarity beyond my ability to provide it, the one who manages to cite historical exceptions that overturn my best generalizations, the one who provides punch lines I never thought of, the ones—all of them—whose learning is deeper and broader than I could ever hope to match. For this volume, Bob White, a friend of nearly fifty years, was especially invaluable. In addition to his editorial fine-tooth comb, he is responsible for the pages on the Greek alphabet, the Pronouncing Glossary, and the Chronology.

I am grateful as well to so many at Doubleday for their unflagging enthusiasm and support: Nan A. Talese above all, but also Katherine Trager, Stephen Rubin, Michael Palgon, Jacqueline Everly, John Pitts, Nicole Dewey, Lorna Owen, Judy Jacoby, Rex Bonomelli, Kim Cacho, Marysarah Quinn, Terry Karydes, Rebecca Holland, Sean Mills, Amy de Rouvray, and the entire, never-to-be-underestimated sales force. Also invaluable has been the assistance of Barbara Flanagan, Chris Carruth, Deborah Bull, and Jennifer Sanfilippo. The supportive team at Anchor—Martin Asher, Anne Messitte, LuAnn Walther, and Jennifer Marshall—is similarly deserving of praise. This time special thanks is owed to CEO Peter Olson, more bellicose than I—at least in his reading—without whose recommendation I might have missed the work of Victor Davis Hanson. Nor can I omit recalling my perennial gratitude to my literary agent, Lynn Nesbit, and her able colleagues Bennett Ashley and Cullen

Stanley, to my assistant Diane Marcus, and to Andrea Ginsky, research librarian of the Selby Public Library in Sarasota, Florida.

Modern Greeks and Greek Americans join hands with their ancient ancestors in the immense value they assign to the pleasures of good conversation. For conversations full of intimate insight, I must thank Athenian friends—Makis Dedes, Despina Gabriel, Nikos Megapanos, Lykourgos V. Papayannopoulos, Takis Theodoropoulos, and Louisa Zaoussi—as well as Olympia Dukakis in New York, and Tedoro and Hera on the great isle of Lesbos.

CREDITS

The author has endeavored to credit all known persons holding copyright or reproduction rights for passages quoted and for illustrations reproduced in this book, especially:

Harcourt, Inc., for the passage from "Ithaca" in *Before Time Could Change Them* by C. P. Cavafy, English translation copyright © 2001 by Theoharis C. Theoharis; and for passages from *The Metamorphoses of Ovid: A New Verse Translation*, English translation copyright © 1993 by Allen Mandelbaum.

Harold Matson Co., Inc., for the passage from "The Hag of Beare" in *The Book of Irish Verse*, English translation copyright © 1974 by John Montague.

Nick Hern Books for the passage from Frederic Raphael and Kenneth McLeish's translation of *Medea* by Euripides, copyright © 1994 by Kenneth McLeish and Volatic Ltd.

Oxford University Press for the passages from *Plato: Republic*, copyright © 1993 by Robin Waterfield, and *Plato: Symposium*, English translation copyright © 1994 by Robin Waterfield.

Random House, Inc., for "The Wanderer" from *Collected Poems* by W. H. Auden, copyright © 1930 by W. H. Auden.

Scribner, an imprint of Simon & Schuster Adult Publishing Group, for the passage from "Sailing to Byzantium" in *The Collected Works of W. B. Yeats, Volume I: The Poems, Revised,* edited by Richard J.

Finneran; copyright © 1928 by The Macmillan Company; copyright renewed © 1956 by Georgie Yeats.

University of Michigan Press, Ann Arbor, for the passages from Hesiod's *Theogony,* English translation copyright © 1959 by Richmond Lattimore.

Viking Penguin, a division of Penguin Group (USA) Inc., for the passages from *The Iliad,* by Homer English translation copyright © 1990 by Robert Fagles, and *The Odyssey* by Homer, English translation copyright © 1996 by Robert Fagles; for the passage from *Agamemnon* in *Aeschylus: The Oresteia,* English translation copyright © 1966, 1967, 1975 by Robert Fagles; and for the passages from *Oedipus the King* in *Sophocles: The Three Theban Plays,* English translation copyright © 1982 by Robert Fagles.

PHOTO CREDITS

20 Nimatallah / Art Resource, NY

21 Museo Archeologico Nazionale, Naples / Bridgeman Art Library

22 Foto Marburg / Art Resource, NY

23 The Art Archive / Acropolis Museum, Athens / Dagli Orti

24 Ashmolean Museum, Oxford

25 Antikensammlung, Staatliche Museen zu Berlin-Preußischer Kulturbesitz / Photo by Jürgen Liepe © bpk, Berlin

26 Erich Lessing / Art Resource, NY

27 Scala / Art Resource, NY

28 Acropolis Museum, Athens / Bridgeman Art Library

29 The Metropolitan Museum of Art, Fletcher Fund, 1927. (27.45)

30 Nimatallah / Art Resource, NY

31 Araldo De Luca, Rome

32 Alinari / Art Resource, NY

33 Giraudon / Art Resource, NY

34 Antikensammlung, Staatliche Museen zu Berlin-Preußischer Kulturbesitz / Photo by Johannes Laurentis © bpk, Berlin

35 Antikensammlung, Staatliche Museen zu Berlin-Preußischer Kulturbesitz / Photo by Ingrid Geske © bpk, Berlin

36 © The British Museum, London

37 Réunion des Musées Nationaux / Art Resource, NY

38 Staatliche Museen zu Berlin-Preußischer Kulturbesitz © bpk, Berlin

39 Antikensammlung, Staatliche Museen zu Berlin-Preußischer Kulturbesitz / Photo by Johannes Laurentis © bpk, Berlin

40 Douris, *Kylix (wine cup) with erotic scene,* ceramic red-figure. Museum of Fine Arts, Boston. Gift of Landon T. Clay (1970.233). Photograph © 2003 Museum of Fine Arts, Boston

41 *Mirror cover with Eros and Symplegma,* bronze. Museum of Fine Arts, Boston. Gift of Edward Perry Warren (RES.08.32c.2). Photograph © 2003 Museum of Fine Arts, Boston

42 *Apulian Red-Figure Bell Krater* by the Name Vase of the Choregos Painter. Courtesy of the J. Paul Getty Museum, Malibu (96.AE.29)

43 British Museum, London / Bridgeman Art Library

44 Vatican Museum, Rome © Bildarchiv Preußischer Kulturbesitz, Berlin

45 Ny Carlsberg Glyptotek, Copenhagen

46 Ny Carlsberg Glyptotek, Copenhagen

47 Erich Lessing / Art Resource, NY

48 Hirmer Fotoarchiv, Munich

49 foto Pedicini / INDEX, Firenze

50 Scala / Art Resource, NY

51 Antikensammlung, Staatliche Museen zu Berlin-Preußischer
Kulturbesitz / Photo by Ingrid Geske © bpk, Berlin

52 Giraudon / Bridgeman Art Library

53 Lauros / Giraudon / Bridgeman Art Library

54 Alinari / Art Resource, NY

55 Alinari / Art Resource, NY

56 Erich Lessing / Art Resource, NY

57 The Metropolitan Museum of Art, Rogers Fund, 1909 (09.39)

58 © The British Museum, London

59 The Art Archive / National Glyptothek, Munich / Dagli Orti

60 Tosi / INDEX, Firenze

61 Photo by Yves Siza © Musée d'art et d'histoire, Ville de Genève
(19026)

62 AKG London

63 Alberti / INDEX, Firenze

64 Private Collection / Bridgeman Art Library

65 Craig Mauzy, Athens

66 Albertinum, Dresden

67 The Walters Art Museum, Baltimore

68 Museum für Kunst und Gewerbe, Hamburg

69 NASA

INDEX

Golden Ass, The (Apuleius), 231–33
Golden Fleece, 131
Good Friday, 254
goodness, 176–77, 183–84
Gospels of Luke and John, 256–58
Graduate, The (Broadway version),
  210*n*
grand unified theory, Einstein's
  attempts at, 151
Great Mother, 10, 14
Greece
  agricultural traditions in, 3, 9, 14,
    19, 109
  chronology of, 285–87
  city-states of, 109–10, 116, 118,
    122, 142–43, 183–84, 188–89,
    213, 220–21
  colonies of, 117–18, 221, 238–39
  cultural revolution in, 58–60,
    81–84, 105, 109, 220
  democracy in, 55, 58–60, 83–84,
    110–19, 122, 182–83, 191, 202,
    239
  landscape of, 204
  language of, 6, 10, 14, 19–20,
    55–60, 62, 96*n*, 157, 199–201,
    222*n*, 256–58, 260, 265–66
  population of, 115–16, 117, 221
  prehistoric, 8, 9–14, 19, 59–60,
    105, 252
  trade in, 10, 14, 109, 115, 116
  warrior culture of, 9, 14, 19–20,
    28–29, 32–34, 42–49, 63, 66,
    81, 98, 116–17, 134–35, 144,
    168, 185, 221
Greek Orthodox Church, 223,
  261
Greeks
  as citizens, 110–11, 134
  classes of, 111–12, 114–15, 158,
    183–84, 219
  cultural superiority felt by,
    128–29, 201–2

Hebrews compared with, 96*n*,
  116, 165, 201
  male-centered ideal of, 206–17,
    221, 224
Gregorian chant, 87
guilt, 122
Gulf War, First, 46
Gulf War, Second, 250*n*
Gulliver's Travels (Swift), 29*n*
Guns, Germs, and Steel (Diamond),
  49
gymnasium, 185, 208

Hades, 3, 53–54, 65–66, 70, 71, 96,
  231, 232
"Hag of Beare, The" (early Irish
  lyric), 261–62, 263
hamartia, 127, 152
Hanson, Victor Davis, 41, 45, 46,
  47, 49
Harvey, Paul, 188
Hebrew language, 56–60, 174*n*, 200,
  256
Hebrews, 38*n*, 57*n*, 58–60, 96*n*, 116,
  165, 174*n*, 200, 201, 255–60
Hector, 34–41, 45, 53, 67, 83, 104,
  134, 259
Hecuba, 34, 104
Hedges, Chris, 28
Hegelochus, 121
Heisenberg, Werner, 150
Helen of Troy, 11, 18, 29–32, 53,
  103
Hellenic period, 214–19, 221–22,
  228
Hellenistic art, 222–28
helots, 117
Henry V (Shakespeare), 210
Hephaestus, 63–64, 252
Hera, 17–18, 24, 25, 63, 252
Heracles (Hercules), 29*n*, 223
Heracles (Euripides), 87

Menelaus, 18, 24, 30, 31, 32, 33, 42,
53, 103, 109
Mercury, 153
Mesopotamia, 10, 38n, 55, 116, 202–3
Metamorphoses (Ovid), 6
metaphors, 236
metempsychōsis, 153, 154
metics, 115, 255
Metropolitan Museum of Art, 7
Michelangelo, 219
mimes, 157–58
Minerva, 252
Minoans, 10–11, 14
Minos, 10, 195
Minotaur, 195
mirrors, 208, 209
Mixolydian mode, 87
moderation, 152, 156
modes, musical, 87
monarchy, 109–10
monasticism, 154, 258
monotheism, 235, 260
monumental buildings, 203–6
morality, 46, 159–63, 165–66
Morte d'Arthur, Le (Malory), 197
mosaics, 96n, 227
Moses, 57n, 58–59
Mother of Sorrows (Christian), 8
Mount Olympus, 17
Mount Parnassus, 204
Mozart, Wolfgang Amadeus, 33
Muses, 79, 80
music, 80, 86–89, 120, 155, 199–201
Music of the Spheres, 155
Mycenae, 11–14, 48, 103–4, 105
Mycenaeans, 11–14, 19, 44, 48, 61,
103, 105
Mysteries (in Greek religion),
254–55, 256, 260
Mysteries of the Snake Goddess
(Lapatin), 10n
mythology, 8, 9, 17–18, 19, 79–80,
235–36

Nagasaki bombing, 46
National Aeronautics and Space
Administration (NASA), 213–14
Nausicaa, 74n
Nero, Emperor of Rome, 256
New Testament, 86, 96n, 109–10,
118, 165, 174n, 182, 256–58
Nicholson, Jack, 195
Nietzsche, Friedrich, 135–36,
141–42, 182, 184
Niobe, 6–7
nouns, 55
nous, 148
novenas, 8
nudity, 207–10, 213–14, 224, 262
nymphs, 226, 228

Odysseus, 6–7, 18, 26, 27, 53–54,
65–75, 81–82, 83, 103, 109, 134
Odyssey (Homer), 14, 19, 43, 53–54,
60–75, 81–82, 83, 134, 167n
Oedipus, 87–88, 124–28, 142, 195,
237–39
Oedipus at Colonnus (Sophocles),
87–88
Oedipus complex, 128
Oedipus Rex (Sophocles), 124–28,
142, 237–39
Olympian gods, 17–18, 19, 24,
25–26, 63–64, 96, 147, 149,
180–81, 218, 223–24, 235–39,
248, 252, 253–54, 260
Olympics, 85
omens, 26–27
On Cheerfulness (Democritus), 149
O'Neill, Eugene, 197
oracles, 125, 152n, 238
oral traditions, 5–6, 19–20, 60–61,
84–85, 103, 235
orchestra, 120
Oresteia (Aeschylus), 105, 123, 127
Orestes, 104, 110

Sparta, 109, 116–17, 189, 190–92,
   220, 223, 242
Sphinx, 124, 125
Stewart, Andrew, 216
stoa, 206
Stoics, 223, 251, 253, 257
Storace, Patricia, 262
Straits of Messina, 65*n*
stratēgos, 48, 119, 130, 248
Strauss, Richard, 197
"Strife Between Odysseus and
   Achilles, The" (*Odyssey*), 66–67
substance, eternal, 145–52, 164, 257
suppliants, 40*n*, 74*n*
Swift, Jonathan, 29*n*, 69, 97
syllogisms, 188
symposia, 97–100, 143, 166–80, 207,
   208
Symposium (Plato), 166–80
Syracuse, 85*n*

Taplin, Oliver, 83–84
taxation, 111
Teiresias, 53, 54
Telemachus, 68, 73*n*, 75, 197
Telesterion, 254
temples, 203–6
Ten Commandments, 57*n*
Tennyson, Alfred, Lord, 69–70, 71,
   83
Teresa of Ávila, 233
Terpsichore, 80
terrorism, 47
Thales, 146, 151, 202
Thalia, 80
theaters, 120–21, 206
theatron, 120, 121
Thebes, 124, 221
Theodosius I, Emperor of Rome, 260
Theognis, 98–99
Theogony (Hesiod), 79–80
theology, 152, 256–58

Thera, 11
Thermopylae, battle of, 189
Theseus, 195, 197, 209
Thespis, 121
thetes, 111, 114
Thetis, 17, 18, 63
Thrasymachus, 163–64
Thucydides, 43, 189–92, 239, 247,
   250*n*–51*n*
Thyestes, 103
Titans, 17, 63
to hellenikon, 144–45, 201–2
Torah, 57*n*, 58–59
torture, 115
tragedy, 119–36, 141–42, 143, 144
tribal societies, 48, 58–59
Trojan Horse, 53, 67, 224
Trojan War, 14, 17–49, 53, 61, 103,
   104, 224
Troy, 11, 18, 25, 28–29, 34, 53, 67,
   82–83, 109, 142, 213, 224
Turner, Kathleen, 210*n*
tympanums, 206
tyrannos, 110, 119, 124, 127, 143

Ulysses (Joyce), 70–72
"Ulysses" (Tennyson), 69–70, 83
uncertainty principle, 150
United Nations, 250*n*
unities, dramatic, 127
universe, nature of, 145–52
Unswept Hall, The (Sosos), 96*n*
Upanishads, 154–55
Urania, 80
urbanization, 109–10
utopias, 82–83, 142, 183–84, 212–13

Vatican, 186
vengeance, 73*n*, 104–5, 110, 122, 125
Venus, 18, 231, 232, 252
verbs, 55–56

A NOTE ABOUT THE AUTHOR ⁊

THOMAS CAHILL is the author of the three previous volumes in the Hinges of History series: *How the Irish Saved Civilization, The Gifts of the Jews,* and *Desire of the Everlasting Hills.* They have been bestsellers, not only in the United States but also in countries ranging from Italy to Brazil. Cahill was recently invited to address members of the U.S. Congress on the Judeo-Christian roots of moral responsibility in American politics. He and his wife, Susan, also a writer, divide their time between New York and Rome.